Handbook of Spirituality, Religion, and Mental Health

Contents

List of contributors

Jonathan S. Abramowitz
Department of Psychology, University of North Carolina at Chapel Hill, Chapel Hill, NC, United States

Michael E. Berrett
Berrett and Company, LLC, Linden, UT, United States

Jennifer L. Buchholz
Department of Psychology, University of North Carolina at Chapel Hill, Chapel Hill, NC, United States

Ying Chen
Human Flourishing Program, Institute for Quantitative Social Science, Harvard University, Cambridge, MA, United States; Department of Epidemiology, Harvard T.H. Chan School of Public Health, Boston, MA, United States

Hilary S. Connery
Division of Alcohol, Drugs, and Addiction, McLean Hospital, Belmont, MA, United States; Department of Psychiatry, Harvard Medical School, Boston, MA, United States

Alexandre de Rezende Pinto
Research Center in Spirituality and Health (NUPES), School of Medicine, Universidade Federal de Juiz de Fora (UFJF), Juiz de Fora, MG, Brazil

Jeff Devido
Department Health and Human Services, Behavioral Health and Recovery Services, Marin County, CA, United States; UCSF Weill Institute for Neurosciences, School of Medicine, University of California, San Francisco, CA, United States

Daniel D. Flint
Department of Psychology, Bowling Green State University, Bowling Green, OH, United States

Jennifer Tegan Grant
Department of Psychology, Bowling Green State University, Bowling Green, OH, United States

Joshua Briggs Grubbs
Department of Psychology, Bowling Green State University, Bowling Green, OH, United States

Randy K. Hardman
Counseling Center, Brigham Young University-Idaho, Rexburg, ID, United States

Philippe Huguelet
Department of Psychiatry, University Hospital of Geneva and University of Geneva, Geneva, Switzerland

Bethany Leidl
Department of Psychiatry, McLean Hospital/Harvard Medical School, Belmont, MA, United States

Annette Mahoney
Department of Psychology, Bowling Green State University, Bowling Green, OH, United States

James S. McGraw
Department of Psychology, Bowling Green State University, Bowling Green, OH, United States

Alexander Moreira-Almeida
Research Center in Spirituality and Health (NUPES), School of Medicine, Universidade Federal de Juiz de Fora (UFJF), Juiz de Fora, MG, Brazil

Bruno Paz Mosqueiro
Postgraduate Program in Psychiatry and Behavioral Sciences (PPGPSQ UFRGS), Universidade Federal do Rio Grande do Sul (UFRGS) and Grupo Hospitalar Conceição, Porto Alegre, RS, Brazil

John Peteet
Department of Psychaitry, Harvard Medical School, Boston, MA, United States

P. Scott Richards
Center for Change of Universal Health Services, Inc., Orem, UT, United States

David H. Rosmarin
Department of Psychiatry, McLean Hospital/Harvard Medical School, Belmont, MA, United States

Christina Rush
Department of Psychology, University of Colorado Denver, Denver, CO, United States

Kaitlyn Vagnini
Department of Psychology, University of Colorado Denver, Denver, CO, United States

Tyler J. VanderWeele
Human Flourishing Program, Institute for Quantitative Social Science, Harvard University, Cambridge, MA, United States; Department of Epidemiology, Harvard T.H. Chan School of Public Health, Boston, MA, United States

Amy Wachholtz
Department of Psychology, University of Colorado Denver, Denver, CO, United States

Sarah Weinberger-Litman
Marymount Manhattan College, Department of Psychology, New York, NY, United States

Foreword

Though my father and mother abandon me, the LORD will take me in

Psalm 27:10

Spirituality and religious experience are reflective of the complex circumstances of human life. While it is not possible to know with any certainty how other species respond to inevitable mortality and suffering, we know as human beings that our time is limited and precious. And if we are attentive, we know that many forms of suffering, pain, and loss are the inevitable accompaniments of being alive. When these are added to a host of other existential dilemmas (what is my purpose in life, what is the best use of my gifts, strengths and weaknesses, how can I live and respond to a world which encompasses great beauty as well as wrenching poverty and pain), it is not surprising that spiritual traditions of various kinds are living and important elements of many people's lives and existence.

The matter becomes more complex and more difficult when the issue of spirituality is linked to medical and especially perhaps to psychiatric care. On the one hand, the practice of medicine broadly construed has a deep and robust connection in its earliest history to religious and priestly functions, many of which were associated or linked to clinical phenomena, which we may see today as psychiatric or psychological. More recently, medicine and psychiatry have both functioned under the standards and ethos of science. To the extent that spiritual questions operate outside of science or are not amenable to resolution by the scientific method may seem to place them in conflict with the standards of medical practice. We also live in a highly pluralistic era when many different religious and spiritual traditions exist side by side. As such, the appeal to a single or dominant spiritual tradition, as may have been true in older cultures, makes reference to a communal standard more difficult at present.

In psychiatry and mental health, there have been other reasons why a discussion about spirituality is complex if not difficult. Both psychiatric disorders and spiritual experiences are mediated in subjective as well as externally observed ways. Since many psychiatric disorders do not have hard biological markers, their demarcation from other conditions can be subject to interpretation and potentially bias. This is particularly true of the many states of mind which can be affected by the challenges of aging, poverty, trauma, and loss: apprehension, demoralization, exhaustion, or loss of purpose. As such, the boundaries between these conditions and some psychiatric disorders can be unclear. While current data do not suggest that religion is implicated in the etiology of psychopathology, this may be even more confusing when dealing with more serious mental disorders where religious delusions or command hallucinations attributed to a deity or demonic force are not uncommon. Likewise, psychiatry and psychology on the one hand, and religious perspectives on the other hand, can appear to be alternative explanatory systems, with different views on the causes, remedies, and treatments of mental distress. These explanations can conflict with one another, and be threatening to the authority of either or both groups. Pharmaceuticals such as psilocybin, some of which are now being studied for their therapeutic benefit, have been used in some traditional cultures for millennia precisely because they can induce profound religious experiences. That some of these experiences can overlap with symptoms seen in serious mental disorders has indeed encouraged a generation of researchers to also see their effects as evidence for the potential neurobiological origins of psychiatric disorders or at least the importance of perturbations in neurochemistry as legitimate targets for study and intervention. Finally, there is the somewhat older explanation of the tension and historic hostility of psychoanalysis and its founder Sigmund Freud to religion, which viewed its persistence as a form of culturally sanctioned neurosis.

However, spirituality and religious experience are too central to human experience and culture for mental health professionals or other clinicians to ignore. Throughout the world, religious institutions are highly integrated into local communities. In many places, they are among the primary social supports available to many individuals. Persons in distress often seek out their religious leaders before they seek medical or other clinical attention. As such, knowing more about the interface between spirituality and mental health becomes a clinical necessity if we are to be of help both within and outside traditional clinical settings.

Writing and thinking about this interface is important if for no other reason than reaching those who are often unseen or unheard, suffering greatly. But as Rosmarin, Koenig, and their colleagues show throughout this essential book, the research—epidemiologic, basic, and clinical—regarding the bidirectional impact of spiritual and religious traditions and mental health care and concerns has advanced far beyond this more traditional view of the field. Bolstered by a new generation of studies and scientists, they and their collaborators carefully dissect what is known—and the limits of that knowledge—in regard to the boundary of spirituality and mental health. They and the authors who have contributed these excellent chapters review the epidemiology of psychiatric disorders in persons with and without spiritual practices, the direct impact of the inclusion of spiritual practices—for good or ill—on those conditions, relevant controlled treatment studies, and data where it exists on the neurobiology which may underlie spiritual experience. Each chapter includes an extensive critical review of the research literature and sets an agenda for future studies. This new edition of the Handbook of Spirituality, Religion, and Mental Health thus not only guides clinicians and religious leaders of all backgrounds in their response to the person seeking help but also provides an essential review of our current knowledge. As such, it is a starting point for future research and clinical care. It deserves wide readership and uses as we all endeavor to listen to, inquire of, and intervene in our patients' illnesses in a respectful and effective manner.

Paul Summergrad
Dr. Frances S. Arkin Professor and Chairman, Department of Psychiatry
Professor of Psychiatry and Medicine, Tufts University School of Medicine
Psychiatrist-in-Chief, Tufts Medical Center, Boston, MA, United States

Introduction

Since the publication of the first edition of this text just over 20 years ago, a wellspring of theory, research, and clinical innovation has poured forth on the subject of spirituality, religion (S/R) and mental health. It is now widely apparent that S/R is strongly tied in both positive and negative ways to depression, suicidality, anxiety, psychosis, obsessions/compulsions, addictions, eating/feeding concerns, psychogenic pain, as well as other facets of behavioral and mental health. These ties reach well beyond social, cultural, or historical significance. The sheer magnitude of amassed data now points to clear implications for public health, in that S/R can clearly inform our understanding of the course and etiology of mental disorders and also enhance methods of clinical treatment.

Despite these welcomed developments, formidable barriers remain for the field of S/R and mental health. In most *other* areas of mental health science, we find mature and well-established conceptual foundations that can support the testing of fine-tuned hypotheses to further our understanding of various processes and mechanisms of action. In general clinical science, state-of-the-art approaches have moved beyond simple randomized controlled methodologies to develop sophisticated treatment models that, in some cases, can be tailored by phenotype to provide targeted, individualized approaches to patient care. In basic and applied research, it is now standard to evaluate symptoms of mental distress at genetic, molecular, cellular, physiological, environmental, and behavioral levels, with an eye toward identifying brain circuits and regions that may mediate or moderate their onset and severity. In contrast, largely owing to a lack of programmatic research support from governmental and private funders, research on S/R and mental health has yet to come of age. More accurately, the field is only beginning to put forth, test, and implement sophisticated scientific models of S/R and mental health.

However, as the 11 chapters in this book make readily apparent, there is light upon the horizon. Each chapter goes far beyond a simple descriptive analysis of *whether* various facets of S/R are tied to emotional processes. Across the board, authors delineate with substantial nuance, aspects of *how* and *why* S/R interfaces so richly with mental health, well-being, and distress. Furthermore, whenever possible, evidence from neurobiological studies is integrated into these discussions. Similarly, chapters reflect on *for whom* spiritual and religious factors are most relevant to mental health, thereby further clarifying mechanisms of association between these variables, and facilitate idiographic tailoring of current models in a way that takes into account individual as well as cultural differences.

Each chapter also reflects on how the extant research can inform evidence-based treatment models for mental disorders and related aspects of behavioral health. Along these lines, chapters describe how integrating S/R into clinical approaches can enhance care and improve efficacy of treatments for various conditions, for some patients. These latter aspects of the present volume are particularly important, since mental health professionals are seldom trained to inquire about S/R, and this domain is often not attended to sufficiently in the context of patient care (Curlin et al., 2007; Rosmarin, Green, Pirutinsky, & McKay, 2013). Our hope for this book, therefore, is to provide an authoritative and up-to-date volume that can inform both mental health research and clinical practice by providing clinically relevant summaries of the extant literature at a high caliber of academic scholarship. In sum, there is but one message across the board: The domain of S/R should not be ignored by the scientists who study, nor the clinicians who treat, mental health and distress. It is hoped that in another 20 years, the field will be so far advanced in its understanding and conceptualization of S/R and mental health that these points will be patently obvious and need not be emphasized.

Definitions

Readers will note that the first edition of this text was published with the title *Handbook of Religion and Mental Health* whereas this second edition includes the word "Spirituality." This reflects three important, current trends. First, while the vast majority of the world's inhabitants continue to profess religious affiliation, Western nations are going through a transition toward less religious identity overall. It is notable that this trend has coincided with a substantial increase in the prevalence and severity of mental disorders across all Western countries in general, and within the United States in particular. Nevertheless, in the current day, experiences that would historically be described as "religious" such as feeling the presence of God or a Higher Power, feeling guided by a Spiritual Force, being grateful for one's blessings, and prayer in its various forms, often occur outside of the context of religion (defined below). Such "spiritual" experiences are common even among individuals who do not profess religious beliefs or affiliations. As but one example, 89% of Americans believe in God, yet only 77% report affiliation with a religious group (Pew Research Center, 2014). We therefore included "spirituality" alongside "religion" in the present edition in order to capture more variance in the inherently diverse nature of this domain in the present day.

Second, despite downward trends in the realm of religion (and historical tensions between S/R and mental health), we seem to be witnessing a spiritual awakening within the combined mental health disciplines. Virtually all medical centers across the United States today offer mindfulness-based stress reduction (MBSR) to patients for a variety of presenting concerns. This is despite the fact that this approach clearly has religious origins in that mindfulness is a distillation of Buddhist meditation practice (the seventh step on the Eightfold Path), and the nearly half of patients' primary reason for attending MBSR is to achieve "spiritual growth" (Greeson et al., 2011). Along these lines, consider that in a 2003 survey of American clinical psychologists – historically one of the *least* religious groups in all of academia – 62% reported studying spiritual material on a monthly or greater basis, and 84% reported having felt "very close to a power spiritual force" at least once in their lifetimes (Delaney, Miller, & Bisono, 2007). However, there remains a stark *religion* gap between mental health practitioners and the general public. In the same survey cited above, psychologists were nearly three times more likely to have no religious affiliation, half as likely to attend religious services on a weekly basis, and 40% less likely to report that "religion" is important in their lives compared to the general populace. Along these lines, the majority of research on religion and mental health today is published using "spiritual" as opposed to "religious" monikers. Therefore, excluding the former would effectively narrow the scope and diminish the utility of this book.

Third, which leads into formal definitions, is that spirituality and religion overlap considerably from an empirical standpoint. The vast majority of individuals in the general population (~65%–85%) identify either as spiritual and religious or neither spiritual nor religious (Rosmarin, 2018). Thus most individuals' spirituality – which refers to any way of relating to that which is perceived to be *sacred* – inherently contains themes of religion – which refers to *institutionalized or culture-bound ways* of relating to that which is perceived to be *sacred* (Pargament, Mahoney, Exline, Jones, & Shafranske, 2013). So, linguistically speaking, spirituality is a broad term that technically refers to any aspect of life that is perceived to have a divine or metaphysical quality, and religion, by contrast, is a specific term referring to such aspects of life that are shared with others within an institutional/cultural group. However, in practice, there is typically little distinction for the majority of individuals. For all of these reasons, the present volume refers to spirituality and religion as a unitary term "S/R," despite the fact that they are theoretically disparate constructs.

Chapters

The present 11-chapter volume is structured quite differently from its preceding first volume, which contained six sections and a total of 26 chapters. In the first volume, dedicated chapters provided detailed accounts of the history of religion in psychiatry/mental health, ethical issues related to this area of study, general research considerations, religious perspectives on mental health from various faith traditions (e.g., Protestantism, Catholicism, Judaism, Buddhism, etc.), clinical applications, and considerations for the education of mental health professionals. In addition, Part III of the first edition contained specific chapters on the relevance of religion to various mental disorders (e.g., depression, anxiety, psychosis, etc.) Indeed, two decades ago there was so little ink on the topic of S/R and mental health that there was a need for a comprehensive approach to this topic that spanned across all of these various topics and issues. As discussed above, in the present day the most pressing priority for the field of S/R and mental health is to focus on elucidating academically rigorous and clinically relevant models to inform future science and clinical practice in this area. To that end, this second edition is organized in a much more focused manner that is akin to Part III in the first edition. Each chapter in this volume addresses how S/R is relevant to a single area of mental health/distress. Furthermore, chapters are organized in a relatively simple fashion. Each provides a densely packed, theoretically integrated, and up-to-date summary of the scientific literature in that specific focus area, as well as a clinically rich discussion of how that extant literature can inform patient care. In many cases, topics such as general research considerations, education, ethics, perspectives of specific religious traditions, and history are addressed in the course of these research and clinical discussions. However, these are clearly secondary considerations within the present volume, given its intended primary scope and purpose.

In Chapter 1, Spirituality, religion, and mood disorders, Bruno Paz Mosqueiro, Alexandre de Rezande Pinto, and Alexander Moreira-Almeida provide a comprehensive current literature review of the vast research findings on the effects of various facets of *S/R and Mood Disorders*, spanning across both depression and mania. This is bolstered by a thoughtful discussion of proposed mechanisms of effect, based on the latest psychosocial and neurobiological data. Their chapter also summarizes the relatively large literature on spiritually integrated treatment approaches to depression and broadly discusses the clinical implications of these data for treating spiritually diverse individuals with mood disorders.

In Chapter 2, Spirituality, religion, and suicide, Ying Chen and Tyler VanderWeele tackle the important public health topic of *S/R and Suicide*. This brief chapter summarizes a consistent and methodologically strong literature evidencing relatively large effects of organized S/R behavior on lower levels of suicidal ideation and completion. The authors discuss potential explanations for such effects and translate their interpretations into models to inform both public health policy as well as clinical practice.

In Chapter 3, Spirituality, religion, and anxiety disorders, David H. Rosmarin and Bethany Leidl address *S/R and Anxiety Disorders*. While a substantial volume of research has been conducted on this topic, there has been great inconsistency in the literature with various studies reporting positive as well as negative associations and many null relationships, as well as considerable variation in effect sizes across the board. The authors synthesize all of these trends to provide an overarching conceptual model of how various aspects of S/R do and do not relate to anxiety symptoms. Their approach has implications for future research on S/R and anxiety, as well as clinical practice in this area.

Chapter 4, Spirituality/religion and obsessive–compulsive-related disorders, authored by Jonathan S. Abramowitz and Jennifer L. Buchholz, addresses *S/R and Obsessive–Compulsive Disorder* (OCD). In a thoughtful and balanced review of the literature, the authors debunk the long-held belief that S/R is a cause of OCD. Instead, the authors share that S/R can coopt the experience of OCD such that symptoms take on religious themes, which can in turn complicate clinical assessment and treatment. Using a cognitive-behavioral framework, the authors review how the scientific literature on S/R and OCD can enhance our understanding and treatment of this disorder, particularly when religious symptoms manifest.

In Chapter 5, Spirituality, religion, and psychotic disorders, Philippe Huguelet addresses *S/R and Psychotic Disorders*. Similar to Chapter 4, Spirituality/religion and obsessive–compulsive-related disorders, the author makes a cogent case that S/R is not a credible risk factor for the development of psychosis, but rather religious delusions and hallucinations simply occur when individuals experience psychotic processes within a latent or active cultural context of religion. The author further discredits long-held fears that addressing S/R issues with psychotic patients could present a risk factor for decompensation or worsening of symptoms. Along these lines, the chapter concludes by describing an evidence-based clinical model for addressing S/R in the treatment of psychotic patients, informed by the extant literature.

Chapter 6, Spirituality, religion, and eating disorders, by P. Scott Richards, Sarah Weinberger-Litman, Michael E. Berrett, and Randy K. Hardman, discusses *S/R and Eating Disorders*. As reviewed in this carefully constructed chapter, the scientific literature on S/R and eating disorders is less developed than other areas of research. Nevertheless, the authors review and integrate the little we know about this topic into a clinically rich and useful model that informs treatment applications for individuals with eating disorders who seek spiritually integrated care.

In Chapter 7, Spirituality, religion, and substance use disorders, Hilary S. Connery and Jeffrey J. DeVido discuss *S/R and Substance Use Disorders* (including alcohol, drugs, and other chemical substances). This well-established topic within the field of mental health science has a large literature base, which the authors summarize and integrate into a theoretically meaningful review. The authors then discuss clinical science in this area and provide a description of how S/R can be successfully integrated into evidence-based assessment and treatment of substance use disorders.

Chapter 8, Spirituality/religion and behavioral addictions, by Joshua Briggs Grubbs and Jennifer Tegan Grant, continues onto a similar theme from the previous chapter and turns our attention to *S/R and Behavioral Addictions*. This important chapter addresses how S/R relates to dysregulated and addictive behaviors such as compulsive gambling, gaming, and sexual behavior. Despite the relative infancy of research on behavioral addictions compared to other areas of psychopathology, consistent trends are already emerging in the burgeoning literature of S/R and behavioral addictions. These are summarized into a clinically useful review, one that also informs future empirical study of this area.

In Chapter 9, Spirituality, religion, and marital/family issues, Annette Mahoney, Daniel Flint, and James McGraw turn our attention beyond psychopathology research into the important topic of *S/R and Marital/Family Issues*. A large and consistent body of research has been conducted on this important topic, which is known to influence the course and severity of a wide range of mental disorders. The authors of this chapter summarize this literature in a clear and concise manner that highlights how and why S/R can functionally impact several important processes for couples, parents, and children, in both positive and negative ways.

Chapter 10, Spirituality/religion, and pain, by Christina Rush, Katie Vagnini, and Amy Wachholtz, discusses *S/R and Pain Disorders*, a topic of particular significance given the current opiate-addiction crisis. This chapter meticulously summarizes a surprisingly large and strong literature tying a variety of facets of S/R to the experience of pain. The authors carefully identify potential "active ingredients" in S/R that may mitigate the experience of pain, in order to inform a clinically useful model of this area of study, and future research.

Finally, in Chapter 11, Spirituality/religion and end-of-life care, John Peteet discusses *S/R and End-of-Life Care*. As his review of the literature teaches us, S/R issues are highly common in the context of life-threatening illnesses and medical decision-making around end-of-life issues. The author integrates this literature into a clinically rich case study, which illustrates how clinicians can go about addressing S/R issues for patients facing such issues. The chapter concludes with an important discussion of ethical issues and training considerations for physicians and other clinicians.

The above chapters go beyond a simple descriptive account to establish basic links between S/R and mental health. They identify that S/R can be functionally relevant to the gamut of mental health symptoms and outcomes for the vast majority of individuals in the general public and clinical populations as well. More broadly, they identify important avenues for clinicians who wish to address S/R in practice and also for researchers who seek to better understand and new vistas within this important area of study. Ultimately, it is our hope that this second edition will continue the trend of its predecessor: To provide an authoritative and up-to-date volume for the academic and clinical communities on S/R and mental health.

References

Curlin, F. A., Lawrence, R. E., Odell, S., Chin, M. H., Lantos, J. D., Koenig, H. G., & Meador, K. G. (2007). Religion, spirituality, and medicine: psychiatrists' and other physicians' differing observations, interpretations, and clinical approaches. *American Journal of Psychiatry*, *164*(12), 1825–1831.

Delaney, H. D., Miller, W. R., & Bisonó, A. M. (2007). Religiosity and spirituality among psychologists: A survey of clinician members of the American Psychological Association. *Professional. Psychology: Research and Practice*, *38*(5), 538.

Greeson, J. M., Webber, D. M., Smoski, M. J., Brantley, J. G., Ekblad, A. G., Suarez, E. C., & Wolever, R. Q. (2011). Changes in spirituality partly explain health-related quality of life outcomes after Mindfulness-Based Stress Reduction. *Journal of behavioral medicine*, *34*(6), 508–518.

Pargament, K.I., Mahoney, A., Exline, J.J., Jones, J.W., & Shafranske, E.P. (2013). Envisioning an integrative paradigm for the psychology of religion and spirituality.

Pew Research Center. (2014). Religion and Public Life. Retrieved April, 2020, from https://www.pewforum.org/2015/11/03/u-s-public-becoming-less-religious/

Rosmarin, D. H. (2018). *Spirituality, religion, and cognitive-behavioral therapy: A guide for clinicians*. Guilford Publications.

Rosmarin, D. H., Green, D., Pirutinsky, S., & McKay, D. (2013). Attitudes toward spirituality/religion among members of the Association for Behavioral and Cognitive Therapies. *Professional Psychology: Research and Practice*, *44*(6), 424.

CHAPTER 1

Spirituality, religion, and mood disorders

Bruno Paz Mosqueiro[1], Alexandre de Rezende Pinto[2] and Alexander Moreira-Almeida[2]
[1]Postgraduate Program in Psychiatry and Behavioral Sciences (PPGPSQ UFRGS), Universidade Federal do Rio Grande do Sul (UFRGS) and Grupo Hospitalar Conceição, Porto Alegre, RS, Brazil
[2]Research Center in Spirituality and Health (NUPES), School of Medicine, Universidade Federal de Juiz de Fora (UFJF), Juiz de Fora, MG, Brazil

Contents

Introduction

ruly, it is in the darkness that one finds this light, so when we are in sorrow and distress, then this light is nearest of all to us"

(Eckhart, 1327)

The study of spirituality/religion (S/R) and mental health touches upon questions about profound human needs, involving the search for understanding, meaning, and purpose in the face of suffering, and the search for transcendence across different cultures and in different periods of human history.

Mood disorders, encompassing bipolar and depressive disorders, are currently evidenced as very common and disabling mental illnesses, with

Handbook of Spirituality, Religion, and Mental Health
DOI: https://doi.org/10.1016/B978-0-12-816766-3.00001-X

serious impact to global health. Major depressive disorder (MDD) affects 300 million people in the world and represents the leading cause of mental health–related diseases worldwide (Herrman et al., 2018). Individuals living with bipolar disorders (BD) experience substantial morbidity and impairment, with an even larger impact in young people, being the sixth leading cause of disability among people aged 10–24 years old in the world (Yatham et al., 2018). The World Mental Health Survey Initiative estimates a lifetime prevalence of BD of around 1.0% (bipolar I and II disorders) and a lifetime prevalence of MDD of 12.8% (Kessler & Bromet, 2013; Merikangas et al., 2011).

S/R represent a very important domain for many, probably most, individuals across different cultures and contexts (Koenig, King, & Carson, 2012). The Pew-Review Templeton Survey identified that 5.8 billion people in the world (84% of the world population) reported a religious affiliation, and for those religious unaffiliated (including atheists, agnostics, and spiritual but not religious people), many held S/R beliefs and practices that often constituted important aspects in their lives (Hackett et al., 2012).

Empirical evidence in the last decades consistently identified mainly positive effects of S/R in mood disorders. S/R beliefs and practices are commonly used coping resources to deal with stressful life events or adversities (Pargament, Koenig, Tarakeshwar, & Hahn, 2004). Furthermore, research indicates that S/R is frequently a source of meaning, resilience, strength, connection, and social support, capable of promoting recovery in many people with MDD and BD. Although less often, S/R may also be a source of conflicts and negative coping (Pargament & Lomax, 2013).

Most patients agreed that health professionals should be sensitive and open to their S/R issues in clinical care (VanderWeele, Balboni, & Koh, 2017). The World Psychiatric Association (WPA) Position Statement on Religion, Spirituality and Psychiatry recommends that S/R should be routinely considered in clinical practice, in a scientifically based, compassionate and culturally sensitive approach (Moreira-Almeida, Sharma, van Rensburg, Verhagen, & Cook, 2016). Understanding how S/R beliefs and practices impact mood disorders, and how to address these issues in a clinical practice, constitutes a central question in mental health care.

The present chapter aims to present an outline of scientific literature regarding the connections between S/R and mood disorders, specifically MDD and BD. In the first section, a comprehensive review of studies including potential psychological and neurobiological pathways to understand how religion and spirituality could affect MDD will be reviewed. Another section will thoughtfully evaluate the impact of S/R issues on BD. Finally, clinical implications and challenges of S/R to mood disorders will be presented and discussed.

Depressive disorders

Depression is a very prevalent condition and prevents many people from fulfilling their potential (Herrman et al., 2018). Multiple factors are thought to play a role in the causality of depressive disorders as a result of an interaction between vulnerable and resilient neurobiological and psychosocial characteristics (Southwick & Charney, 2012). Nevertheless, despite all the advances in psychiatric research, most people with major depression experience a course with recurrent episodes (Hardeveld, Spijker, De Graaf, Nolen, & Beekman, 2009). Furthermore, around 12% of patients present a chronic unremitting course (Cleare et al., 2015). Nearly 35% of patients experience recurrent thoughts of death or suicide ideation, and around 13% may report a lifetime suicide attempt, with serious implications to mental health (Hasin et al., 2018). Antidepressants, and other available treatments, represent very useful and effective treatment strategies for MDD (Cipriani et al., 2018; Ijaz et al., 2018). However, further strategies and renewed interventions are needed to increase full recovery and to prevent relapses and other complications (Cleare et al., 2015).

Spirituality/religion and depressive disorders

In the last decades, an increased number of scientific publications emerged, attempting to understand the relationship between S/R and depressive episodes and how S/R might contribute in the treatment of depression.

In a systematic review, 67% of 178 methodologically most rigorous studies found inverse associations between S/R and depression, while 7% of such studies found positive associations (Bonelli, Dew, Koenig, Rosmarin, & Vasegh, 2012). The comprehensive review of the Handbook of Religion and Health in the first and the second editions identified 443 published studies examining the relationship between S/R and depression prior to 2012. The overall quality of studies, ranging from 1 to 10, averaged 6.4 across studies, with 47% of publications being defined as high-quality studies (rating of 7 or higher). Generally, more religiousness was associated with less depression in 58% of studies, more depression in 7%, mixed findings in 11%, and no association in 22%. Strictly evaluating the high-quality studies, including 148 publications, higher religious involvement was associated with less depression in 68% of studies (Koenig et al., 2012). The complexity of the relationships between S/R and depression confirms the fact that spirituality or religiosity is not a single construct or measure, but rather a multidimensional construct with different domains (Pargament & Lomax, 2013). These multiple aspects of patients' S/R can have different impacts on depression (Moreira-Almeida, Neto, & Koenig, 2006).

A metanalysis investigating 147 studies on S/R and depression involving 98,975 individuals found a predominantly inverse correlation between religiosity and depression. The magnitude of association was consistent through gender, age, and ethnicity and the protective effect size was higher among people under severe life stress (e.g., recent divorce or being the victim of a crime). However, extrinsic religiousness and negative religious coping were associated with more depressive symptoms (Smith, McCullough, & Poll, 2003).

A few studies investigated the impact of S/R in recovery of depressive symptoms. They have found positive effects in different clinical settings. Higher intrinsic religiosity predicted faster remission of depressive symptoms in 87 medically ill elderly patients after hospital discharge in the US (Koenig, George, & Peterson, 1998). In another study in Brazil, in a sample of 143 severely depressed inpatients prospectively evaluated from admission to discharge in a psychiatric care unit, intrinsic religiosity was associated with a higher improvement of depressive symptoms, fewer suicide attempts, and higher reported resilience, social support and quality of life (Mosqueiro, da Rocha, & Fleck, 2015).

S/R also presents a significant protective effect to incident depression. Among high-risk individuals for depression, those who reported a high S/R importance presented one-tenth the risk of having a depressive episode during the ten-year follow-up (Miller et al., 2012). In a recent very well designed longitudinal study, involving 48,984 women, higher frequency of religious service attendance decreased the risk of incidence of depression over up to 12 years of follow-up by about 30% (Li, Okereke, Chang, Kawachi, & VanderWeele, 2016). In the same cohort, evaluating 89,708 women, weekly religious attendance also predicted seven times lower suicide deaths over a 14-year follow-up compared to those who never attended (VanderWeele, Li, Tsai, & Kawachi, 2016).

Impact of spirituality/religion on depression

Numerous studies have found an inverse association between S/R and depression. However, the mechanisms by which S/R impact depressive symptoms and personal well-being are still poorly understood. Several mediators postulated to explain the effects of S/R on depression are discussed below.

Religious coping

Religious coping is one of the strongest and most studied potential mediators of the impact of S/R on mental health outcomes (see Table 1.1). We performed a brief systematic review of studies in the PubMed database to evaluate the impact of positive and negative religious coping strategies in depressive symptoms or MDD. Potential eligible articles in the PubMed database from inception to November 2018 that evaluated positive and negative religious coping and depressive symptoms as outcomes were evaluated. For the purpose of this chapter, a general search was conducted with the terms "religious coping" and "depression." From the 133 potential articles yielded in the search, 48 were selected after a comprehensive evaluation. Religious coping studies evaluating depression as an outcome were identified in 10 different countries, covering different regions and cultures worldwide (Brazil, Chile, England, India, Iran, Malaysia, Netherlands, Nigeria, Pakistan, Tanzania). A diversity of populations was studied, from community and clinical samples, adolescents, and elderly and from different settings (oncology, psychiatry, primary care, HIV/AIDS, rheumatology, cardiology, surgery, health professionals, students, trauma survivors, and prisoners). Most studies (72%) performed multivariate analysis; 77% were cross-sectional studies; and 33% were longitudinal studies. Negative religious coping strategies were the most correlated to depressive symptoms, being positively correlated with greater depression in 89% of studies. However, positive religious coping strategies were inversely correlated to depression in 37% of studies and presented no association in 62% of studies. A metanalysis, with 13,512 individuals across 47 studies, supported the significant effects of religious coping in mental health and depression. The majority of patients who turned to religious coping resources predominantly presented positive outcomes and benefits (Ano & Vasconcelles, 2005).

Although positive religious coping strategies are usually much more commonly used than negative ones, they seem to have a stronger impact

Table 1.1 Positive and negative religious coping strategies.

To find meaning
(P) Benevolent religious reappraisal (redefining the stressor as benevolent and beneficial through religion)
(N) Punishing God reappraisal (redefining the stressor as punishing from God, sin)
(N) Demonic reappraisal (redefining the stressor as an act of Devil)
(N) Reappraisal of God's power (redefining beliefs in God's power, not sufficient in face of stressful events)
To gain control
(P) Collaborative religious coping (problem solving partnership with God)
(P) Active religious surrender (active giving up control to God)
(N) Passive religious deferral (passive waiting for God to solve situation)
(N) Pleading for direct intercession (waiting for a miracle or direct divine intervention)
(N) Self-directing religious coping (search control individually rather than through God intervention)
To gain comfort and closeness to god
(P) Seeking spiritual support (comfort and reassurance through God's love and care)
(P) Religious focus (engage in religious activities to shift from problems)
(P) Religious purification (search for religious actions to spiritual cleansing)
(P) Spiritual connection (search for a sense of connection with transcendent forces)
(N) Spiritual discontent (confusion and dissatisfaction with God in stressful situations)
(N) Marking religious boundaries (demark strict right/wrong or acceptable/unacceptable religious behaviors)
To Achieve intimacy with others and closeness to God
(P) Seeking Support from Clergy or Members (comfort and reassurance through love and care in religious members)
(P) Religious Helping (Provide spiritual support and comfort to others)
(N) Interpersonal Religious Discontent (confusion and dissatisfaction with clergy/religion members in stressful situations)
To achieve a life transformation
(P) Seeking a Religious Direction (assistance in finding new direction when needed)
(P) Religious Conversion (search for a religion to a radical change in life)
(P) Religious Forgiving (religious support to achieve a state of peace from an offense feelings of anger, hurt and fear)

Notes: P, positive religious coping strategies; *N*, negative religious coping strategies.
Source: Adapted from Brief RCOPE instrument. Pargament, K., Feuille, M., & Burdzy, D. (2011). The Brief RCOPE: Current psychometric status of a short measure of religious coping. *Religions*, *2*(1), 51–76. Available from https://doi.org/10.3390/rel2010051; Pargament, K. I., Koenig, H. G., Tarakeshwar, N., & Hahn, J. (2004). Religious coping methods as predictors of psychological, physical and spiritual outcomes among medically ill elderly patients: A two-year longitudinal study. *Journal of Health Psychology*, *9*(6), 713–730. Available from https://doi.org/10.1177/1359105304045366.

on depressive disorders. Alternatively, negative religious coping may just be a transient adaptive strategy to stressful situations. The main source of concern is probably persistent negative religious coping (see Table 1.2). One important clinical target may be to help patients find more adaptive coping resources, replacing negative for positive religious coping strategies.

Spirituality/religion social support

Social support is a mediator often proposed to explain the relation between S/R and health, since religious involvement is often social in nature. However, evidence has varied (George, Ellison, & Larson, 2002). Although S/R is usually associated with increased levels of general social support, it has often failed in tests for mediation of S/R and depression relationships (Corrêa, Moreira-Almeida, Menezes, Vallada, & Scazufca, 2011; Koenig et al., 1997; Mosqueiro et al., 2015). One possible explanation is that S/R social support (e.g., church-based social support such as worshiping together and sharing values and beliefs), as opposed to secular ones, may be an important specific mediator that differs from secular forms of social support (Krause, 2017). Congregation-based support and greater clergy-based support were associated with fewer reported depressive symptoms in African-American cocaine users in the United States (Montgomery, Stewart, Bryant, & Ounpraseuth, 2014). Religiosity and social support independently led to fewer depressive symptoms in a sample of HIV patients (Kudel, Cotton, Szaflarski, Holmes, & Tsevat, 2011). In summary, the benefits of S/R in depressive disorders cannot be explained exclusively by social support. However, religious support is usually a source of comfort to patients and should therefore be thoroughly considered in clinical practice (Cipriani et al., 2018; Vicente, Castro-Costa, Firmo, Lima-Costa, & Loyola Filho, 2018).

Religious/spiritual worldviews and sense of coherence

Religious and spiritual beliefs may provide a worldview or cognitive framework that may be protective to mental health and depressive disorders (Koenig et al., 1998). Religious involvement can prevent the onset of depression by helping individuals deal with precipitating stressors or, if depression sets in, S/R can facilitate faster adaptation to underlying stressors and thus speed recovery from a depressive disorder (Koenig et al., 2012). S/R beliefs could also be related to the "sense of coherence" (SC), a dispositional way of perceiving and dealing with stressful life events which includes

Table 1.2 PubMed database systematic review about religious coping and depression.

	Study	Year	Country	Sample	+ RCOPE	− RCOPE	Design	Analysis
1	Garcia, FE	2018	Chile	244 work accident	NA	+ dep	6-month L	Regression
2	Vitorino, L	2017	Brazil	160 pregnant women	NA	+ dep	CS	Regression
3	Vitorino, L	2018	Brazil	98 caregivers older adults	NA	+ dep	CS	Regression
4	Santos, PR	2017	Brazil	161 end-stage renal disease	− dep	+ dep	CS	Regression
5	Grover, S	2016	India	109 self-harm	− dep	+ dep	CS	Correlation
6	Shariff, S	2018	Iran	482 cancer hospital	− dep	+ dep	CS	Regression
7	Ng, GC	2017	Malaysia	200 cancer hospital	NA	+ dep	CS	Regression
8	Amadi, K U	2015	Nigeria	224 outpatients DM, MDD	NA	+ dep	CS	Correlation
9	Roberts, L R	2016	United States	350 community Sikh immigrants	NA	+ dep	CS	Regression
10	Freitas, TH	2015	Brazil	147 inflammatory bowel disease	− dep	+ dep	CS	Regression
11	Rahnama, P	2015	Iran	213 spinal cord injury	NA	+ dep	CS	Regression
12	Brewer, G	2014	United Kingdom	256 community religious events	NA	NA	CS	Regression
13	Henslee, AM	2015	United States	810 community Hurricane Katrina	− dep	+ dep	CS	Regression
14	Watt, M	2015	Tanzania	54 women obstetric fistula	NA	+ dep	CS	Regression
15	Rathier, LA	2015	United States	191 caregivers dementia	− dep	+ dep	CS	Regression
16	Reynolds, N	2014	United States	128 adolescents chronic illness	− dep	NA	2-year L	Regression
17	Montgomery, B	2014	United States	223 African-American cocaine users	NA	+ dep	CS	Correlation
18	Dalmida, SG	2013	United States	292 HIV/AIDS patients	− dep	+ dep	CS	Regression
19	Lee, M	2014	United States	198 AIDS patients	NA	+ dep	CS	Regression
20	Rosmarin, DH	2014	United States	34 geriatric mood disorder patients	NA	+ dep	CS	Regression
21	Fernandez A	2014	United States	247 Mexican-American students	− dep	+ dep	CS	Regression
22	Haghighi, F	2013	Iran	150 cancer hospital patients	− dep	+ dep	CS	Correlation
23	Braam, AW	2014	The Netherlands	343 depressive older patients	NA	+ dep	12-year L	Regression
24	Johansson, G	2013	United States	17 African-American women breast cancer	NA	+ dep	CS	Correlation
25	Feder, A	2013	Pakistan	200 community earthquake survivors	NA	+ dep	CS	Regression
26	Allen, RS	2013	United States	94 older prisoners	− dep	+ dep	CS	Regression

27	Thuné-Boyle, IC	2013	United Kingdom	155 breast newly diagnosed cancer women	NA	+ dep	CS	Regression
28	Ramirez, SP	2012	Brazil	170 end-stage renal disease	NA	+ dep	CS	Regression
29	Park, CL	2012	United States	202 congestive heart failure patients	NA	NA	6-month L	Regression
30	Rand KL	2012	United States	86 men advanced cancer	− dep	+ dep	CS	Regression
31	Pirutinsky S	2011	United States	80 orthodox Jews	-	+ dep	2-week L	Regression
32	Park CL	2012	United States	56 acute myocardical infarction patients	− dep	+ dep	4-week L	Regression
33	Sternthal, MJ	2010	United States	3150 community Chicago adults	NA	+ dep	CS	Regression
34	Braam, AW	2010	The Netherlands	776 individuals different ethnic groups	− dep	+ dep	CS	Regression
35	Ahrens, CE	2010	United States	100 sexual assault survivors women	− dep	+ dep	CS	Regression
36	Herbert, R	2009	United States	284 breast cancer women	NA	+ dep	8- to 12-month L	Regression
37	Herrera, AP	2009	United States	66 Mexican-American caregivers older relatives	NA	+ dep	CS	Regression
38	Sherman, AC	2008	United States	94 myeloma transplantation patients	NA	+ dep	3- to 4-month L	Regression
39	Trevino, KM	2010	United States	429 HIV/AIDS patients	NA	+ dep	12- to 18-month L	Regression
40	Desrosiers, A	2007	United States	615 community adolescents	− dep	–	CS	Regression
41	Yi, MS	2006	United States	450 HIV/AIDS patients	NA	NA	CS	Regression
42	McConnel, KM	2006	United States	1629 individuals national sample	NA	+ dep	CS	Regression
43	Yi, MS	2006	United States	227 primary care medical residents	NA	+ dep	CS	Regression
44	Sherman, AC	2005	United States	213 multiple myeloma patients	NA	+ dep	CS	Regression
45	Wilvliet, CV	2004	United States	213 help-seeking veterans with PTSD	NA	+ dep	CS	Regression
46	VanderCreek, L	2004	United States	181 rheumatoid arthritis	NA	+ dep	CS	Regression
47	Bosworth, HB	2003	United States	114 depressed elderly patients	− dep	NA	6-month L	Regression
48	Koenig, H	1998	United States	577 hospitalized older patients	NA	+ dep	CS	Regression

CS, Cross-sectional design; *− dep*, less depression; *+ dep*, more depression; *L*, longitudinal design; *NA*, no association.

cognitive, behavioral, and motivational aspects. The literature reports that religiosity is inversely associated with depressive symptoms and that SC is a recognized mediator of effect in some populations (Anyfantakis et al., 2015).

Relational spirituality

The relational spirituality framework comprises different definitions and theoretical orientations (Tomlinson, Glenn, Paine, & Sandage, 2016). One of its most studied concepts is based on attachment styles and evaluates the way an individual develops a relationship to the sacred, God or spirituality. For instance, "insecure attachment to God" predicted higher levels of depression in US students, and disappointment with God was a mediator of this relationship (Paine & Sandage, 2016). A stronger "relationship with God" predicted fewer depressive and anxiety symptoms in North Ireland adolescents (Goeke-Morey, Taylor, Merrilees, Shirlow, & Cummings, 2014), and a "loving relationship with God" was a strong predictor of lower depressed affect in 205 primary care patients, controlling for multiple social and health measures (Levin, 2002).

Spirituality/religion and positive psychology

Another promising approach to understand how S/R beliefs and practices may impact mood disorders is the positive mental health measures (Jeste, Palmer, Rettew, & Boardman, 2015). S/R may be directly correlated with positive emotions and characteristics, such as awe, love, trust/faith, compassion, gratitude, forgiveness, and hope, that could positively impact mood disorders (Cloninger, 2006; Vaillant, 2013). Higher religious involvement was associated with purpose, optimism, generosity and gratefulness in chronic medically ill-depressed patients (Koenig et al., 2014). Religiosity is also positively correlated with posttraumatic growth in people undergoing stressful events (Jeon, Park, & Bernstein, 2017) and resilience in depressed patients (Southwick & Charney, 2012).

Spirituality/religion can promote healthy behaviors

Religiously affiliated people are also more likely to adopt healthy behaviors that can impact mood disorders (Krause, Hill, Emmons, Pargament, & Ironson, 2016). Research indicates that encouragement from religious groups could play a role in decisions to lead a healthy lifestyle (Hill, Ellison, Burdette, & Musick, 2007). Regular exercise, for instance, has a defined protective factor to incident depression and promotes a better recovery from depressive symptoms (Schuch et al., 2018). Previous studies identified that religious people may be more likely to engage in physical activities (Kim & Sobal, 2004); however, inverse findings were also identified in other studies (Krause et al., 2016). S/R may influence other healthy behaviors that recognizably impact mood disorders, such as healthier sleep routines (Krause et al., 2016) or lower alcohol and drug abuse (Moreira-Almeida et al., 2006), which are clearly associated with worse outcomes in MDD and BD (Yatham et al., 2018).

Consistent adherence to psychiatric treatments, such as antidepressants and mood stabilizers, represents another important condition to long-term outcomes in mood disorders. To the best of our knowledge, no previous study evaluated the impact of S/R in the use of medications in MDD or BD. In a sample of black women in the United States, S/R beliefs contributed to adherence to other continuous medications such as antihypertensives (Abel, Joyner, Cornelius, & Greer, 2017). Additionally, negative religious coping was associated with lower adherence to treatment in Brazilian inflammatory bowel disease patients (Freitas et al., 2015).

Private spirituality/religion practices

Recent studies reported the benefits of meditation, mindfulness, and self-compassion practices to depressive symptoms and stress (Snaith, Schultz, Proeve, & Rasmussen, 2018). A systematic review reported that private prayer frequency was associated with lower depression. Nonetheless, most studies in prayer and MDD were cross-sectional and observational and conclusive data is limited (Anderson & Nunnelley, 2016). Some cross-sectional studies have found direct associations between private religious practices, such as prayer, and worse mental and physical health (Koenig et al., 2012). However, it is necessary to be careful in assessing these associations, since they probably reflect a turning to religion during stressful situations or when there are physical impairments that may prevent attendance to public religious meetings.

Neurobiological correlates of spirituality/religion and depression

Several studies have tried to identify biological correlates for S/R experiences and how they relate to mental disorders. Functional neuroimaging studies of healthy adults revealed that the intensity of self-evoked religious experiences was associated with increased blood flow in several subregions of the prefrontal and parietal cortex (Azari et al., 2001). Other data points to bilateral increased blood flow in the frontal cortex, cingulate gyros, and thalamus and reduced blood flow in the upper part of the parietal cortex (responsible for body representation) during prayer and religious meditation (Newberg, 2006).

A recent retrospective cohort study, with a sample of 103 adults, found that attributing higher importance to S/R was associated with thicker cortices at the superior parietal and occipital brain regions. Thickness in these regions was inversely correlated to depressive symptoms, especially among subjects with a high risk for depression (Miller et al., 2014). Additionally, higher S/R importance predicted decreased default mode network (DMN) connectivity in the depression high-risk group in the same cohort. Higher DMN connectivity was positively associated with depressive symptoms, suggesting neurobiological pathways that could mediate the protective effect of S/R (Svob, Wang, Weissman, Wickramaratne, & Posner, 2016).

If prayer and other religious practices, such as meditation, activate various areas of the brain, including frontal lobe structures, this activation may help regulate the immune system and the autonomic nervous system (with decreased blood pressure, heart rate, and levels of cortisol) (Seybold, 2007). Considering the well-known long-term cardiovascular, metabolic, and immunological effects, religious practices that improve the body's responses to stress may have positive effects on health and mood disorders (Seybold, 2007).

Authors raised a hypothesis that higher importance to S/R might also form a pattern of kindling with protective effects against depression (Kendler, Thornton, & Gardner, 2001; Miller et al., 2012). Developmental psychopathology studies showed that increases in genetic heritable contribution of personal religiosity were associated concomitantly with a decreased risk of MDD (Miller et al., 2012).

Negative effects of spirituality/religion and depression

Despite the predominant positive aspects of S/R, there is a growing body of research demonstrating that there is also a downside to this relationship with health and that religion can be a major source of stress for many people (view Table 1.3). A systematic review indicated that, in up to 11% of studies, religiosity may be associated with more depression (Bonelli et al., 2012). For some individuals, S/R could be connected to or hide unresolved psychological conflict (Exline & Rose, 2013).

Table 1.3 *"Red Flags"* in the relationship of religiosity and mental health.

Self-neglect
(e.g., decide to devote all time to religion, sacrifice all interests, realize that the World is not important, stop taking care of self, and focus only in God)
Self-worship
(e.g., decide to turn away from God and live alone, nothing accounts in the world, no longer worry about morality, focus only on personal pleasures)
Religious apathy
(e.g., lost in interest in God, other people, self, life is pointless, stop caring about what happens)
God's punishment
(e.g., lack of spirituality was responsible for an event, expectative of punishment for bad thoughts and actions, interpretation of an event as a message from God telling about a failure)
Religious passivity
(e.g., surrender to God since nothing personal can make a difference, wait for a sign of God to take a decision, let the Church handle a situation, feeling of total helplessness without God)
Religious vengeance
(e.g., realize or pray for God to punish the true sinners, ask God to make others hurt, believe that God will have his vengeance on those who sin)
Religious denial
(e.g., refuse to feel bad, bothered, or upset because of faith teachings or God will or plans)
Interpersonal religious conflicts
(e.g., argue with family or friends about religion or faith, feel that the Church did not support in time of need or angry with church members)
Conflicts with church dogma
(e.g., disagreement with clergy about faith, God, religion, the way to handle specific situations or the views of Church about personal events)
Anger at God
(e.g., angry with God concerning bad events, for God not hear personal prayer, or letting something happen)
Religious doubt
(e.g., questions about whether God exists, about faith, religion, beliefs, difficulty gaining comfort)

Source: Adapted from Pargament, K. I., Zinnbauer, B. J., Scott, A. B., Butter, E. M., Zerowin, J., & Stanik, P. (1998). Red flags and religious coping: Identifying some religious warning signs among people in crisis. *Journal of Clinical Psychology*, *54*, 77–89. doi:CCC0021-9762/98/010077-13.

The concept of spiritual struggle can be defined as any dysfunctional religious or spiritual belief that is capable of generating or exacerbating suffering (Rosmarin, Malloy, & Forester, 2014). The definition of spiritual struggle encompasses three major types of areas involving: supernatural agents (the divine, the evil, the demonic), interpersonal conflicts with S/R institutions, and intrapersonal conflicts involving internal questions about the sacred, moral concerns, doubts about S/R and perception of the lack of meaning of life (Pargament, Murray-Swank, Magyar, & Ano, 2005). Thus, spiritual struggle may include anger toward God (Exline, Park, Smyth, & Carey, 2011), religious guilt, belief that God is malicious (Rosmarin, Pargament, & Mahoney, 2009) and fear of retribution (Pargament, Koenig, & Perez, 2000). This construct is also commonly referred to as "negative religious coping" (Pargament et al., 2005).

Negative psychological outcomes associated with S/R may be related to spiritual struggle, lack of understanding of spiritual experiences and negative religious beliefs (Weber & Pargament, 2014). Spiritual struggles usually arise in response to psychosocial stressors, constituting an important risk factor for mental disorders, notably depression and suicide (Ironson et al., 2011). For example, some moral remarks of religion may contribute to a pathological sense of guilt and, consequently, predispose to depression (Bonelli & Koenig, 2013). Religious struggles are strongly associated with depression (Rosmarin et al., 2014) and are negatively associated with happiness (Abu-Raiya, Pargament, & Krause, 2015). The correlation of negative religious coping to depression is not restricted to a religious denomination and has been identified across different ethnic groups (Braam et al., 2010).

This dual nature of the effects of religion on mental health demands increased awareness of religious issues by mental health professionals, as well as increased psychiatric research on this subject (Weber & Pargament, 2014). The identification of S/R variables that moderate the impact of spiritual struggles could lead to the development of programs that assist people experiencing periods of spiritual difficulties in their lives (Abu-Raiya et al., 2015).

Bipolar disorders

Bipolar Disordered patients usually present with significant functional impairments and repeated mood episodes, sometimes leading to cognitive impairments and clinical deterioration even after remission of acute symptoms. Behavioral and psychosocial experiences that help promote recovery, including improvements of symptoms, functionality and quality of life, are undoubtedly very important to management of BD (Yatham et al., 2018).

Spirituality/religion and bipolar disorders

Understanding how S/R are related to bipolar disorder (BD) symptoms represents a key challenge to clinical practice. Clinical psychiatry textbooks often report that S/R experiences can be commonly identified in BD episodes; however, there have been few high-quality empirical studies that evaluated this information (Stroppa & Moreira-Almeida, 2009). S/R is very prevalent among BD patients in different cultures and is also a common source of coping (Stroppa, Colugnati, Koenig, & Moreira-Almeida, 2018). Not only may S/R impact BD, but the experience of having BD may also impact S/R. A study in New Zealand found that two fifths of 81 BD patients reported that their mental illness resulted in a decrease in their faith (Mitchell & Romans, 2003). Alternatively, a study reported an increase of intrinsic religiosity and positive religious coping among 158 Brazilian bipolar patients over 2 years of treatment (Stroppa et al., 2018).

A few studies evaluated the impact of S/R beliefs and practices in BD outcomes. A US study found an association of higher rates of private religious practices in BD patients with mixed mood symptoms; however, as a cross-sectional study, it was not possible to assess whether private religious activity (such as prayer or meditation) caused the symptoms, were consequences of BD psychopathology or if they were coping strategies to deal with BD symptoms (Cruz et al., 2010). A relevant minority of BD patients (around one quarter) reported religious disagreement with psychiatric treatment in New Zealand (Mitchell & Romans, 2003) and in Brazil (Stroppa & Moreira-Almeida, 2013). In a study of 185 euthymic patients from India, positive religious coping and private religious practices were positively associated with recovery from BD (Grover et al., 2016).

Two Brazilian studies found positive and negative associations between S/R and relevant BD outcomes such as depression, quality of life, and suicidal behavior. Among 164 BD euthymic outpatients, private religious activities and intrinsic religiosity were both inversely correlated with a history of suicide attempts, even after controlling for several sociodemographic and clinical variables (Caribe et al., 2015). A cross-sectional analysis of 168 BD outpatients found that high levels of intrinsic religiosity and positive religious coping were associated with four to five lower rates of depression (Stroppa & Moreira-Almeida, 2013). At the 2-year follow-up, in a mainly euthymic sample, positive religious coping strongly predicted higher quality of life across all domains. Alternatively, negative religious coping, although less frequent than the positive coping, was a stronger predictor of poor quality of life in patients with Bipolar Disorder. The significant impact of S/R over quality of life in euthymic BD patients suggests that S/R might play an important role in a full mental health recovery process for many BD patients (Stroppa et al., 2018).

In summary, the limited available evidence suggests that S/R is a frequent coping strategy among BD patients, most commonly with positive impacts on several aspects, ranging from suicide to quality of life. However, although less frequent, negative religious coping and religious opposition to treatment pose some challenges to be addressed regarding S/R in BD.

Clinical practice

Assessment of spirituality/religion in mood disorders

Given the previously reported relationships between S/R and mental health, different professional associations, such as the WPA, the American Psychological Association, the American Psychiatric Association, and the Royal College of Psychiatrists, have sections dedicated to S/R. However, applying research results to clinical practice is always a challenge (Moreira-Almeida, Koenig, & Lucchetti, 2014). In 2016, the WPA published a Position Statement, recommending that the taking of spiritual history should be an essential component of the assessment in order to understand the S/R beliefs and practices of the patients (Moreira-Almeida et al., 2016). Most doctors have not included this subject in clinical practice, and most patients still do not have their spiritual needs detected. Many reasons might explain the religious and spiritual neglect by mental health professionals, such as a lack of knowledge about available evidence and the treatment gap in how to deal with S/R in clinical practice (Moreira-Almeida et al., 2014).

Some practical guidelines on the integration of S/R in the treatment of patients with mental disorders are suggested: show genuine interest and respect to the S/R beliefs and values of the patients, take a patient-centered approach, not imposing spiritual and antispiritual visions, and to consider that the spiritual or secular beliefs and values of professionals can influence clinical practice (Moreira-Almeida et al., 2014). A few symptoms of mood disorders could overlap with S/R and should be carefully evaluated. An increased focus on S/R content and religious delusions can be identified in individuals with BD experiencing an acute manic episode.

Depressed mood or sadness and feelings of guilt may have a connection to S/R beliefs or struggles. Otherwise, additional symptoms of mood disorders would not be expected regardless of patient's S/R, including a persistent euphoric or irritable mood, increased energy, agitation and decreased need for sleep in BD or a markedly diminished interest or pleasure, feelings of worthlessness, suicidal thoughts, loss of energy, changes in sleep, appetite, concentration or psychomotor disturbances in MDD. Incidentally, the emergence of sacred or spiritual experiences for many people could be a source of meaning, growth, and healing but are not uncommonly preceded or followed by feelings of distress, anxiety, and sadness. Sometimes patients could be reluctant to discuss these experiences since they can be concerned about criticisms or that it could not be well understood or appropriate. Mental health professionals should be aware and well trained to identify these S/R issues and sensitively address them in clinical practice and psychotherapy (Lomax, Kripal, & Pargament, 2011).

Integrating spirituality/religion in treatment for mood disorders

Many studies have demonstrated benefits when S/R are appropriately incorporated into mental health assessment and treatment (Weber & Pargament, 2014). A systematic metaanalysis of randomized clinical trials (RCTs) to assess the impact of S/R interventions, including psychotherapy based on S/R issues, meditation and pastoral services, such as prayers, showed a significant reduction in anxiety levels and a tendency to improve depression (Gonçalves, Lucchetti, Menezes, & Vallada, 2015). Another systematic review of nine RCTs and one quasiexperimental study compared the efficacy of religiously modified cognitive behavioral therapy (CBT) to standard CBT or other treatments for depressive disorders, generalized anxiety disorder, and schizophrenia. Most of the studies found no differences in efficacy, so the fusion of religious content with CBT may be an acceptable treatment modality for religious individuals (Lim, Sim, Renjan, Sam, & Quah, 2014).

A metaanalysis of 97 studies with 7181 patients examined the efficacy of psychotherapy adaptation to S/R beliefs and values compared to untreated controls and conventional treatments. Psychotherapy with S/R influence was equally effective, compared to other approaches, in reducing psychological distress and resulted in greater spiritual well-being (Captari et al., 2018). Regarding S/R and depression, one study evaluated the accessibility and effectiveness of two interventions delivered over the Internet: conventional CBT and religious-based CBT. A total of 79 patients were randomly assigned to active treatment or control group waiting list and self-reported measures of depression, anxiety, and quality of life were collected before, immediately after and 6 months after the intervention. There were no differences between the conventional and religious-based forms. However, the addition of religious components to CBT contributed to initial adherence to treatment for religious participants, increasing treatment accessibility (Tulbure, Andersson, Salagean, Pearce, & Koenig, 2018).

Another systematic review with metaanalysis evaluated the efficacy of psychological therapies for depression or anxiety with faith-based adaptations, choosing 16 studies using traditional or faith-adapted cognitive and behavioral models. There seems to be a suggestion that CBT adapted to the faith could overcome standard CBT and control conditions (waiting list or usual treatment) (Anderson et al., 2015). A study compared religiously integrated CBT (RCBT) with conventional CBT (CCBT) in increasing daily spiritual experiences (DSE) in depressive disorder and chronic medical illness. A total of 132 patients aged 18–85 years were randomized to RCBT ($n = 65$) or CCBT ($n = 67$). Participants received 10 sessions of 50 minutes each (mostly by telephone) for 12 weeks. RCBT tended to be more effective than CCBT in increasing DSE, especially in those with low religiousness. A higher initial DSE predicted a decrease in depressive symptoms, independent of the treatment group, and an increase in SDS with treatment was correlated with a decrease in depressive symptoms (Koenig, Pearce, Nelson, & Erkanli, 2016).

RCBT is based on the cognitive model as it contextualizes interventions within the patient's religious structure. The psychotherapist makes use of the patient's own S/R as an important basis for identifying distorted thoughts and behaviors to reduce depressive symptoms. Some of the key RCBT tools include (Captari et al., 2018):

1. Renewing the minds of patients by replacing negative speech with positive messages from the sacred scriptures.
2. Meditate on sacred texts and participate in contemplative prayer.
3. Consider religious beliefs and resources.
4. Cultivate forgiveness, hope, gratitude, and generosity through daily religious practices.
5. Identify S/R resources according to the patient's faith tradition.
6. Altruistic involvement in the religious community.

S/R could also be integrated in interpersonal psychotherapy (IPT), a time-limited, structured and evidence-based psychotherapy for MDD. IPT aims to help patients to solve interpersonal crisis, reduce symptoms, deal with interpersonal effects of depression, improve communication skills, and increase social support (Cuijpers, Donker, Weissman, Ravitz, & Cristea, 2016). S/R would also work as a resource to deal with different interpersonal problems (grief, role disputes, role transitions, and interpersonal deficits), improving social support and depressive symptoms (Mastropieri, Schussel, Forbes, & Miller, 2015).

Discussion

S/R represent a relevant aspect to assessment, treatment, and prevention of mood disorders. Studies in BD patients identify that S/R place a great deal of importance in disease recovery and promotion of well-being and quality of life. Mental health professionals should be aware of potential religious struggles or eventual disagreements between religious beliefs. Spirituality-integrated psychotherapies are promising strategies to improve recovery and prevention of mood disorders.

References

Abel, W. M., Joyner, J., Cornelius, J., & Greer, D. B. (2017). Self-care management strategies used by Black women who self-report consistent adherence to antihypertensive medication. *Patient Preference and Adherence*, *11*, 1401–1412. Available from https://doi.org/10.2147/ppa.S138162.

Abu-Raiya, H., Pargament, K. I., & Krause, N. (2015). Religion as problem, religion as solution: Religious buffers of the links between religious/spiritual struggles and well-being/mental health. *Quality of Life Research*, *25*(5), 1265–1274. Available from https://doi.org/10.1007/s11136-015-1163-8.

Anderson, J. W., & Nunnelley, P. A. (2016). Private prayer associations with depression, anxiety and other health conditions: An analytical review of clinical studies. *Postgraduate Medicine*, *128*(7), 635–641. Available from https://doi.org/10.1080/00325481.2016.1209962.

Anderson, N., Heywood-Everett, S., Siddiqi, N., Wright, J., Meredith, J., & McMillan, D. (2015). Faith-adapted psychological therapies for depression and anxiety: Systematic review and meta-analysis. *Journal of Affective Disorders*, *176*, 183–196. Available from https://doi.org/10.1016/j.jad.2015.01.019.

Ano, G. G., & Vasconcelles, E. B. (2005). Religious coping and psychological adjustment to stress: A meta-analysis. *Journal of Clinical Psychology*, *61*(4), 461–480. Available from https://doi.org/10.1002/jclp.20049.

Anyfantakis, D., Symvoulakis, E. K., Linardakis, M., Shea, S., Panagiotakos, D., & Lionis, C. (2015). Effect of religiosity/spirituality and sense of coherence on depression within a rural population in Greece: The Spili III project. *BMC Psychiatry*, *15*, 173. Available from https://doi.org/10.1186/s12888-015-0561-3.

Azari, N. P., Nickel, J., Wunderlich, G., Niedeggen, M., Hefter, H., Tellmann, L., ... Seitz, R. J. (2001). Neural correlates of religious experience. *European Journal of Neuroscience*, *13*(8), 1649–1652. Available from https://doi.org/10.1046/j.0953-816x.2001.01527.x.

Bonelli, R., Dew, R. E., Koenig, H. G., Rosmarin, D. H., & Vasegh, S. (2012). Religious and spiritual factors in depression: Review and integration of the research. *Depression Research and Treatment*, *2012*, 1–8. Available from https://doi.org/10.1155/2012/962860.

Bonelli, R. M., & Koenig, H. G. (2013). Mental disorders, religion and spirituality 1990 to 2010: A systematic evidence-based review. *Journal of Religion and Health*, *52*(2), 657–673. Available from https://doi.org/10.1007/s10943-013-9691-4.

Braam, A. W., Schrier, A. C., Tuinebreijer, W. C., Beekman, A. T., Dekker, J. J., & de Wit, M. A. (2010). Religious coping and depression in multicultural Amsterdam: A comparison between native Dutch citizens and Turkish, Moroccan and Surinamese/Antillean migrants. *Journal of Affective Disorders*, *125*(1–3), 269–278. Available from https://doi.org/10.1016/j.jad.2010.02.116.

Captari, L. E., Hook, J. N., Hoyt, W., Davis, D. E., McElroy-Heltzel, S. E., & Worthington, E. L., Jr. (2018). Integrating clients' religion and spirituality within psychotherapy: A comprehensive meta-analysis. *Journal of Clinical Psychology*, *74*(11), 1938–1951. Available from https://doi.org/10.1002/jclp.22681.

Caribe, A. C., Studart, P., Bezerra-Filho, S., Brietzke, E., Nunes Noto, M., Vianna-Sulzbach, M., ... Miranda-Scippa, A. (2015). Is religiosity a protective factor against suicidal behavior in bipolar I outpatients? *Journal of Affective Disorders*, *186*, 156–161. Available from https://doi.org/10.1016/j.jad.2015.07.024.

Cipriani, A., Furukawa, T. A., Salanti, G., Chaimani, A., Atkinson, L. Z., Ogawa, Y., ... Geddes, J. R. (2018). Comparative efficacy and acceptability of 21 antidepressant drugs for the acute treatment of adults with major depressive disorder: A systematic review and network meta-analysis. *The Lancet*, *391*(10128), 1357–1366. Available from https://doi.org/10.1016/s0140-6736(17)32802-7.

Cleare, A., Nutt, D. J., Blier, P., Pariante, C. M., Young, A. H., Anderson, I. M., ... Uher, R. (2015). Evidence-based guidelines for treating depressive disorders with antidepressants: A revision of the 2008 British Association for Psychopharmacology guidelines. *Journal of Psychopharmacology*, *29*(5), 459–525. Available from https://doi.org/10.1177/0269881115581093.

Cloninger, C. R. (2006). The science of well-being: An integrated approach to mental health and its disorders. *World Psychiatry*, *5*, 71–76.

Corrêa, A. A. M., Moreira-Almeida, A., Menezes, P. R., Vallada, H., & Scazufca, M. (2011). Investigating the role played by social support in the association between religiosity and mental health in low income older adults: Results from the São Paulo Ageing & Health Study (SPAH). *Brazilian Journal of Psychiatry*, *33*, 157–164.

Cruz, M., Pincus, H. A., Welsh, D. E., Greenwald, D., Lasky, E., & Kilbourne, A. M. (2010). The relationship between religious involvement and clinical status of patients with bipolar disorder. *Bipolar Disorders*, *12*(1), 68–76. Available from https://doi.org/10.1111/j.1399-5618.2009.00772.x.

Cuijpers, P., Donker, T., Weissman, M. M., Ravitz, P., & Cristea, I. A. (2016). Interpersonal psychotherapy for mental health problems: A comprehensive meta-analysis. *American Journal of Psychiatry*, *173*(7), 680–687. Available from https://doi.org/10.1176/appi.ajp.2015.15091141.

Diagnostic and Statistical Manual of Mental Disorders, 5th Edition: DSM-5 (Fifth Edition ed.): American Psychiatric Association.

Eckhart, M. (1327). The complete mystical works of meister eckhart, sermon eighty-three (2009). New York: The Crossroad Publishing Company.

Exline, J. J., Park, C. L., Smyth, J. M., & Carey, M. P. (2011). Anger toward God: Social-cognitive predictors, prevalence, and links with adjustment to bereavement and cancer. *Journal of Personality and Social Psychology*, *100*(1), 129–148. Available from https://doi.org/10.1037/a0021716.

Exline, J. J., & Rose, E. D. (2013). Religious and spiritual struggles. In R. F. P. C. L. Park (Ed.), *Handbook of the psychology of religion and spirituality* (2 ed., pp. 380–398). New York: Guilford Press.

Freitas, T. H., Hyphantis, T. N., Andreoulakis, E., Quevedo, J., Miranda, H. L., Alves, G. S., … Carvalho, A. F. (2015). Religious coping and its influence on psychological distress, medication adherence, and quality of life in inflammatory bowel disease. *Revista Brasileira de Psiquiatria*, *37*(3), 219–227. Available from https://doi.org/10.1590/1516-4446-2014-1507.

George, L. K., Ellison, C. G., & Larson, D. B. (2002). Explaining the relationships between religious involvement and health. *Psychological Inquiry*, *13*(3), 190–200. Available from https://doi.org/10.1207/s15327965pli1303_04.

Goeke-Morey, M. C., Taylor, L. K., Merrilees, C. E., Shirlow, P., & Cummings, E. M. (2014). Adolescents' relationship with God and internalizing adjustment over time: The moderating role of maternal religious coping. *Journal of Family Psychology*, *28*(6), 749–758. Available from https://doi.org/10.1037/a0037170.

Gonçalves, J. P. B., Lucchetti, G., Menezes, P. R., & Vallada, H. (2015). Religious and spiritual interventions in mental health care: A systematic review and meta-analysis of randomized controlled clinical trials. *Psychological Medicine*, *45*(14), 2937–2949. Available from https://doi.org/10.1017/s0033291715001166.

Grover, S., Hazari, N., Aneja, J., Chakrabarti, S., Sharma, S., & Avasthi, A. (2016). Recovery and its correlates among patients with bipolar disorder: A study from a tertiary care centre in North India. *International Journal of Social Psychiatry*, *62*(8), 726–736. Available from https://doi.org/10.1177/0020764016676214.

Hackett, C., Grim, B. J., Cooperman, A., Ochoa, J. C., Gao, C., Shi, A. F., … Lugo, L. (2012). The global religious landscape. A report on the size and distribution of the world's major religious groups as of 2010. *Pew Research Center*, 3–82.

Hardeveld, F., Spijker, J., De Graaf, R., Nolen, W. A., & Beekman, A. T. F. (2009). Prevalence and predictors of recurrence of major depressive disorder in the adult population. *Acta Psychiatrica Scandinavica*, *122*(3), 184–191. Available from https://doi.org/10.1111/j.1600-0447.2009.01519.x.

Hasin, D. S., Sarvet, A. L., Meyers, J. L., Saha, T. D., Ruan, W. J., Stohl, M., & Grant, B. F. (2018). Epidemiology of adult DSM-5 major depressive disorder and its specifiers in the United States. *JAMA Psychiatry*, *75*(4), 336–346. Available from https://doi.org/10.1001/jamapsychiatry.2017.4602.

Herrman, H., Kieling, C., McGorry, P., Horton, R., Sargent, J., & Patel, V. (2018). Reducing the global burden of depression: A Lancet–World Psychiatric Association Commission. *The Lancet*, *393*, e42–e43. Available from https://doi.org/10.1016/s0140-6736(18)32408-5.

Hill, T. D., Ellison, C. G., Burdette, A. M., & Musick, M. A. (2007). Religious involvement and healthy lifestyles: Evidence from the survey of Texas adults. *Annals of Behavioral Medicine*, *34*(2), 217–222. Available from https://doi.org/10.1007/BF02872676.

Ijaz, S., Davies, P., Williams, C. J., Kessler, D., Lewis, G., & Wiles, N. (2018). Psychological therapies for treatment-resistant depression in adults. *Cochrane Database of Systematic Reviews*, *5*. Available from https://doi.org/10.1002/14651858.CD010558.pub2, Cd010558.

Ironson, G., Stuetzle, R., Ironson, D., Balbin, E., Kremer, H., George, A., … Fletcher, M. A. (2011). View of God as benevolent and forgiving or punishing and judgmental predicts HIV disease progression. *Journal of Behavioral Medicine, 34*(6), 414–425. Available from https://doi.org/10.1007/s10865-011-9314-z.

Jeon, G. S., Park, S. Y., & Bernstein, K. S. (2017). Socio-demographic and psychological correlates of posttraumatic growth among Korean Americans with a history of traumatic life experiences. *Archives of Psychiatric Nursing, 31*(3), 256–262. Available from https://doi.org/10.1016/j.apnu.2016.12.002.

Jeste, D. V., Palmer, B. W., Rettew, D. C., & Boardman, S. (2015). Positive psychiatry: Its time has come. *The Journal of Clinical Psychiatry, 76*(6), 675–683. Available from https://doi.org/10.4088/JCP.14nr09599.

Kendler, K. S., Thornton, L. M., & Gardner, C. O. (2001). Genetic risk, number of previous depressive episodes, and stressful life events in predicting onset of major depression. *American Journal of Psychiatry, 158*(4), 582–586. Available from https://doi.org/10.1176/appi.ajp.158.4.582.

Kessler, R. C., & Bromet, E. J. (2013). The epidemiology of depression across cultures. *Annual Review of Public Health, 34*(1), 119–138. Available from https://doi.org/10.1146/annurev-publhealth-031912-114409.

Kim, K. H.-c, & Sobal, J. (2004). Religion, social support, fat intake and physical activity. *Public Health Nutrition, 7*(6), 773–781. Available from https://doi.org/10.1079/phn2004601.

Koenig, H. G., Berk, L. S., Daher, N. S., Pearce, M. J., Bellinger, D. L., Robins, C. J., ... King, M. B. (2014). Religious involvement is associated with greater purpose, optimism, generosity and gratitude in persons with major depression and chronic medical illness. *Journal of Psychosomatic Research, 77*(2), 135–143. Available from https://doi.org/10.1016/j.jpsychores.2014.05.002.

Koenig, H. G., George, L. K., & Peterson, B. L. (1998). Religiosity and remission of depression in medically ill older patients. *American Journal of Psychiatry, 155*(4), 536–542. Available from https://doi.org/10.1176/ajp.155.4.536.

Koenig, H. G., Hays, J. C., George, L. K., Blazer, D. G., Larson, D. B., & Landerman, L. R. (1997). Modeling the cross-sectional relationships between religion, physical health, social support, and depressive symptoms. *The American Journal of Geriatric Psychiatry, 5*(2), 131–144.

Koenig, H. G., King, D. E., & Carson, V. B. (2012). *Handbook of religion and health*. New York: Oxford University Press.

Koenig, H. G., Pearce, M. J., Nelson, B., & Erkanli, A. (2016). Effects on daily spiritual experiences of religious versus conventional cognitive behavioral therapy for depression. *Journal of Religion and Health, 55*(5), 1763–1777. Available from https://doi.org/10.1007/s10943-016-0270-3.

Krause, N. (2017). Invited commentary: Explaining the relationship between attending worship services and mortality—A brief excursion into the contribution of social relationships in religious institutions. *American Journal of Epidemiology, 185*(7), 523–525. Available from https://doi.org/10.1093/aje/kww180.

Krause, N., Hill, P. C., Emmons, R., Pargament, K. I., & Ironson, G. (2016). Assessing the relationship between religious involvement and health behaviors. *Health Education & Behavior, 44*(2), 278–284. Available from https://doi.org/10.1177/1090198116655314.

Kudel, I., Cotton, S., Szaflarski, M., Holmes, W. C., & Tsevat, J. (2011). Spirituality and religiosity in patients with HIV: A test and expansion of a model. *Annals of Behavioral Medicine, 41*(1), 92–103. Available from https://doi.org/10.1007/s12160-010-9229-x.

Levin, J. (2002). Is depressed affect a function of one's relationship with God?: Findings from a study of primary care patients. *The International Journal of Psychiatry in Medicine, 32*(4), 379–393. Available from https://doi.org/10.2190/3183-wpyv-3kyy-k3v7.

Li, S., Okereke, O. I., Chang, S.-C., Kawachi, I., & VanderWeele, T. J. (2016). Religious service attendance and lower depression among women—A Prospective Cohort Study. *Annals of Behavioral Medicine, 50*(6), 876–884. Available from https://doi.org/10.1007/s12160-016-9813-9.

Lim, C., Sim, K., Renjan, V., Sam, H. F., & Quah, S. L. (2014). Adapted cognitive-behavioral therapy for religious individuals with mental disorder: A systematic review. *Asian Journal of Psychiatry, 9*, 3–12. Available from https://doi.org/10.1016/j.ajp.2013.12.011.

Lomax, J. W., Kripal, J. J., & Pargament, K. I. (2011). Perspectives on "sacred moments" in psychotherapy. *American Journal of Psychiatry, 168*, 12–18.

Mastropieri, B., Schussel, L., Forbes, D., & Miller, L. (2015). Inner resources for survival: Integrating interpersonal psychotherapy with spiritual visualization with homeless youth. *Journal of Religion and Health, 54*(3), 903–921. Available from https://doi.org/10.1007/s10943-015-0044-3.

Merikangas, K. R., Jin, R., Kessler, R. C., Lee, S., Sampson, N. A., Viana, M. C., ... Zarkov, Z. (2011). Prevalence and correlates of bipolar spectrum disorder in the world mental health survey initiative. *Archives of General Psychiatry, 68*(3), 241–251. Available from https://doi.org/10.1001/archgenpsychiatry.2011.12.

Miller, L., Bansal, R., Wickramaratne, P., Hao, X., Tenke, C. E., Weissman, M. M., & Peterson, B. S. (2014). Neuroanatomical correlates of religiosity and spirituality: A study in adults at high and low familial risk for depression. *JAMA Psychiatry, 71*(2), 128–135. Available from https://doi.org/10.1001/jamapsychiatry.2013.3067.

Miller, L., Wickramaratne, P., Gameroff, M. J., Sage, M., Tenke, C. E., & Weissman, M. M. (2012). Religiosity and major depression in adults at high risk: A ten-year prospective study. *American Journal of Psychiatry, 169*(1), 89–94. Available from https://doi.org/10.1176/appi.ajp.2011.10121823.

Mitchell, L., & Romans, S. (2003). Spiritual beliefs in bipolar affective disorder: Their relevance for illness management. *Journal of Affective Disorders, 75*(3), 247–257. Available from https://doi.org/10.1016/s0165-0327(02)00055-1.

Montgomery, B. E., Stewart, K. E., Bryant, K. J., & Ounpraseuth, S. T. (2014). Dimensions of religion, depression symptomatology, and substance use among rural African American cocaine users. *Journal of Ethnicity in Substance Abuse, 13*(1), 72–90. Available from https://doi.org/10.1080/15332640.2014.873605.

Moreira-Almeida, A., Koenig, H. G., & Lucchetti, G. (2014). Clinical implications of spirituality to mental health: Review of evidence and practical guidelines. *Revista Brasileira de Psiquiatria, 36*(2), 176–182. Available from https://doi.org/10.1590/1516-4446-2013-1255.

Moreira-Almeida, A., Neto, F. L., & Koenig, H. G. (2006). Religiousness and mental health: A review. *Revista Brasileira de Psiquiatria, 28*, 242–250.

Moreira-Almeida, A., Sharma, A., van Rensburg, B. J., Verhagen, P. J., & Cook, C. C. H. (2016). WPA position statement on spirituality and religion in psychiatry. *World Psychiatry, 15*(1), 87–88. Available from https://doi.org/10.1002/wps.20304.

Mosqueiro, B. P., da Rocha, N. S., & Fleck, M. P. (2015). Intrinsic religiosity, resilience, quality of life, and suicide risk in depressed inpatients. *Journal of Affective Disorders, 179*, 128–133. Available from https://doi.org/10.1016/j.jad.2015.03.022.

Newberg, A. B. (2006). Religious and spiritual practices: A neurochemical perspective. In P. McNamara (Ed.), *Where God and science meet: The neurology of religious experience* (Vol. 2, pp. 15–31). Westport CT: Praege.

Paine, D. R., & Sandage, S. J. (2016). Religious involvement and depression: The mediating effect of relational spirituality. *Journal of Religion and Health, 56*(1), 269–283. Available from https://doi.org/10.1007/s10943-016-0282-z.

Pargament, K., Feuille, M., & Burdzy, D. (2011). The Brief RCOPE: Current psychometric status of a short measure of religious coping. *Religions*, *2*(1), 51–76. Available from https://doi.org/10.3390/rel2010051.

Pargament, K. I., Koenig, H. G., & Perez, L. M. (2000). The many methods of religious coping: Development and initial validation of the RCOPE. *Journal of Clinical Psychology*, *56*, 519–543.

Pargament, K. I., Koenig, H. G., Tarakeshwar, N., & Hahn, J. (2004). Religious coping methods as predictors of psychological, physical and spiritual outcomes among medically ill elderly patients: A two-year longitudinal study. *Journal of Health Psychology*, *9* (6), 713–730. Available from https://doi.org/10.1177/1359105304045366.

Pargament, K. I., & Lomax, J. W. (2013). Understanding and addressing religion among people with mental illness. *World Psychiatry*, *12*(1), 26–32. Available from https://doi.org/10.1002/wps.20005.

Pargament, K. I., Murray-Swank, N., Magyar, G. M., & Ano, G. G. (2005). Spiritual struggle: A phenomenon of interest to psychology and religion. In W. R. Miller, & H. Delaney (Eds.), *Judeo-Christian perspectives on psychology: Human nature, motivation, and change* (pp. 245–268). Washington, DC: APA Books.

Pargament, K. I., Zinnbauer, B. J., Scott, A. B., Butter, E. M., Zerowin, J., & Stanik, P. (1998). Red flags and religious coping: Identifying some religious warning signs among people in crisis. *Journal of Clinical Psychology*, *54*, 77–89. Available from https://doi.org/CCC0021-9762/98/010077-13.

Rosmarin, D. H., Malloy, M. C., & Forester, B. P. (2014). Spiritual struggle and affective symptoms among geriatric mood disordered patients. *International Journal of Geriatric Psychiatry*, *29*(6), 653–660. Available from https://doi.org/10.1002/gps.4052.

Rosmarin, D. H., Pargament, K. I., & Mahoney, A. (2009). The role of religiousness in anxiety, depression, and happiness in a Jewish community sample: A preliminary investigation. *Mental Health, Religion & Culture*, *12*(2), 97–113. Available from https://doi.org/10.1080/13674670802321933.

Schuch, F. B., Vancampfort, D., Firth, J., Rosenbaum, S., Ward, P. B., Silva, E. S., ... Stubbs, B. (2018). Physical activity and incident depression: A meta-analysis of prospective cohort studies. *American Journal of Psychiatry*, *175*(7), 631–648. Available from https://doi.org/10.1176/appi.ajp.2018.17111194.

Seybold, K. S. (2007). Physiological mechanisms involved in religiosity/spirituality and health. *Journal of Behavioral Medicine*, *30*(4), 303–309. Available from https://doi.org/10.1007/s10865-007-9115-6.

Smith, T. B., McCullough, M. E., & Poll, J. (2003). Religiousness and depression: Evidence for a main effect and the moderating influence of stressful life events. *Psychological Bulletin*, *129*(4), 614–636. Available from https://doi.org/10.1037/0033-2909.129.4.614.

Snaith, N., Schultz, T., Proeve, M., & Rasmussen, P. (2018). Mindfulness, self-compassion, anxiety and depression measures in South Australian yoga participants: Implications for designing a yoga intervention. *Complementary Therapies in Clinical Practice*, *32*, 92–99. Available from https://doi.org/10.1016/j.ctcp.2018.05.009.

Southwick, S. M., & Charney, D. S. (2012). The science of resilience: Implications for the prevention and treatment of depression. *Science*, *338*(6103), 79–82. Available from https://doi.org/10.1126/science.1222942.

Stroppa, A., Colugnati, F. A., Koenig, H. G., & Moreira-Almeida, A. (2018). Religiosity, depression, and quality of life in bipolar disorder: A two-year prospective study. *Revista Brasileira de Psiquiatria*, *40*(3), 238–243. Available from https://doi.org/10.1590/1516-4446-2017-2365.

Stroppa, A., & Moreira-Almeida, A. (2009). Religiosidade e espiritualidade no transtorno bipolar de humor. *Archives of Clinical Psychiatry (São Paulo)*, *36*, 190–196.

Stroppa, A., & Moreira-Almeida, A. (2013). Religiosity, mood symptoms, and quality of life in bipolar disorder. *Bipolar Disorders*, *15*(4), 385–393. Available from https://doi.org/10.1111/bdi.12069.

Svob, C., Wang, Z., Weissman, M. M., Wickramaratne, P., & Posner, J. (2016). Religious and spiritual importance moderate relation between default mode network connectivity and familial risk for depression. *Neuroscience Letters*, *634*, 94–97. Available from https://doi.org/10.1016/j.neulet.2016.10.009.

Tomlinson, J., Glenn, E. S., Paine, D. R., & Sandage, S. J. (2016). What is the "relational" in relational spirituality? A review of definitions and research directions. *Journal of Spirituality in Mental Health*, *18*(1), 55–75. Available from https://doi.org/10.1080/19349637.2015.1066736.

Tulbure, B. T., Andersson, G., Salagean, N., Pearce, M., & Koenig, H. G. (2018). Religious versus conventional internet-based cognitive behavioral therapy for depression. *Journal of Religion and Health*, *57*(5), 1634–1648. Available from https://doi.org/10.1007/s10943-017-0503-0.

Vaillant, G. E. (2013). Psychiatry, religion, positive emotions and spirituality. *Asian Journal of Psychiatry*, *6*(6), 590–594. Available from https://doi.org/10.1016/j.ajp.2013.08.073.

VanderWeele, T. J., Balboni, T. A., & Koh, H. K. (2017). Health and spirituality. *JAMA*, *318*(6), 519–520. Available from https://doi.org/10.1001/jama.2017.8136.

VanderWeele, T. J., Li, S., Tsai, A. C., & Kawachi, I. (2016). Association between religious service attendance and lower suicide rates among US women. *JAMA Psychiatry*, *73*(8), 845–851. Available from https://doi.org/10.1001/jamapsychiatry.2016.1243.

Vicente, A. R. T., Castro-Costa, É., Firmo, J. d. O. A., Lima-Costa, M. F., & Loyola Filho, A. I. d (2018). Religiousness, social support and the use of antidepressants among the elderly: A population-based study. *Ciência & Saúde Coletiva*, *23*(3), 963–971. Available from https://doi.org/10.1590/1413-81232018233.05922016.

Weber, S. R., & Pargament, K. I. (2014). The role of religion and spirituality in mental health. *Current Opinion in Psychiatry*, *27*(5), 358–363. Available from https://doi.org/10.1097/YCO.0000000000000080.

Yatham, L. N., Kennedy, S. H., Parikh, S. V., Schaffer, A., Bond, D. J., Frey, B. N., ... Berk, M. (2018). Canadian Network for Mood and Anxiety Treatments (CANMAT) and International Society for Bipolar Disorders (ISBD) 2018 guidelines for the management of patients with bipolar disorder. *Bipolar Disorders*, *20*(2), 97–170. Available from https://doi.org/10.1111/bdi.12609.

CHAPTER 2

Spirituality, religion, and suicide

Ying Chen[1,2] and Tyler J. VanderWeele[1,2]
[1]Human Flourishing Program, Institute for Quantitative Social Science, Harvard University, Cambridge, MA, United States
[2]Department of Epidemiology, Harvard T.H. Chan School of Public Health, Boston, MA, United States

Contents

Introduction

Suicide is the 10th leading cause of death in the United States and is also one of the three leading causes that have been on the rise (CDC, 2018). In 2016 nearly 45,000 Americans died by suicide, with approximately one death occurring per 12 minutes. In addition, 9.8 million American adults seriously considered suicide, 2.8 million made a plan, and 1.3 million actually attempted suicide in 2016 (Substance Abuse & Mental Health Services Administration, 2017). The estimated national cost, largely due to lost productivity, of suicides and suicide attempts, exceeded $90 billion in 2013 (Shepard, Gurewich, Lwin, Reed, & Silverman, 2016). In a recent report, the World Health Organization called for prioritizing suicide prevention on the global health agenda (World Health Organization, 2014). Suicides are preventable, and a number of risk factors have been identified such as unemployment, relationship problems or loss, substance

Handbook of Spirituality, Religion, and Mental Health
DOI: https://doi.org/10.1016/B978-0-12-816766-3.00002-1

misuse, previous suicidality, mental illness, and physical health problems (Sinclair & Leach, 2017). Nevertheless, there has been little progress in reducing suicide rates in the United States over the past decades, despite improvements in mental health overall (Jones, Podolsky, & Greene, 2012). Suicide prevention efforts have largely focused on providing treatment for individuals with mental illness. However, a considerable proportion of suicidal behaviors actually occurred in individuals without a formally diagnosed mental disorder (Nock et al., 2009). To improve primary suicide prevention, the Centers for Disease Control and Prevention (CDC) has recently called for a comprehensive public health approach to reducing suicide, focusing not only on reducing risk factors but also on promoting protective factors at all levels (Stone et al., 2017). A number of protective factors for reducing suicide have been proposed, and participation in religion is potentially one such factor (Sinclair & Leach, 2017).

Most major world religions consider life as a sacred gift from God and have strong sanctions against suicide (Koenig, King, & Carson, 2012; VanderWeele, 2017). One of the earliest empirical studies on religion and suicide dates back to Durkheim in the 19th century, in which he found suicide rates lower in Catholic countries compared to Protestant regions at the aggregate level (Durkheim, 1897). Since then, there have been hundreds of studies examining the association between various aspects of religion (e.g., religious affiliation, religious importance, service attendance, spirituality) and suicide (suicide ideation, suicide attempts, and completed suicide), and the majority of these suggest that religion is a protective factor against suicidality (Koenig et al., 2012). A few potential mechanisms for the inverse association between religion and suicide have also been proposed, such as the religious moral objections against suicide; religion providing social control and social integration; religious teaching about leading a healthy lifestyle (e.g., negative attitudes toward substance use); religion reducing risk of depression, aggression, and hostility; and providing a sense of hope, meaning, and purpose (Durkheim, 1897; Gearing & Lizardi, 2009; Koenig et al., 2012; O'Reilly & Rosato, 2015). Theological and ethical reasons sometimes given for prohibitions against suicide include life being a gift from God, suicide being against the natural order, suicide causing injury to the community, suicide encouraging others to follow a similar course, and death being this life's greatest evil (Aquinas, 1948; Catholic Church, 2000).

While there have been an increasing number of empirical studies on religion and suicide, the most robust evidence comes from only a few studies. For instance, most studies, especially on suicide ideation and attitudes, are cross-sectional; a number used ecological data (including Durkheim's) that are unable to control for individual-level confounding factors; and a majority of studies examined suicide ideation or attempts as the outcome, whereas evidence on completed suicide remains relatively limited (VanderWeele, 2017). Koenig et al. (2012) have conducted a comprehensive review of studies on religion and suicide prior to 2010. In that review, of studies on suicide published in the prior 10 years, 67% reported associations of religious participation with less suicide, ideation, and attempts; 6% reported associations with more; and 24% reported no association. It was also noted that there is considerable variability in the rigor of the methodology in these studies. For the purposes of this review, we will, therefore, focus here on the few methodologically strong studies (e.g., longitudinal, large sample size, rigorous confounding control) or more recent studies. As will be seen, and as is the case with many other mental and physical health outcomes, religious service attendance is one of the strongest predictors of subsequent suicide among factors related to religion and spirituality.

Religion, suicide ideation, and suicide attempts

Religious affiliation

We only identified one longitudinal study that examined the association of religious affiliation with suicide ideation and attempts. Kuo, Gallo, and Tien (2001) analyzed prospective data of 3481 adults from the Baltimore sample of the NIMH Epidemiologic Catchment Area survey (1981–94). Over the 13-year follow-up, 89 incident cases of suicide ideation and 34 new cases of suicide attempts occurred. In both univariate and adjusted analyses (controlling for age, socioeconomic status, ethnicity, and marital status), religious affiliation was not associated with either incident suicide ideation or incident suicide attempt (Kuo et al., 2001).

There is, however, some evidence from cross-sectional studies suggesting that religious affiliation may protect against suicide attempts, although the associations may vary by the culture-dependent instantiations and implications of specific religious affiliations (Lawrence, Oquendo, & Stanley, 2016). Also, as discussed below, a very large study found protective associations between religious affiliation and completed suicide.

Religious importance

Thompson, Ho, and Kingree (2007) analyzed prospective data of 15,034 adolescents from the National Longitudinal Study on Adolescent Health. There was no association between religious importance and incident suicide ideation or suicide attempts, but greater religious importance was associated with lower likelihood of requiring medical care after a suicide attempt at the 7-year follow-up, adjusting for sociodemographic factors, problematic drinking, self-esteem, impulsivity, depression, and delinquency (Thompson et al., 2007). Svob et al. (2018) examined the associations stratified by sex using longitudinal data from a multigeneration family study at the New York State Psychiatric Institute and Columbia University with a sample size of 214 offspring aged 6–18 years from 112 nuclear families. Offspring religious importance was inversely associated with suicide ideation/attempts only in girls [odds ratio (OR) = 0.48, 95% CI: 0.33, 0.70] but not in boys (OR = 1.15, 95% CI: 0.74, 1.80), controlling for age and risk of depression. Parental religious importance was also inversely associated with offspring suicidal ideation and attempts even independently of offspring religious importance (OR = 0.61, 95% CI: 0.39, 0.96), while adjusting for parental depression, suicide ideation, and marital status (Svob et al., 2018).

Of note, there is some suggestive evidence from cross-sectional studies that greater religious importance may substantially increase the risk of suicidal behaviors in sexual minority groups (Lytle, Blosnich, De Luca, & Brownson, 2018), though other cross-sectional studies suggest a potential protective effect among sexual minority groups (Kralovec, Fartacek, Fartacek, & Ploderl, 2014) and this may vary by cultural and country context and religious practice. Further rigorous research is, therefore, needed. We are not aware of any studies to date that examined religion and suicide among sexual minorities using longitudinal data.

Religious service attendance

Rasic, Robinson, Bolton, Bienvenu, and Sareen (2011) analyzed prospective data of 1091 adults aged 30 years and older from waves 3 and 4 of the Baltimore Epidemiologic Catchment Area study. There was no evident association between religious service attendance and subsequent suicidal ideation. However, religious service attendance (less than once per month to more than once per week vs never attendance) was related to 67% lower risk of subsequent suicide attempts

(OR = 0.33, 95% CI: 0.13, 0.84), adjusting for sociodemographic factors, baseline suicidal ideation/attempts, comorbid mental disorders, social support, and chronic physical health conditions (Rasic et al., 2011). Interestingly, the same study also suggested that spirituality (measured with a question on frequency of seeking spiritual comfort) was inversely associated with suicidal ideation (OR = 0.55, 95% CI: 0.31, 0.98) but not with suicidal attempts. Svob et al.'s study using data from a multigeneration family study (2018) further examined the association between service attendance and suicidal behaviors stratified by sex. It suggested that offspring service attendance was only associated with lower risk of suicidal ideation/attempts in girls (OR = 0.64, 95% CI: 0.49, 0.84) but not in boys, and there was no association between parental religious service attendance and offspring suicidal behaviors (Svob et al., 2018).

Summary

There is no clear evidence that religious affiliation is associated with subsequent suicidal ideation or attempts. In comparison, there is some evidence suggesting that religious importance may protect against suicidal behaviors, and that the protective effects may extend into the next generation. Spirituality may also reduce the risk of suicidal ideation, whereas the evidence is perhaps somewhat stronger that religious service attendance protects against suicidal attempts. However, religious affiliation may be a limited measure of religiosity. For instance, even within a single affiliation, the degree of adherence to religious teachings and practices may vary widely. Moreover, given the recent secularization trends, religious affiliation may have a weakened correspondence with religious beliefs and practices on average (Lawrence et al., 2016; O'Reilly & Rosato, 2015). In comparison, religious importance may be a better indicator of intrinsic religiosity and adherence to religious values and traditions. The communal form of religious participation, such as service attendance, can also help reinforce the social regulatory function of religious networks and connect individuals to a broader community, which in turn may reduce risk of suicidal behaviors (Koenig et al., 2012).

Religion and completed suicide

Wu, Wang, and Jia (2015) performed a metaanalysis of nine retrospective cohort or case–control studies on religion and completed suicide published prior to 2015. It suggested an overall protective effect of religiosity on suicide (pooled OR = 0.38, 95% CI: 0.21, 0.71). Subanalyses further suggest that the associations were stronger in western countries, in regions with religious homogeneity, and among older versus younger groups. Here we will focus on reviewing evidence from a few longitudinal or more recent studies.

Religious affiliation

Spoerri et al. (2010) linked the 2000 national census data of 3.7 million individuals (46% Catholics, 42% Protestant, and 12% with no religious affiliation) to death records through 2005 in Switzerland. Compared to Protestants, risk of suicide was substantially lower in Catholics and higher in individuals with no religious affiliation, adjusting for age, marital status, education, type of household, language, and degree of urbanization. The associations were modified by both age and gender and were stronger in older versus younger groups for both men and women. For instance, compared to Protestants aged 65 or older, the risk was lower among Catholic counterparts by 40% in men [hazard ratio (HR) = 0.60, 95% CI: 0.53, 0.67] and 33% in women (HR = 0.67, 95% CI: 0.59, 0.77) and was substantially higher among nonaffiliate counterparts by 96% in men (HR = 1.96, 95% CI: 1.69, 2.27) and by 2.63-fold in women (HR = 2.63, 95% CI: 2.22, 3.12). Moreover, the associations were particularly strong for assisted suicide (legal in Switzerland) (Spoerri et al., 2010). This study thus suggests that Durkheim's observation may persist in modern societies, at least in Switzerland, and does so using individual-level data.

Despite the general sanction against suicide, those who are religious will sometimes still consider ending life to avoid terminal suffering or despair (Engelhardt & Iltis, 2005; Panczak et al., 2013). As a follow-up to Spoerri et al.'s study (2010), Panczak et al. (2013) thus further examined whether the association between religious affiliation and suicide was modified by concomitant mental illness or malignant diseases. They used the same longitudinal data in Switzerland as Spoerri et al.'s study but with a longer follow-up through 2008. The results suggested that the protective effect of a Catholic affiliation and the increased risk among those with no religious affiliation were stronger if a diagnosis of cancer was present and were weaker if the individual had a comorbid mental disorder. For example, among males aged 65 or above without a comorbid condition, Catholics had 39% lower risk and nonaffiliates had 2.06 times higher risk of suicide compared to Protestants. In comparison, among cancer patients, the corresponding figures were 65% lower risk in Catholics and 2.29 times higher risk in the nonaffiliates, whereas when comorbid mental disorders were present, the risk was 28% lower in Catholics and 1.76 times higher in nonaffiliates. Patterns were similar in younger groups and among women (Panczak et al., 2013).

O'Reilly and Rosato (2015) also examined religious affiliation and suicide in the setting of the United Kingdom. Longitudinal data from the Northern Ireland Mortality Study were derived from the 2001 UK census returns and linked with the registered death up to 2009. Over the 9-year follow-up of 1,106,104 individuals aged 15–74, 1119 cases of death from suicide occurred. The risk of suicide was similar among Roman Catholics, Protestants and those reporting no religious affiliation. However, Conservative Christians had 29% lower risk of suicide compared to Roman Catholics (HR = 0.71, 95% CI: 0.52, 0.97), adjusting for age, gender, marital status, household composition, socioeconomic status, and area of residence. Further analyses stratified by age suggested that the protective effect of affiliation with Conservative Christian was only present among those aged 35–54 years.

Religious service attendance

Kleiman and Liu (2014) used the longitudinal data of 20,014 participants from the third National Health and Nutrition Examination Survey (NHANES III). Over the follow-up from between 1988 and 1994 through 2006, 25 cases of suicide occurred. Frequent religious service attendance (at least twice per month vs less frequently) was associated with 68% lower risk of death by suicide (HR = 0.32, 95% CI: 0.01, 0.99), adjusting for sociodemographic characteristics, marijuana use, and previous suicidal behaviors (Kleiman & Liu, 2014). This study was, however, not able to control for baseline depressive symptoms or examine the association stratified by religious denominations due to the lack of data.

Tsai, Lucas, Sania, Kim, and Kawachi (2014) analyzed longitudinal data of 34,901 US male health professionals from the Health Professionals Follow-Up Study from 1988 through 2012 to examine the association between social integration and death by suicide. Social integration was measured with a multiitem index with questions on marital status, social network size, frequency of contact with social ties, religious service attendance, and participation in other community or social groups. Over a

24-year follow-up, there were 147 cases of suicide. The highest versus lowest social integration category was associated with 59% lower risk of suicide, adjusting for a wide range of covariates including sociodemographic factors, smoking, alcohol consumption, caffeine intake, physical activity, antidepressant use, body mass index, health care use, and baseline physical health problems. When components of the social integration index were examined separately and were mutually adjusted for, religious service attendance (at least once per week vs less frequently) was associated with substantially lower risk of suicide by 51% (HR = 0.49, 95% CI: 0.49, 95% CI: 0.33, 0.73). As with Kleiman and Liu's study (2014), this study was, however, unable to adjust for baseline depressive symptoms due to lack of data (Tsai et al., 2014).

VanderWeele, Li, Tsai, and Kawachi (2016) examined longitudinal data of 89,708 US female nurses (mostly white) from the Nurses' Health Study from 1996 through 2010. During the 14-year follow-up, 36 cases of suicide occurred. At least weekly religious service attendance versus never attendance was associated with more than fivefold lower rate of suicide (HR = 0.16, 95% CI: 0.06, 0.46), adjusting for a wide range of covariates including sociodemographic characteristics, depressive symptoms, other aspects of social integration, lifestyle factors (body mass index, physical activity, alcohol consumption, caffeine intake, smoking), physical health (history of hypertension, diabetes, cancer, hypercholesterolemia), and prior religious service attendance. The associations were stronger for Catholics (HR = 0.05, 95% CI: 0.006, 0.48) than for Protestants (HR = 0.34, 95% CI: 0.10, 1.10); the *P*-value for heterogeneity = .05. The lower rates of suicide were partly mediated by social integration, depressive symptoms, and alcohol consumption for those who attended services occasionally but not among those who attended services more frequently (VanderWeele et al., 2016).

Using a classic approach for calculating population attributable risk, the authors estimated the proportion of the increase in suicide cases that could be attributable to the decline in religious service attendance in the general population. Specifically, between 1999 and 2014, there was a 24% increase in suicide in the United States, based on a report from the CDC. During the same period, there was a 7% decrease in weekly religious service attendance, according to the Gallup Poll. If strength of the association between service attendance and suicide observed in this study was to be extrapolated to the general population, approximately 40% of the increase in suicide rates could be attributed to the decline in service attendance (VanderWeele, Li, & Kawachi, 2017).

Given the recent secularization trends, Kleiman and Liu (2018) further examined whether the association between service attendance and suicide might be subject to period effects. They analyzed longitudinal data of 30,650 participants from the 1978 to 2010 General Social Survey linked to the National Death Index through 2014. Over the study period, there were 465 cases of suicide. Weekly service attendance (vs less frequent attendance) was only associated with lower risk of death by suicide in more recent (2000–10, HR = 0.39, 95% CI: 0.16, 0.90) but not earlier (prior to 1998, HR = 0.82, 95% CI: 0.34, 1.98) data collection periods, though the confidence interval in this earlier period is quite wide. The authors hypothesized that within the broader context of secularization, motives to attend religious services may have changed. For instance, individuals may attend services increasingly for expanding social connections and searching for life purpose and meaning, rather than as a social convention and tradition (Kleiman & Liu, 2018). There was some evidence, however, from another study also using data from the General Social Survey suggesting that belief in afterlife and acceptance of suicide may be stronger predictors of completed suicide compared to religious affiliation and religious service attendance, adjusting for age and gender (Feigelman, Rosen, & Gorman, 2014).

Summary

There is some evidence that religious affiliations may be associated with lower risk of suicide, but the associations vary across religious denominations and social contexts. In comparison, there was stronger evidence suggesting that frequent religious service attendance may reduce risk of death by suicide, and the associations remain robust even after adjusting for baseline depressive symptoms, physical health problems, other aspects of social integration, and prior religious service attendance. The association between religion and suicide needs to be understood within the broader context of secularization and shift in the age distribution of suicide from older to younger groups in many modern societies. In terms of knowledge gaps, there remains limited evidence on the associations between religion and suicide in Eastern countries and in regions with less religious homogeneity; whether participation in other forms of structured social activities (e.g., community groups, volunteering) may confer similar protection against suicide also remains unclear; further, potential mechanisms underlying religion/spirituality and suicide remain poorly understood. While there has been some evidence indicating that psychosocial and behavioral factors may partly mediate the associations (VanderWeele et al., 2016), to the best of our knowledge there is little prior work directly examining potential biological pathways. Recent evidence from neuroscience studies, however, suggested that religious/spiritual experiences and suicidal behaviors may share some common neurological changes. For instance, some postmortem studies suggested that suicide was related to a higher level of serotonin (e.g., more serotonin neurons, greater serotonin-related gene expression, and higher serotonin concentration) (Van Heeringen & Mann, 2014), while other genomic and neuroimaging studies found that religious/spiritual belief was correlated with lower serotonin receptor binding potentials (Yaden, Iwry, & Newberg, 2016). While such evidence has been mostly preliminary and various methodological challenges remain, future neuroscience research may help provide critical evidence for understanding the biological basis linking religious/spiritual experiences to suicidality and the potential epigenetic mechanisms whereby religious/spiritual practices influence individuals' predisposition to suicidal behaviors.

Implications for clinical practice

Most world major religions consider caring for the sick and the relief of suffering of central importance, and many leading medical institutions also have a religious history. There has been, however, comparatively less frequent formal collaboration between clinicians and religious and spiritual leaders in modern societies (VanderWeele, Balboni, & Koh, 2017). Although a substantial proportion of patients report having a spiritual life and consider their spiritual well-being as equally important as, or more important than, physical health, patients' spiritual needs are often ignored and not satisfied (Koenig, 2000; Mueller, Plevak, & Rummans, 2001). There are several major challenges for strengthening spiritual care in medical practice. For instance, clinical practice is dominated by a biomedical model in which spiritual well-being is of little relevance. Clinicians may also have limited time, skills, and confidence for engaging religiously diverse patients in meaningful conversations about spiritual well-being (Mueller et al., 2001). In fact, clinicians often do not receive medical training in spiritual care. Although most medical schools in the United States do offer such training, much of the material appears elective courses (Koenig et al., 2012; Koenig, Hooten, Lindsay-Calkins, & Meador, 2010).

Despite increasing empirical evidence on religion and spirituality as a potential protective factor against suicidality, information on patients' spiritual history is generally not included in suicide risk assessment in clinical practice. Such information may help psychiatrists better evaluate risk of suicide, prevent suicidal behaviors, and improve treatment. Questions such as "Are religion or spirituality important to you in thinking about health and illness, or at other times?" or "Do you have, or would you like to have, someone to talk to about religious or spiritual matters?" can help in assessing such information. Furthermore, for patients who hold religious beliefs and positively self-identify with a religious tradition but have stopped attending services, encouraging their return to a faith community and reconnecting to the religious network if they also desire so, may help reduce risk of suicide, particularly for those who are socially isolated (Koenig, 2016). The college position statement has provided some general recommendations for psychiatrists on spirituality and religion to guide clinical practice (Cook, 2013). It would be wise, however, to always proceed with caution as patients contemplating suicide might be particularly vulnerable. Special attention should be given to past negative religious experiences or potential abuse in religious contexts and these should be taken into discussion with referral made as appropriate. The questions about what to discuss with patients in relation to religion and spirituality and how, and where, to best draw boundaries in clinical practice also remain to be addressed (Cook, 2014).

Discussion

Empirical evidence to date generally suggests religion, particularly religious service attendance, as a potential protective factor for reducing completed suicide and possibly also suicide attempts. Although there is a growing number of empirical studies on religion and suicide, the majority are cross-sectional from which causality cannot be inferred. Longitudinal evidence to further understand the relationship between religion and suicide across religious denominations, in Eastern countries, in regions with less religious homogeneity and within the broader context of secularization, is needed. Further studies on potential neurobiological, psychosocial, and behavioral pathways linking religious/spiritual involvement to lower risk of suicide will be helpful for informing suicide prevention programs and interventions. For individuals with no religious beliefs, evidence is needed to understand whether other forms of structured social participation (e.g., volunteering) may confer similar protection against suicidality.

Although various challenges remain in strengthening spiritual care in clinical practice, incorporation of information from a spiritual history in suicide risk assessment may be particularly helpful for preventing suicidal behaviors and improving treatment in psychiatric practice. Evidence on the feasibility of such an approach and potential effectiveness (or harm) of religious and spiritual interventions in psychiatric practice remains scarce and is much needed (Cook, 2014). Religion and spirituality may be a potentially important but underappreciated resource that may be explored in primary prevention and clinical practice for reducing suicide, as appropriate.

References

Aquinas, T. (1948). *Summa theologica. Complete English translation in five volumes*. Notre Dame, IN: Ave Maria Press. (Original work published 1274).

Catholic Church. (2000). *Catechism of the Catholic Church*. Chicago, IL: Libreria Editrice Vaticana Loyola University Press.

CDC. (2018). *Web-based injury statistics query and reporting system (WISQARS)*. Retrieved from <https://www.cdc.gov/injury/wisqars/index.html>.

Cook, C.C. (2013). *Recommendations for psychiatrists on spirituality and religion: Position statement PS03/2013*. London. Retrieved from <http://dro.dur.ac.uk/9872/>.

Cook, C. C. (2014). Suicide and religion. *The British Journal of Psychiatry*, *204*, 254–255. Available from https://doi.org/10.1192/bjp.bp.113.136069.

Durkheim, E. (1897). *Suicide: A study in sociology* (p. 1951) New York: Free Press.

Engelhardt, H. T., Jr., & Iltis, A. S. (2005). End-of-life: The traditional Christian view. *Lancet*, *366*(9490), 1045–1049. Available from https://doi.org/10.1016/S0140-6736(05)67383-7.

Feigelman, W., Rosen, Z., & Gorman, B. S. (2014). Exploring prospective predictors of completed suicides: Evidence from the general social survey. *Crisis*, *35*(4), 233–244. Available from https://doi.org/10.1027/0227-5910/a000257.

Gearing, R. E., & Lizardi, D. (2009). Religion and suicide. *Journal of Religion and Health*, *48*(3), 332–341. Available from https://doi.org/10.1007/s10943-008-9181-2.

Jones, D. S., Podolsky, S. H., & Greene, J. A. (2012). The burden of disease and the changing task of medicine. *The New England Journal of Medicine*, *366*(25), 2333–2338. Available from https://doi.org/10.1056/NEJMp1113569.

Kleiman, E. M., & Liu, R. T. (2014). Prospective prediction of suicide in a nationally representative sample: Religious service attendance as a protective factor. *The British Journal of Psychiatry*, *204*, 262–266. Available from https://doi.org/10.1192/bjp.bp.113.128900.

Kleiman, E. M., & Liu, R. T. (2018). An examination of the prospective association between religious service attendance and suicide: Explanatory factors and period effects. *Journal of Affective Disorders, 225*, 618–623. Available from https://doi.org/10.1016/j.jad.2017.08.083.

Koenig, H. G. (2000). MSJAMA: Religion, spirituality, and medicine: Application to clinical practice. *The Journal of the American Medical Association, 284*(13), 1708.

Koenig, H. G. (2016). Association of religious involvement and suicide. *JAMA Psychiatry, 73*(8), 775–776. Available from https://doi.org/10.1001/jamapsychiatry.2016.1214.

Koenig, H. G., Hooten, E. G., Lindsay-Calkins, E., & Meador, K. G. (2010). Spirituality in medical school curricula: Findings from a national survey. *International Journal of Psychiatry in Medicine, 40*(4), 391–398. Available from https://doi.org/10.2190/PM.40.4.c.

Koenig, H. G., King, D., & Carson, V. B. (2012). *Handbook of religion and health*. New York: Oxford University Press.

Kralovec, K., Fartacek, C., Fartacek, R., & Ploderl, M. (2014). Religion and suicide risk in lesbian, gay and bisexual Austrians. *Journal of Religion and Health, 53*(2), 413–423. Available from https://doi.org/10.1007/s10943-012-9645-2.

Kuo, W. H., Gallo, J. J., & Tien, A. Y. (2001). Incidence of suicide ideation and attempts in adults: The 13-year follow-up of a community sample in Baltimore, Maryland. *Psychological Medicine, 31*(7), 1181–1191.

Lawrence, R. E., Oquendo, M. A., & Stanley, B. (2016). Religion and suicide risk: A systematic review. *Archives of Suicide Research: Official Journal of the International Academy for Suicide Research, 20*(1), 1–21. Available from https://doi.org/10.1080/13811118.2015.1004494.

Lytle, M. C., Blosnich, J. R., De Luca, S. M., & Brownson, C. (2018). Association of religiosity with sexual minority suicide ideation and attempt. *American Journal of Preventive Medicine, 54*(5), 644–651. Available from https://doi.org/10.1016/j.amepre.2018.01.019.

Mueller, P. S., Plevak, D. J., & Rummans, T. A. (2001). Religious involvement, spirituality, and medicine: Implications for clinical practice. *Mayo Clinic Proceedings, 76*(12), 1225–1235. Available from https://doi.org/10.4065/76.12.1225.

Nock, M. K., Hwang, I., Sampson, N., Kessler, R. C., Angermeyer, M., Beautrais, A., ... Williams, D. R. (2009). Cross-national analysis of the associations among mental disorders and suicidal behavior: Findings from the WHO World Mental Health Surveys. *PLoS Medicine, 6*(8), e1000123. Available from https://doi.org/10.1371/journal.pmed.1000123.

O'Reilly, D., & Rosato, M. (2015). Religion and the risk of suicide: Longitudinal study of over 1 million people. *The British Journal of Psychiatry, 206*(6), 466–470. Available from https://doi.org/10.1192/bjp.bp.113.128694.

Panczak, R., Spoerri, A., Zwahlen, M., Bopp, M., Gutzwiller, F., Egger, M., & Swiss National Cohort, S. (2013). Religion and suicide in patients with mental illness or cancer. *Suicide & Life-Threatening Behavior, 43*(2), 213–222. Available from https://doi.org/10.1111/sltb.12009.

Rasic, D., Robinson, J. A., Bolton, J., Bienvenu, O. J., & Sareen, J. (2011). Longitudinal relationships of religious worship attendance and spirituality with major depression, anxiety disorders, and suicidal ideation and attempts: Findings from the Baltimore epidemiologic catchment area study. *Journal of Psychiatric Research, 45*(6), 848–854. Available from https://doi.org/10.1016/j.jpsychires.2010.11.014.

Shepard, D. S., Gurewich, D., Lwin, A. K., Reed, G. A., Jr., & Silverman, M. M. (2016). Suicide and suicidal attempts in the United States: Costs and policy implications. *Suicide & Life-Threatening Behavior, 46*(3), 352–362. Available from https://doi.org/10.1111/sltb.12225.

Sinclair, L., & Leach, R. (2017). Exploring thoughts of suicide. *British Medical Journal, 356*, j1128. Available from https://doi.org/10.1136/bmj.j1128.

Spoerri, A., Zwahlen, M., Bopp, M., Gutzwiller, F., Egger, M., & Swiss National Cohort Study. (2010). Religion and assisted and non-assisted suicide in Switzerland: National Cohort Study. *International Journal of Epidemiology*, *39*(6), 1486–1494. Available from https://doi.org/10.1093/ije/dyq141.

Stone, D. M., Holland, K. M., Bartholow, B., Crosby, A. E., Davis, S., & Wilkins, N. (2017). *Preventing suicide: A technical package of policies, programs, and practices*. Atlanta, GA. Retrieved from <https://www.cdc.gov/violenceprevention/pdf/suicideTechnicalPackage.pdf>.

Substance Abuse and Mental Health Services Administration. (2017). *Key substance use and mental health indicators in the United States: Results from the 2016 National Survey on Drug Use and Health (HHS Publication No. SMA 17-5044, NSDUH Series H-52)*. Retrieved from <https://www.samhsa.gov/data/>.

Svob, C., Wickramaratne, P. J., Reich, L., Zhao, R., Talati, A., Gameroff, M. J., ... Weissman, M. M. (2018). Association of parent and offspring religiosity with offspring suicide ideation and attempts. *JAMA Psychiatry*. Available from https://doi.org/10.1001/jamapsychiatry.2018.2060.

Thompson, M. P., Ho, C. H., & Kingree, J. B. (2007). Prospective associations between delinquency and suicidal behaviors in a nationally representative sample. *The Journal of Adolescent Health*, *40*(3), 232–237. Available from https://doi.org/10.1016/j.jadohealth.2006.10.016.

Tsai, A. C., Lucas, M., Sania, A., Kim, D., & Kawachi, I. (2014). Social integration and suicide mortality among men: 24-Year cohort study of U.S. health professionals. *Annals of Internal Medicine*, *161*(2), 85–95. Available from https://doi.org/10.7326/M13-1291.

Van Heeringen, K., & Mann, J. J. (2014). The neurobiology of suicide. *Lancet Psychiatry*, *1*(1), 63–72. Available from https://doi.org/10.1016/S2215-0366(14)70220-2.

VanderWeele, T. J. (2017). Religion and health: A synthesis. In J. R. Peteet, & M. J. Balboni (Eds.), *Spirituality and religion within the culture of medicine: From evidence to practice*. New York: Oxford University Press.

VanderWeele, T. J., Balboni, T. A., & Koh, H. K. (2017). Health and spirituality. *The Journal of the American Medical Association*, *318*(6), 519–520. Available from https://doi.org/10.1001/jama.2017.8136.

VanderWeele, T. J., Li, S., & Kawachi, I. (2017). Religious service attendance and suicide rates—Reply. *JAMA Psychiatry*, *74*(2), 197–198. Available from https://doi.org/10.1001/jamapsychiatry.2016.2780.

VanderWeele, T. J., Li, S., Tsai, A. C., & Kawachi, I. (2016). Association between religious service attendance and lower suicide rates among US women. *JAMA Psychiatry*, *73*(8), 845–851. Available from https://doi.org/10.1001/jamapsychiatry.2016.1243.

World Health Organization. (2014). *Preventing suicide: A global imperative*. Geneva, Switzerland. Retrieved from <http://www.who.int/mental_health/suicide-prevention/world_report_2014/en/>.

Wu, A., Wang, J. Y., & Jia, C. X. (2015). Religion and completed suicide: a meta-analysis. *PLoS One*, 10(6), e0131715.

Yaden, D., Iwry, J., & Newberg, A. (2016). Neuroscience and religion: Surveying the field. In N. K. Clements (Ed.), *Religion: Mental religion* (pp. 277–299). New York: Macmillan Reference.

CHAPTER 3

Spirituality, religion, and anxiety disorders

David H. Rosmarin and Bethany Leidl
Department of Psychiatry, McLean Hospital/Harvard Medical School, Belmont, MA, United States

Contents

Introduction

Anxiety disorders are more common than any other mental health condition. In the United States, 18.1% of adults experience clinically significant symptoms of anxiety in each and every year (Kessler & Wang, 2008), and 41.7% have a diagnosable anxiety disorder over their life span (Kessler, Petukhova, Sampson, Zaslavsky, & Wittchen, 2012). For these reasons, the modern era has been dubbed the "Age of Anxiety" (Horwitz, 2010). As discussed in the introduction to this volume, mental health professionals seldom inquire about spirituality/religion (S/R) in the context of patient care (Curlin et al., 2007), despite the fact that more than 9 in 10 Americans believe in God, more than half report that religion is "very important" in their lives (Gallup, 2011), and more than half of psychotherapy patients wish to discuss spiritual/religious matters in treatment (Rosmarin, Forester, Shassian, Webb, & Björgvinsson, 2015). Given these trends regarding S/R and the prevalence of anxiety disorders in the general population and clinical settings, it is essential for mental health professionals to understand how S/R is related to anxiety. The present chapter addresses this question, with the hope of informing conceptual models, research, and clinical practice.

Handbook of Spirituality, Religion, and Mental Health
DOI: https://doi.org/10.1016/B978-0-12-816766-3.00003-3

Over the past 20 years, over 100 empirical studies have investigated associations between S/R and symptoms of anxiety. As discussed elsewhere in this volume, previous research tying S/R to other areas of mental health is generally consistent, showing that positive aspects of S/R buffer against incidence and severity of such symptoms (to varying degrees) whereas negative aspects of S/R are risk factors for mental distress. By contrast, the extant research on S/R and anxiety is decisively mixed (Shreve-Neiger & Edelstein, 2004). Initially, in our own reading and review of this body of literature, the relationship between S/R and anxiety seemed spurious or perhaps simply an artifact of measurement error. However, as the present chapter illustrates, S/R and anxiety relate to each other in relatively predictable ways once it is recognized that S/R is a multifaceted construct (Hill & Pargament, 2003).

More specifically, S/R can be broken down into two broad categories. On the one hand, S/R can involve observable behaviors such as religious service attendance, prayer, S/R study, participating in religious rituals, and the like. From our vantage point, generally speaking, behavioral facets of S/R are poor predictors of anxiety. Published studies commonly find positive, negative, and/or no associations between these variables, and effect sizes tend to be small. Put simply, it is very hard to predict meaningful levels of anxiety from crude indices of S/R behavior (e.g., church attendance). On the other hand, S/R can involve cognitive or emotional states such as beliefs, motivations, a sense of gratitude or attachment to God, and other S/R thoughts and feelings. The extant literature consistently shows that S/R cognitions and emotions can be further divided into positive states (e.g., faith/trust in God) and negative states (e.g., appraisals that God is punitive or unfair). Generally speaking, positive cognitive or emotional aspects of S/R life are consistently associated with less anxiety, whereas negative internal facets of S/R are associated with more anxiety, and effect sizes to be moderate to large.

In sum, as can be seen in Fig. 3.1, cognitive and emotional facets of S/R are strongly and consistently (large arrows) associated with anxiety in two directions: Positive S/R thoughts and emotions predict less anxiety, and negative internal S/R is associated with greater anxiety symptoms. By contrast, observable S/R behaviors are weakly associated with anxiety and directions of effect are hard to predict a priori. The remainder of this chapter will further detail this overarching conceptual framework by summarizing the literature on S/R and anxiety.

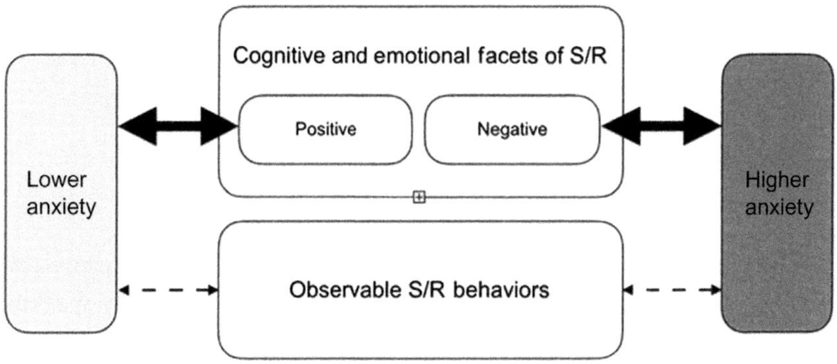

Figure 3.1 Spirituality/religion & anxiety: an overarching conceptual model.

Spiritual/religious behaviors and anxiety

A comprehensive nationwide 2014 study found that many Americans regularly engage in a number of S/R behaviors (Pew Research Center, 2014). Americans most commonly pray (55% pray at least once a day), attend religious services (36% attend service at least once a week), and participate in religious groups (24% attend a prayer or scripture study group at least once a week). Some researchers define these activities as "organizational religiosity" (Krause, 1993), but more accurately they can be characterized as observable S/R behaviors, in that they occur in spiritual as well as religious contexts (see the introduction of this volume for definitions of these terms). Behavioral dimensions of S/R are more easily measured and quantified than cognitive and emotional dimensions. Perhaps for this reason, both physical and mental health research works have historically focused more on S/R behaviors than internal aspects of S/R (Rosmarin, Wachholtz, & Ai, 2011). However, published studies on S/R behavior and anxiety have mixed findings across the board. For example, as mentioned below, the same behavioral S/R variables (e.g., church attendance) are associated with greater anxiety in some studies and less anxiety in others. In fact, often even within studies, different behavioral facets of S/R are positively and negatively correlated with anxiety symptoms for different individuals or groups of individuals. Furthermore, effect sizes tend to be relatively small in both directions; while some studies demonstrate a weak positive association between religious behaviors and anxiety, others show small negative associations, and still other studies show no association at all. These effects can be summarized in Fig. 3.2.

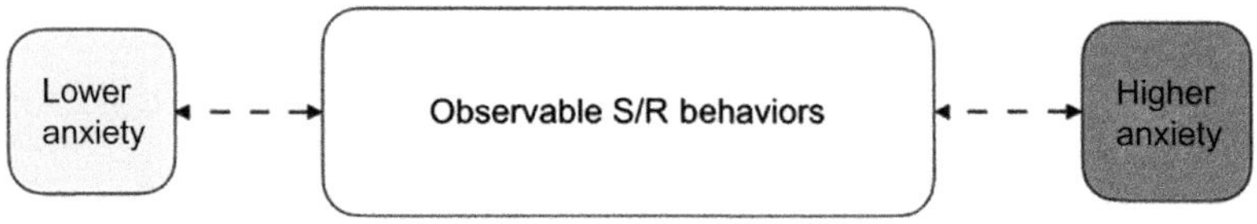

Figure 3.2 Spiritual/religious behaviors & anxiety.

What might account for this pattern of seemingly spurious low-level correlations between S/R behavior and anxiety? Psychologically speaking, S/R behavior can serve an anxiolytic effect by activating positive cognitive schemas, facilitating emotion regulation, and serving a coping function (Rosmarin, 2018). It is therefore common for individuals with anxiety symptoms to engage in S/R behaviors; that is, the experience of anxiety symptoms can activate or increase levels of S/R behavior through negative reinforcement (reduction of anxiety). Perhaps for this reason, soldiers who have had negative or frightening experiences during combat are more likely to attend religious services than noncombat veterans (Wansink & Wansink, 2013). On the other hand, engagement in S/R behaviors can also decrease the experience of anxiety through a similar mechanism. Utilizing S/R to cope or create positive spiritual experiences can, in turn, provide solace and hope, or at least distraction from anxiety symptoms. Observed correlations between S/R behaviors and anxiety may therefore simply be a function of when these variables are assessed: Did the anxiety precede the (increase in) S/R behavior, or did the S/R behavior precede a (decrease) in anxiety? Thus, in cross-sectional (or even longitudinal) studies, S/R behavior may be correlated with *less or more* anxiety, since directions of effect in such research designs cannot be assessed and it is not possible to gauge whether S/R behavior is a function of anxiety, or vice versa. To make matters even more complicated, S/R behaviors can also directly increase anxiety, by creating a context for spiritual struggles, which can engender shame, guilt and other negative emotions (Exline, Yali, & Sanderson, 2000). Furthermore, the statistical effects of positive and negative associations between S/R behaviors and anxiety may cancel each other out, leading to conflicting findings and small or even null associations. Along these lines, it could be said that S/R afflicts the comforted and comforts the afflicted. The following brief sections review some of the literature on S/R behaviors and anxiety.

A handful of research studies have found that S/R behaviors are associated with higher levels of anxiety, albeit with very modest effect sizes.

For example, Peterman, LaBelle, and Steinberg (2014) found that attending religious services and belonging to religious youth groups was associated with slightly but significantly greater anxiety ($r = 0.07-0.08$). Similarly, a less recent but well-cited study found that watching religious television shows predicted greater levels of anxiety (Koenig, Ford, George, Blazer, & Meador, 1993). A third study showed that more frequent church attendance is related to one specific subset of anxiety: death anxiety (Wen, 2010). Regarding all of these findings, it is unclear whether greater S/R precedes or perhaps causes anxiety, or vice versa. For example, individuals with greater fears of death may attend religious services in order to create a sense of eternality during their lifetimes. Alternatively, it is possible that attending services is a cue for thinking and thus developing concerns about death-related themes such as salvation. Similarly, several studies have found that prayer is associated with greater anxiety (Byrd & Boe, 2001; Sternthal, Williams, Musick, & Buck, 2010). Here too, the nature of these effects is unclear. It is possible that the act of prayer increases anxiety through the avenues of worry, or that praying creates spiritual strain when individuals perceive that their prayers are unanswered. Alternatively, anxiety could simply negatively reinforce the act of prayer through the avenues of coping, reframing, or distraction, as suggested above. Unfortunately, the vast majority of research on S/R behavior and anxiety is correlational in nature; however, several notable longitudinal, prospective studies in this area have found that baseline S/R behaviors predict greater subsequent levels of anxiety (Korenromp, Page-Christiaens, Bout, Multer, & Visser, 2009; Peterman et al.; Trevino, Naik, & Moye, 2016).

On the other hand, many reports have found negative correlations between S/R behaviors and anxiety. Attending religious events has been tied to fewer anxiety symptoms (Ellison, Burdette, & Hill, 2009; Jansen, Motley, & Hovey, 2010; Koenig, George, Blazer, & Pritchett, 1993; Ng, Mohamed, Sulaiman, & Zainal, 2017; Schieman, Pudrovska, Pearlin, & Ellison, 2006). For example, in a national sample size of 37,000 Canadians, Baetz and colleagues found that participants who attended more religious services also reported fewer panic disorders and social phobia disorders (Baetz, Bowen, Jones, & Koru-Sengul, 2006). Similarly, in a large 2009 study based on a US national sample, Ellison and colleagues reported that church attendance was associated with slightly less anxiety ($r = -0.09$). Notably, Sternthal and colleagues (2010) found that weekly service attendance predicted less anxiety, but that greater attendance did not account for any additional variance in anxiety. This latter finding suggests that at best, religious participation beyond a certain threshold does not confer additional protective effects against anxiety. Regarding prayer, a handful of studies have found negative associations with anxiety (e.g., Ai et al., 2007; Ai, Tice, Peterson, & Huang, 2005; Dehghani et al., 2012; Rosmarin, Krumrei, & Andersson, 2009), but many have shown the reverse (Masters & Spielmans, 2007). Similarly, several studies have found that reciting the Catholic rosary is associated with lower levels of worry (Anastasi & Newberg, 2008; Dehghani et al., 2012; Gaudette & Jankowski, 2013). Across all of these studies, however, negative relationships between S/R behavior and anxiety tend to be very small.

Other studies have found no relationships between S/R behaviors and anxiety symptoms. In contrast to above findings, Vasegh and Mohammadi (2007) reported that no measures of S/R behavioral engagement among Iranian medical students were associated with greater or less anxiety. Similarly, in a recent investigation by Neal Krause (2015), church attendance was not related to death anxiety. Similar findings have been reported by many other laboratories (e.g., Hale & Clark, 2013; Park, Hong, Park, & Cho, 2012). Interestingly, the three best-designed studies on S/R behaviors and anxiety all revealed no relationships between these variables. In 2009, Ellison and colleagues found that frequency of prayer had no association with either anxiety or tranquility in a sample of 961 US adults participating in the General Social Survey (Ellison et al., 2009). More recently, a prominent study based on a large epidemiological dataset ($n = 1091$) found that religious service attendance was not associated with greater or less odds for any anxiety disorder (Rasic, Robinson, Bolton, Bienvenu, & Sareen, 2011). Similarly, a population-based study of 16,415 Latinos in four US cities found that Church attendance was not associated with anxiety for any age group (Lerman et al., 2018). It is unclear whether these null findings suggest that S/R behaviors and anxiety are unrelated, or that positive and negative effects described above cancel each other out in large-scale, well-conducted studies. However, a failure to identify positive or negative effects of S/R behaviors on anxiety in cross-sectional and longitudinal population-based investigations clearly suggests, at a minimum, that S/R behaviors are a poor predictor of anxiety symptoms.

We propose that several mechanisms may explain the above positive, negative, and null relationships between S/R behaviors and anxiety. Regarding positive associations, first, as discussed above, anxious individuals may seek out S/R behaviors as a means of anxiety relief. Most commonly, when individuals face distress, they may turn to S/R behaviors in order to cope (Pargament, 1997; Zwingmann, Müller, Körber, & Murken, 2008). As such, anxiety can serve as an unpleasant internal activating event for individuals to increase their level of S/R behavior (negative reinforcement). Second, religious cultural systems may be a context for spiritual and/or social pressures that lead to greater anxiety; S/R activity may increase one's own or other's expectations of oneself, which can increase demands on time and other resources, leading to greater stress, tension, and anxiety symptoms. Relatedly, S/R behaviors may be borne from death anxiety, as reviewed above. Regarding negative associations, S/R behaviors can protect against anxiety by facilitating hope, optimism, gratitude, and other positive emotions, which may buffer against anxiety symptoms. S/R behavior in a communal context can also enhance or even facilitate social support, which can help individuals suffering from anxiety. Regarding null associations, there are two possibilities: First, all of these and other potential effects may be present within or between studies, and therefore cross-sectional positive and negative effects of S/R behavior on anxiety may cancel each other out. Second, S/R behaviors may simply not be good predictors of anxiety symptoms. This latter possibility seems most likely, given that studies showing positive and/or negative associations tend to have small effect sizes, as reviewed above. In summary, the research on S/R behaviors is clearly mixed, with low-level or even null effects almost across the board. This seems to be because S/R behavior has a variety of psychological functions vis-à-vis anxiety, and therefore indices of S/R behavior are simply not specific enough to account for these many functions. Further, and more important for the present chapter, while some associations are statistically significant (in both directions), observed effect sizes tend to be very small. In fact, no studies have revealed *clinically* significant correlations between S/R behaviors and anxiety or suggested that S/R behaviors can buffer against or predict clinical levels of anxiety. In other words, it is very hard to predict meaningful levels of anxiety from S/R behavior alone.

Spiritual/religiouscognitions, emotions, and anxiety

Cognitive and emotional facets of S/R include beliefs, motivations, and attitudes. Generally speaking, these aspects of S/R can be divided into two categories: (1) positive internal states such as faith or trust in God, secure religious attachment, intrinsic religious motivation, and religious gratitude; and (2) negative states such as appraisals that God is being punitive, anger or mistrust toward God, insecure or avoidant religious attachment, extrinsic religious motivation, and the like. In contrast with the literature on S/R behaviors and anxiety, which shows conflicting results and weak ties overall, research on S/R cognitions and emotions and anxiety is far more consistent: Positive cognitive and emotional aspects of S/R tend to consistently buffer against anxiety, whereas negative cognitive and emotional facets of S/R generally predict greater anxiety. Furthermore, the extant literature shows strong effects of both positive and negative facets of S/R cognition and emotion on anxiety that are clinically significant in many cases. Our conceptual framework is summarized below (Fig. 3.3).

S/R thoughts and feelings have robust (large arrows) relationships with anxiety. Positive beliefs, motivations, emotions, and attachments appear to be salutary, whereas negative facets appear to be detrimental. The following paragraphs highlight pertinent literature that supports this model.

Beliefs about God encompass far more than the classic binary Yes/No responses of believers and atheists, or even a gray scale ranging from "Yes, very much" to "not at all." Beliefs about God may be anthropomorphic (e.g., fatherly, loving), deistic (e.g., creator, judge), or nontraditional (e.g., force, energy). Broadly speaking though, beliefs about God range from positive (e.g., loving, caring, benevolent, kind, generous) to negative (e.g., critical, punitive, destructive, malevolent), depending on the individual believer, their religious affiliation, and their life experiences, among other factors. Consistent research from the early 1990s (e.g., Schaefer & Gorsuch, 1991) through the current day shows that beliefs in a "benevolent" God are associated with fewer worries and fears. Recently, using

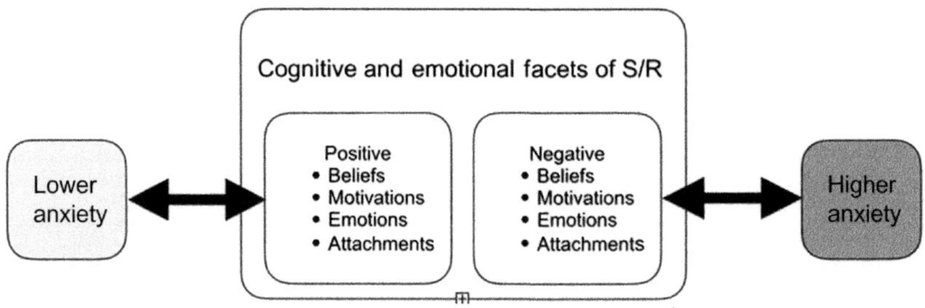

Figure 3.3 Spiritual/religious cognitions, emotions & anxiety.

data from a large survey of 1426 US adults, Silton, Flannelly, Galek, and Ellison (2014) found that belief in a benevolent God was negatively associated with a host of anxiety-related concerns such as worry, social apprehension, paranoia, obsessions, and compulsions. More importantly, benevolent God appraisals predicted between 4.1% and 9.4% of total variance (r^2 values) in these factors. In a similar national study with 1306 US adults, Flannelly, Galek, Ellison, and Koenig (2010) found that belief in a "close and loving" God predicted substantially less generalized anxiety, social anxiety, paranoid ideation, and obsessionality/compulsivity, with large and clinically, as well as statistically, significant salutary effects across the board, whereas frequency of religious service attendance was not associated with any indicators of anxiety. Conversely, negative beliefs about God consistently predict greater anxiety. Silton's research above found that belief in a punitive God was associated with greater social anxiety and paranoia, with large effect sizes. Further, in a large-scale and well-cited national study on spiritual struggles, believers who viewed God as adversarial were more likely to experience anxiety (McConnell, Pargament, Ellison, & Flannelly, 2006). Similarly, in a series of studies with Jewish and Christian community samples, Rosmarin, Krumrei, and Andersson (2009) and Rosmarin, Pirutinsky, Pargament, and Krumrei (2009), found that mistrust in God—characterized by beliefs in God's inability to assist and/or malevolence—strongly predicted greater stress, anxiety, and worry, accounting for up to 7.8% of the variance in these factors. In subsequent clinical research, reductions in mistrust in God over a 2-week period were associated with statistically and clinically significant decreases in stress and worry (Rosmarin, Pargament, Pirutinsky, & Mahoney, 2010).

What might explain these findings? In a 2008 experimental study, 47 subjects completed an anxiety-provoking visualization procedure, but only half were randomized to an experimental manipulation designed to lower beliefs in their personal sense of control (Laurin, Kay, & Moscovitch, 2008). Among experimental participants (whose sense of personal control was threatened), anxiety symptoms were associated with increased levels of belief in God after the experiment. These findings suggest that the experience of lacking personal control can, at least temporarily, increase belief in God. They further suggest that belief in God can serve as an anxiolytic by compensating for a perceived lack of control. Rosmarin, Pirutinsky, Auerbach, et al. (2011) and Rosmarin, Pirutinsky, Cohen, et al. (2011) similarly found that trust and mistrust in God appear to relate to anxiety through the mechanism of intolerance of uncertainty—a known cognitive vulnerability for anxiety, in which individuals struggle to accept situations in which the outcome is uncertain or unreliable. Specifically, trust in a loving and supportive God seems to be an adaptive cognitive schema that supports greater acceptance and tolerance of uncertainty, and thereby predicts less worry. Conversely, mistrust in an impotent or malevolent God is a ripe context for intolerance of uncertain situations, which in turn is associated with greater worry, stress, and tension. Like the findings of Laurin et al., above, this suggests that when one lacks certainty or control over life, belief in a loving God can buffer against anxiety.

Recent neurobiological research supports these notions. In 2009, in a series of fascinating experimental studies, Michael Inzlicht and colleagues found that during cognitive-stress tasks, belief in God was associated with less firing of the anterior cingulate cortex (ACC)—a brain region that is known to relate to anxiety—even after controlling for personality factors and cognitive ability. In a follow-up study, Inzlicht and Tullett (2010) found that when believers focused on religion during an experimental task, they demonstrated decreased error-related negativity in the ACC in response to self-generated errors. Summarizing these findings, Inzlicht, Tullet, and Good (2011) concluded that belief in God seems to attenuate ACC activity specifically by providing meaning and promoting greater tolerance of uncertainty. In sum, considerable evidence shows that positive beliefs about God predict and perhaps even lead to less anxiety, whereas negative Divine beliefs predict greater anxiety. More specifically, positive beliefs about God appear to provide psychologically adaptive cognitive if not neural effects during uncertain times when one lacks perceived control, which in turn buffers against anxiety symptoms. It is therefore not surprising that effect sizes across the board for this body of literature are large and clinically, as well as statistically, significant.

Just as children form psychologically healthy or unhealthy attachments to their parents, believers can form healthy or unhealthy attachments to God (Rowatt & Kirkpatrick, 2002). Developmental and clinical psychology research consistently highlight that secure attachment—feeling important to one's caregivers and knowing that one can depend on them for security and support—is psychologically adaptive and healthy. By contrast, anxious or avoidant attachment—which involves bonds that are contaminated by fear or rejection—predict a host of negative psychological outcomes including relationship failure and clinical distress (see Waters, Merrick, Treboux, Crowell, & Albersheim, 2000 for a comprehensive review). Similarly, secure versus anxious/avoidant attachment to God robustly differentiate individuals on a host of mental health variables, including anxiety. In 2010, drawing on data from a national study of elders and members of the US Presbyterian Church, Bradshaw, Ellison, and Marcum found that secure attachment to God predicted substantially less distress ($r^2 = -0.05$) even after controlling for age, gender, race, socioeconomic and marital status, and even church attendance and frequency of prayer. Conversely, anxious attachment to God predicted significantly more distress ($r^2 = 0.05$). In a follow-up study within a national sample ($n = 1511$), anxious attachment to God predicted 17%–22% of the variance in (greater) worry, social apprehension, obsessions, and compulsions (Ellison, Bradshaw, Flannelly, & Galek, 2014). Furthermore, prayer was inversely associated with anxiety disorders, but only for individuals who reported secure attachment to God. This latter finding suggests that secure attachment can moderate the effects of S/R behaviors on anxiety. In a recent 3-year longitudinal study with 325 individuals from the Jewish community, Pirutinsky, Rosmarin, & Kirkpatrick (2019) found that, of all aspects of Jewish S/R life, secure attachment to God emerged as a better predictor of (less) anxiety than any other factor including religious social support, religious practice, intrinsic religiosity, and religious coping. In other research, avoidant attachment to God, which represents viewing God as impersonal, cold, or distant, is associated with substantially higher traits of neuroticism, as well as greater anxiety (Rowatt & Kirkpatrick, 2002). In sum, the way in which one perceives their relationship to God is a consistent predictor of anxiety symptoms: Secure, loving, connected bonds with the Divine appear to buffer against anxiety, whereas anxious or avoidant connections with God predict psychogenic distress.

Another aspect of S/R cognition and emotion relates to the motivation to engage in religion. Like all facets of human motivation, S/R motivations are complex but are widely thought to essentially involve two approaches (which can co-occur in some individuals): (1) intrinsic S/R motivations involve adhering to spiritual or religious standards because they represent deeply held higher-order internal values; (2) extrinsic S/R motivations involve spiritual or religious identities or activities that are aimed toward self-interest, such as status, sociability, recreation, self-justification, or even solace or security. To contrast these further, intrinsic S/R motivation involves personal beliefs or values, whereas extrinsic S/R motivation involves social or other functional benefits from faith.

Regarding anxiety, over 30 years of research has consistently shown that among Protestant Christians, intrinsic S/R motivations predict less distress whereas extrinsic S/R is associated with greater distress (e.g., Davis, Kerr, & Robinson-Kurpius, 2003; Maltby, Lewis, & Day, 1999; Park, Cohen, & Herb, 1990). Specifically, intrinsic religiosity is associated with substantially less exam-related anxiety among college students (McMahon & Biggs, 2012), less death anxiety (Hui & Fung, 2008; Thorson & Powell, 1990), and less state and trait anxiety among at-risk male high school students (Davis et al., 2003). By contrast, extrinsic religious motivation is associated with higher levels of trait anxiety and worry (Baker & Gorsuch, 1982; Bergin, Masters, & Richards, 1987; Tapanya, Nicki, & Jarusawad, 1997), with consistent and large effect sizes.

However, in a well-conducted and often-cited study by Cohen et al. (2005), intrinsic and extrinsic religiosity predicted less and greater death anxiety (respectively) among Protestant Christians, but not Catholics. Similarly, research by Crystal Park and colleagues from the late 1980s (Park, Cohen, & Herb, 1990) found that Protestants and Catholics differed substantially in how intrinsic/extrinsic religious orientations related to anxiety. Cohen et al. (2005) explained these differences by illustrating that "different religious communities see the relative value of private motivations for religiosity and social motivations for religiosity differently" (p. 310). More specifically, while American Protestantism values private, intrinsic religious motivation as a "gold standard," other religious cultures—including Catholicism, and to some extent Judaism and Islam—intrinsically value behavioral and collectivistic/social facets of religion. Measures of extrinsic religious motivation may therefore tap into aspects of intrinsically motivated religious activity among non-Protestant groups. More broadly, intrinsic and extrinsic religiosity does not appear to represent positive vs. negative cognitive and emotional aspects of S/R (respectively), across all religious cultures. Notwithstanding these important limitations and the need for further research on religious motivations and anxiety across different religious groups, this much seems clear: Among Protestants, believers with intrinsic S/R motivation appear to experience less anxiety, whereas extrinsic motivation predicts greater levels of anxiety.

In the past decade, the psychology of S/R has turned its attention toward direct study of S/R emotions, including gratitude toward God and anger toward God. This body of research, which is broadly informed by emotion regulation theory (Gross, 1998), is a significant development for the field in that it provides clear theoretical and empirical links to clinical science. Regarding religious gratitude, Neal Krause (2006) has done substantial work in this area, including one research study in a large sample of older adults ($n = 906$), which found that gratitude to God predicted substantially less negative psychological impact of stressful living conditions. Further developing this line of research, Rosmarin, Pirutinsky, Cohen, et al. (2011) found that religious gratitude accounted for additional variance in (lower) anxiety, over-and-above general (nonreligious) gratitude, particularly for religious individuals. A relatively recent study of Iranian students similarly found that gratitude to God was associated with less anxiety and greater emotional stability (Aghababaei, 2013). It is possible that gratitude toward God facilitates greater tolerance of uncertainty, secure attachment to God, or even psychologically adaptive religious motivations, since feeling appreciation toward God can engender positive appraisals of distress and greater spiritual connection.

However, like all aspects of life, S/R emotions can be negative as well as positive. Feelings such as anger or fear toward God have historically fallen under the category of negative religious coping (Pargament, Koenig, & Perez, 2000; Pargament, Smith, Koenig, & Perez, 1998), though these may occur inside or outside the context of life stress. Numerous studies have found that these facets of S/R life are strongly associated with greater anxiety (e.g., Chapman & Steger, 2010; Ramirez et al., 2012; Sherman, Plante, Simonton, Latif, & Anaissie, 2009; Trenholm, Trent, & Compton, 1998). Specifically, when believers fear they will be punished for their sins, they are substantially more likely to have general worries and fear (Ellison et al., 2009). These findings are not surprising, since core negative emotions toward God may engender, or be an artifact, of anxiety, as well as other facets of emotional distress.

Call to action: Clinical implications

The above literature underscores that S/R cognitions and emotions, including the nature of one's beliefs about God, attachments to God, religious motivations, and S/R emotions such as religious gratitude and anger toward God are robust and strong predictors of anxiety symptoms. In contrast, S/R behaviors such as attending religious services, prayer, S/R study or exposure to religious media, are poor predictors of anxiety. At a surface level, these general trends suggest that clinicians working with anxious patients should give more consideration to internal facets of S/R in clinical assessment and treatment, relative to behavioral facets. More specifically, clinicians (and researchers) should not simply assess for patients' religious identities or adherence to religious rituals, or even whether or not they believe in God, but rather provide patients with opportunities to explore the nature of their beliefs (e.g., positive or negative), their sense of connection to S/R, their internal reasons for engaging in S/R, and any pertinent S/R emotions they may experience regularly or from time to time. While many clinicians lack basic training in how to effectively integrate these aspects of patients' lives into evidence-based care (Rosmarin, 2018), assessing for these factors and providing patients with time and space to explore their relationship to presenting problems is part and parcel of culturally and spiritually sensitive clinical practice. Taking things one step further: When patients identify S/R themes related to symptoms of anxiety (or other presenting concerns), clinicians should consider collaboration with S/R leaders such as clergy in supporting patients' spiritual and religious needs, alongside standard clinical interventions.

There is growing research support that the above approaches and other methods of spiritually integrated psychotherapy can be effective for individuals presenting with anxiety disorders. In 2010, Koszycki and colleagues conducted a small randomized controlled trial of one-on-one spiritually integrated versus conventional cognitive behavioral therapy (CBT), for Canadian adults presenting with anxiety concerns (Koszycki, Raab, Aldosary, & Bradwejn, 2010). Spiritually integrated CBT in this study included concepts such as forgiveness, gratitude, and ethical priorities, alongside other aspects of treatment (e.g., cognitive restructuring, behavioral experimentation, exposure). Results demonstrated that spiritually integrated treatment was just as effective as standard CBT, suggesting that patients who wish to harness spirituality in treatment may do so without compromising efficacy. Also, in 2010, Rosmarin and colleagues conducted a randomized controlled trial with 125 Jewish individuals, comparing the efficacy of a spiritually integrated treatment delivered via the Internet, to progressive muscle relaxation and a waitlist control condition, for anxiety symptoms (worry and stress). Results suggested that effects of the spiritually integrated treatment—which was aimed at helping individuals develop greater trust in God through a series of readings and structured exercises (25–30 min/day for 2 weeks) —on reduced worry, stress, and intolerance of uncertainty were greater than those of progressive muscle relaxation, which in turn was equivalent to the waitlist control condition. In yet another study, Paukert et al. (2009) found that patients with generalized anxiety disorder receiving spiritually integrated treatment demonstrated reductions in symptoms at a faster rate than those receiving traditional treatment. Furthermore, in nonclinical experimental research, Amy Wachholtz and colleagues showed remarkable effects of engagement in spiritual versus secular meditation on anxiety, as well as other symptoms. Specifically, patients who practiced spiritual meditation (e.g., repetition of the phrase "God is good") on a daily basis for 30 days reported less postexperiment anxiety compared to individuals who practiced secular meditation or relaxation exercises (Wachholtz & Pargament, 2005, 2008). In other nonclinical experimental research, a more recent randomized controlled trial found that six weekly 1-hour prayer sessions, but not a control condition, were associated with reduced anxiety (Boelens, Reeves, Replogle, & Koenig, 2010), which was sustained both 1-month and 1-year following the final prayer session (Boelens, Reeves, Replogle, & Koenig, 2012).

While the above results are promising, this body of study remains in its infancy, and therefore it remains unclear how S/R can be harnessed clinically in the treatment of anxiety disorders. With that said, the above research review clarifies several potential avenues, including efforts to cultivate positive beliefs about God, attachment-based treatments to promote secure connections with the Divine, strategies to enhance psychologically adaptive aspects of religious motivation, and efforts to promote positive religious emotions. Conversely, efforts to understand, validate, and target negative S/R beliefs, anxious or avoidant attachments to God, selfishly motivated religious activity, and negative S/R emotions such as anger toward God or excessive fear of God may be fruitful clinical activities when treating individuals with anxiety or other disorders. To these ends, there is a pressing need for innovation in this area of study, including development and syndication of tried and tested methods to assess for and address S/R in both research and treatment ofanxiety symptoms.

Discussion

Let us return to our original question: How is S/R related to anxiety? In a nutshell, *S/R behaviors* are generally unrelated to anxiety, seemingly because the internal and external contexts for such behaviors vary widely from person to person, and situation to situation. By contrast, *S/R cognitions and emotions* are strongly connected to anxiety in two ways: Positive S/R beliefs and feelings predict less anxiety, whereas negative S/R mindsets and sentiments are associated with greater anxiety. Clinically speaking, there is a growing empirical basis to include S/R cognitions and emotions into treatment of individuals with anxiety concerns, and substantial clinical reason to do so (when such approaches are desired by patients). However, more innovation in this area is needed to identify guidelines and techniques for broaching S/R matters in treatment, and to better measure aspects of S/R that are functionally related to anxiety in research applications.

References

Aghababaei, N. (2013). Between you and God, where is the general factor of personality? Exploring personality-religion relationships in a Muslim context. *Personality and Individual Differences*, *55*(2), 196–198.

Ai, A. L., Peterson, C., Tice, T. N., Huang, B., Rodgers, W., & Bolling, S. F. (2007). The influence of prayer coping on mental health among cardiac surgery patients: The role of optimism and acute distress. *Journal of Health Psychology*, *12*(4), 580–596.

Ai, A. L., Tice, T. N., Peterson, C., & Huang, B. (2005). Prayers, spiritual support, and positive attitudes in coping with the September 11 national crisis. *Journal of Personality*, *73*(3), 763–792.

Anastasi, M. W., & Newberg, A. B. (2008). A preliminary study of the acute effects of religious ritual on anxiety. *The Journal of Alternative and Complementary Medicine*, *14*(2), 163–165.

Baetz, M., Bowen, R., Jones, G., & Koru-Sengul, T. (2006). How spiritual values and worship attendance relate to psychiatric disorders in the Canadian population. *Canadian Journal of Psychiatry*, *51*(10), 654–661.

Baker, M., & Gorsuch, R. (1982). Trait anxiety and intrinsic-extrinsic religiousness. *Journal for the Scientific Study of Religion*, 119–122.

Bergin, A. E., Masters, K. S., & Richards, P. S. (1987). Religiousness and mental health reconsidered: A study of an intrinsically religious sample. *Journal of Counseling Psychology*, *34*(2), 197.

Boelens, P. A., Reeves, R. R., Replogle, W. H., & Koenig, H. G. (2010). A randomized trial of the effect of prayer on depression and anxiety. *International Journal of Psychiatry in Medicine*, *39*(4), 377–392.

Boelens, P. A., Reeves, R. R., Replogle, W. H., & Koenig, H. G. (2012). The effect of prayer on depression and anxiety: Maintenance of positive influence one year after prayer intervention. *International Journal of Psychiatry in Medicine*, *43*(1), 85–98.

Byrd, K. R., & Boe, A. (2001). The correspondence between attachment dimensions and prayer in college students. *The International Journal for the Psychology of Religion*, *11*(1), 9–24.

Center, P. R. (2014). *Religious landscape study (RLS-II)—Main survey of nationally representative sample of adults*. Washington, DC: Pew Research Center.

Chapman, L. K., & Steger, M. F. (2010). Race and religion: Differential prediction of anxiety symptoms by religious coping in African American and European American young adults. *Depression and Anxiety*, *27*(3), 316–322.

Cohen, A. B., Pierce, J. D., Jr, Chambers, J., Meade, R., Gorvine, B. J., & Koenig, H. G. (2005). Intrinsic and extrinsic religiosity, belief in the afterlife, death anxiety, and life satisfaction in young Catholics and Protestants. *Journal of Research in Personality, 39*(3), 307–324.

Curlin, F. A., Lawrence, R. E., Odell, S., Chin, M. H., Lantos, J. D., Koenig, H. G., & Meador, K. G. (2007). Religion, spirituality, and medicine: Psychiatrists' and other physicians' differing observations, interpretations, and clinical approaches. *The American Journal of Psychiatry, 164*(12), 1825–1831.

Davis, T. L., Kerr, B. A., & Kurpius, S. E. R. (2003). Meaning, purpose, and religiosity in at-risk youth: The relationship between anxiety and spirituality. *Journal of Psychology and Theology, 31*(4), 356–365.

Dehghani, K., Rahimabadi, A. Z., Pourmovahed, Z., Dehghani, H., Zarezadeh, A., & Namjou, Z. (2012). The effect of prayer on level of anxiety in mothers of children with cancer. *Iranian Journal of Pediatric Hematology and Oncology, 2*(2).

Ellison, C. G., Bradshaw, M., Flannelly, K. J., & Galek, K. C. (2014). Prayer, attachment to God, and symptoms of anxiety-related disorders among US adults. *Sociology of Religion, 75*(2), 208–233.

Ellison, C. G., Burdette, A. M., & Hill, T. D. (2009). Blessed assurance: Religion, anxiety, and tranquility among US adults. *Social Science Research, 38*(3), 656–667.

Flannelly, K. J., Galek, K., Ellison, C. G., & Koenig, H. G. (2010). Beliefs about God, psychiatric symptoms, and evolutionary psychiatry. *Journal of Religion and Health, 49*(2), 246–261.

Gallup. (2011). *Religion [Gallup Historical Trends]*. Retrieved from <www.gallup.com/poll/1690/religion.aspx>.

Gaudette, H., & Jankowski, K. R. (2013). Spiritual coping and anxiety in palliative care patients: A pilot study. *Journal of Health Care Chaplaincy, 19*(4), 131–139.

Hale, M. A., & Clark, D. A. (2013). When good people have bad thoughts: Religiosity and the emotional regulation of guilt-inducing intrusive thoughts. *Journal of Psychology and Theology, 41*(1), 24–35.

Hill, P. C., & Pargament, K. I. (2003). Advances in the conceptualization and measurement of religion and spirituality: Implications for physical and mental health research. *The American Psychologist, 58*(1), 64.

Horwitz, A. V. (2010). How an age of anxiety became an age of depression. *The Milbank Quarterly, 88*(1), 112–138.

Hui, V. K. Y., & Fung, H. H. (2008). Mortality anxiety as a function of intrinsic religiosity and perceived purpose in life. *Death Studies, 33*(1), 30–50.

Inzlicht, M., & Tullett, A. M. (2010). Reflecting on God: Religious primes can reduce neurophysiological response to errors. *Psychological Science, 21*(8), 1184–1190.

Jansen, K. L., Motley, R., & Hovey, J. (2010). Anxiety, depression and students' religiosity. *Mental Health, Religion & Culture, 13*(3), 267–271.

Kessler, R. C., Petukhova, M., Sampson, N. A., Zaslavsky, A. M., & Wittchen, H. U. (2012). Twelve-month and lifetime prevalence and lifetime morbid risk of anxiety and mood disorders in the United States. *International Journal of Methods in Psychiatric Research, 21*(3), 169–184.

Kessler, R. C., & Wang, P. S. (2008). The descriptive epidemiology of commonly occurring mental disorders in the United States. *Annual Review of Public Health, 29*, 115–129.

Koenig, H. G., Ford, S. M., George, L. K., Blazer, D. G., & Meador, K. G. (1993). Religion and anxiety disorder: An examination and comparison of associations in young, middle-aged, and elderly adults. *Journal of Anxiety Disorders*.

Koenig, H. G., George, L. K., Blazer, D. G., & Pritchett, J. T. (1993). The relationship between religion and anxiety in a sample of community-dwelling older adults. *Journal of Geriatric Psychiatry*.

Korenromp, M. J., Page-Christiaens, G., Bout, J., Multer, E. J. H., & Visser, G. H. A. (2009). Adjustment to termination of pregnancy for fetal anomaly: A longitudinal study in women at 4, 8, and 16 months. *American Journal of Obstetrics & Gynecology, 201*(160), e1–e7.

Koszycki, D., Raab, K., Aldosary, F., & Bradwejn, J. (2010). A multifaith spiritually based intervention for generalized anxiety disorder: A pilot randomized trial. *Journal of Clinical Psychology, 66*(4), 430–441.

Krause, N. (1993). Measuring religiosity in later life. *Research on Aging, 15*(2), 170–197.

Krause, N. (2006). Gratitude toward God, stress, and health in late life. *Research on Aging, 28*(2), 163–183.

Krause, N. (2015). Trust in God, forgiveness by God, and death anxiety. *OMEGA – Journal of Death and Dying, 72*(1), 20–41.

Laurin, K., Kay, A. C., & Moscovitch, D. A. (2008). On the belief in God: Towards an understanding of the emotional substrates of compensatory control. *Journal of Experimental Social Psychology, 44*(6), 1559–1562.

Lerman, S., Jung, M., Arredondo, E. M., Barnhart, J. M., Cai, J., Castañeda, S. F., ... Perreira, K. (2018). Religiosity prevalence and its association with depression and anxiety symptoms among Hispanic/Latino adults. *PLoS One, 13*(2).

Maltby, J., Lewis, C. A., & Day, L. (1999). Religious orientation and psychological well-being: The role of the frequency of personal prayer. *British Journal of Health Psychology, 4(Part, 4*, 363–378. Available from: https://doi.org/10.1348/135910799168704.

Masters, K. S., & Spielmans, G. L. (2007). Prayer and health: Review, meta-analysis, and research agenda. *Journal of Behavioral Medicine, 30*, 329–338.

McConnell, K. M., Pargament, K. I., Ellison, C. G., & Flannelly, K. J. (2006). Examining the links between spiritual struggles and symptoms of psychopathology in a national sample. *Journal of Clinical Psychology, 62*(12), 1469–1484.

McMahon, B. T., & Biggs, H. C. (2012). Examining spirituality and intrinsic religious orientation as a means of coping with exam anxiety. *Vulnerable Groups & Inclusion, 3.*

Ng, G. C., Mohamed, S., Sulaiman, A. H., & Zainal, N. Z. (2017). Anxiety and depression in cancer patients: The association with religiosity and religious coping. *Journal of Religion and Health, 56*(2), 575–590.

Park, C., Cohen, L. H., & Herb, L. (1990). Intrinsic religiousness and religious coping as life stress moderators for Catholics versus Protestants. *Journal of Personality and Social Psychology, 59*(3), 562–574.

Pargament, K. I., Koenig, H. G., & Perez, L. M. (2000). The many methods of religious coping: Development and initial validation of the RCOPE. *Journal of Clinical Psychology, 56*(4), 519–543.

Pargament, K. I., Smith, B. W., Koenig, H. G., & Perez, L. (1998). Patterns of positive and negative religious coping with major life stressors. *Journal for the Scientific Study of Religion, 37*, 710–724.

Pirutinsky, S., Rosmarin, D. H., & Kirkpatrick, L. A. (2019). Is attachment to God a unique predictor of mental health?: Test in a Jewish sample. *International Journal of Psychological Religious, 29*(3), 161–171.

Pargament, K. I. (1997). *The psychology of religion and coping: Theory, research, practice.* Guilford Press.

Park, J. I., Hong, J. P., Park, S., & Cho, M. J. (2012). The relationship between religion and mental disorders in a Korean population. *Psychiatry Investigation, 9*(1), 29–35.

Paukert, A. L., Phillips, L., Cully, J. A., Loboprabhu, S. M., Lomax, J. W., & Stanley, M. A. (2009). Integration of religion into cognitive-behavioral therapy for geriatric anxiety and depression. *Journal of Psychiatric Practice, 15*(2), 103–112.

Peterman, J. S., LaBelle, D. R., & Steinberg, L. (2014). Devoutly anxious: The relationship between anxiety and religiosity in adolescence. *Psychology of Religion and Spirituality, 6*(2), 113.

Ramirez, S. P., Macêdo, D. S., Sales, P. M. G., Figueiredo, S. M., Daher, E. F., Araújo, S. M., ... Carvalho, A. F. (2012). The relationship between religious coping, psychological distress and quality of life in hemodialysis patients. *Journal of Psychosomatic Research*, *72*(2), 129–135.

Rasic, D., Robinson, J. A., Bolton, J., Bienvenu, O. J., & Sareen, J. (2011). Longitudinal relationships of religious worship attendance and spirituality with major depression, anxiety disorders, and suicidal ideation and attempts: Findings from the Baltimore epidemiologic catchment area study. *Journal of Psychiatric Research*, *45*(6), 848–854.

Rosmarin, D. H. (2018). Spirituality, religion, and cognitive-behavioral therapy: A guide for clinicians. Guilford Publications.

Rosmarin, D. H., Krumrei, E. J., & Andersson, G. (2009). Religion as a predictor of psychological distress in two religious communities. *Cogn Behav Ther*, *38*(1), 54–64, 2009.

Rosmarin, D. H., Pirutinsky, S., Pargament, K. I., & Krumrei, E. J. (2009). Are religious beliefs relevant to mental health among Jews? *Psychological Religious Spiritual*, *1*(3), 180–190.

Rosmarin, D. H., Forester, B. P., Shassian, D. M., Webb, C. A., & Björgvinsson, T. (2015). Interest in spiritually integrated psychotherapy among acute psychiatric patients. *Journal of Consulting and Clinical Psychology*, *83*(6), 1149–1153.

Rosmarin, D. H., Krumrei, E. J., & Andersson, G. (2009). Religion as a predictor of psychological distress in two religious communities. *Cognitive Behaviour Therapy*, *38*(1), 54–64.

Rosmarin, D. H., Pargament, K. I., Pirutinsky, S., & Mahoney, A. (2010). A randomized controlled evaluation of a spiritually integrated treatment for subclinical anxiety in the Jewish community, delivered via the Internet. *Journal of Anxiety Disorders*, *24*(7), 799–808.

Rosmarin, D. H., Pirutinsky, S., Auerbach, R. P., Björgvinsson, T., Bigda-Peyton, J., Andersson, G., ... Krumrei, E. J. (2011). Incorporating spiritual beliefs into a cognitive model of worry. *Journal of Clinical Psychology*, *67*(7), 691–700.

Rosmarin, D. H., Pirutinsky, S., Cohen, A. B., Galler, Y., & Krumrei, E. J. (2011). Grateful to God or just plain grateful? A comparison of religious and general gratitude. *The. Journal of Positive Psychology*, *6*(5), 389–396.

Rosmarin, D. H., Wachholtz, A., & Ai, A. (2011). Beyond descriptive research: Advancing the study of spirituality and health. *Journal of Behavioral Medicine*, *34*(6), 409–413.

Rowatt, W., & Kirkpatrick, L. A. (2002). Two dimensions of attachment to God and their relation to affect, religiosity, and personality constructs. *Journal for the Scientific Study of Religion*, *41*(4), 637–651.

Schaefer, C. A., & Gorsuch, R. L. (1991). Psychological adjustment and religiousness: The multivariate belief-motivation theory of religiousness. *Journal for the Scientific Study of Religion*, 448–461.

Schieman, S., Pudrovska, T., Pearlin, L. I., & Ellison, C. G. (2006). The sense of divine control and psychological distress: Variations across race and socioeconomic status. *Journal for the Scientific Study of Religion*, *45*(4), 529–549.

Sherman, A. C., Plante, T. G., Simonton, S., Latif, U., & Anaissie, E. J. (2009). Prospective study of religious coping among patients undergoing autologous stem cell transplantation. *Journal of Behavioral Medicine*, *32*(1), 118–128.

Shreve-Neiger, A. K., & Edelstein, B. A. (2004). Religion and anxiety: A critical review of the literature. *Clinical Psychology Review*, *24*(4), 379–397.

Silton, N. R., Flannelly, K. J., Galek, K., & Ellison, C. G. (2014). Beliefs about God and mental health among American adults. *Journal of Religion and Health*, *53*(5), 1285–1296.

Sternthal, M. J., Williams, D. R., Musick, M. A., & Buck, A. C. (2010). Depression, anxiety, and religious life: A search for mediators. *Journal of Health and Social Behavior, 51* (3), 343–359.

Tapanya, S., Nicki, R., & Jarusawad, O. (1997). Worry and intrinsic/extrinsic religious orientation among Buddhist (Thai) and Christian (Canadian) elderly persons. *The International Journal of Aging and Human Development, 44*(1), 73–83.

Thorson, J. A., & Powell, F. C. (1990). Meanings of death and intrinsic religiosity. *Journal of Clinical Psychology, 46*(4), 379–391.

Trenholm, P., Trent, J., & Compton, W. C. (1998). Negative religious conflict as a predictor of panic disorder. *Journal of Clinical Psychology, 54*(1), 59–65.

Trevino, K. M., Naik, A. D., & Moye, J. (2016). Perceived and actual change in religion/spirituality in cancer survivors: Longitudinal relationships with distress and perceived growth. *Psychology of Religion and Spirituality, 8*(3), 195–205.

Vasegh, S., & Mohammadi, M. R. (2007). Religiosity, anxiety, and depression among a sample of Iranian medical students. *The International Journal of Psychiatry in Medicine, 37* (2), 213–227.

Waters, E., Merrick, S., Treboux, D., Crowell, J., & Albersheim, L. (2000). Attachment security in infancy and early adulthood: A twenty-year longitudinal study. *Child Development, 71*(3), 684–689.

Wachholtz, A. B., & Pargament, K. I. (2005). Is spirituality a critical ingredient of meditation? Comparing the effects of spiritual meditation, secular meditation, and relaxation on spiritual, psychological, cardiac, and pain outcomes. *Journal of Behavioral Medicine, 28*(4), 369–384.

Wachholtz, A. B., & Pargament, K. I. (2008). Migraines and meditation: Does spirituality matter? *Journal of Behavioral Medicine, 31*(4), 351–366.

Wansink, B., & Wansink, C. S. (2013). Are there atheists in foxholes? Combat intensity and religious behavior. *Journal of Religion and Health, 52*(3), 768–779.

Wen, Y. H. (2010). Religiosity and death anxiety. *The Journal of Human Resource and Adult Learning, 6*(2), 31–37.

Zwingmann, C., Müller, C., Körber, J., & Murken, S. (2008). Religious commitment, religious coping and anxiety: A study in German patients with breast cancer. *European Journal of Cancer Care, 17*(4), 361–370.

CHAPTER 4

Spirituality/religion and obsessive–compulsive-related disorders

Jonathan S. Abramowitz and Jennifer L. Buchholz
Department of Psychology, University of North Carolina at Chapel Hill, Chapel Hill, NC, United States

Contents

Introduction

Obsessive–compulsive disorder (OCD) is an anxiety-based psychological condition characterized by intrusive thoughts that provoke subjective anxiety and distress (obsessions) and avoidance, rituals, and other behaviors (compulsions) performed deliberately to neutralize the distress or remove unwanted thoughts (American Psychiatric Association, 2013). With an estimated prevalence of 1%–3% of the population, OCD is a common mental health concern (Ruscio, Stein, Chiu, & Kessler, 2010). In severe instances, obsessions and compulsions lead to impairment in several domains of functioning, such as work and school, family and relationships,

Handbook of Spirituality, Religion, and Mental Health
DOI: https://doi.org/10.1016/B978-0-12-816766-3.00004-5

and leisure time. OCD is a heterogeneous condition as the themes of obsessions and compulsions might concern topics such as contamination, responsibility for causing harm, symmetry or exactness, violence, sex, and, especially relevant to this chapter, religion (McKay et al., 2004).

At the intersection of OCD, spirituality, and religion is *scrupulosity*, which literally means *fearing sin where there is none*. Common religious obsessions include recurrent senseless doubts that one has committed a sin (e.g., "Did I cheat on the test when I gazed quickly around the room?"), intrusive blasphemous thoughts (e.g., "The devil is stronger than God"), concerns that one is not faithful, moral, or pious enough ("What if I don't really love God as much as I should?"), fears that one didn't perform a religious prayer or ceremony properly ("What if my mind wandered while I was praying?"), and thoughts of punishment from God ("What if I'm not saved?"). Common compulsive rituals include excessive praying, repetition of religious rituals and scriptures until they are done or said "perfectly," unnecessary reassurance seeking from clergy or loved ones about salvation or other religious matters, and excessive or inappropriate confession. Individuals with scrupulosity often avoid situations and stimuli that trigger their obsessions and compulsions such as places of worship, books of scripture and other religious icons, listening to sermons, reading religious literature, and antireligious or sinful materials (e.g., pornography, books about atheism). Evidence suggests that the presence of scrupulosity predicts poorer outcomes in OCD treatment, which may be attributed to limited knowledge among clinicians about this symptom presentation, as well as inadvertent reinforcement of subtle rituals by members of religious communities (Huppert & Siev, 2010).

Scrupulosity versus normal religious practice

It may be challenging to distinguish (pathological) scrupulosity from healthy religious practices, especially since the content of scrupulous obsessions and compulsions often has some basis in conventional religious belief and practice. Moreover, some members of an individual's religious community might encourage scrupulous behavior, perceiving it simply as fervent religious devotion. The person with scrupulosity, however, typically has excessive and rigid concerns regarding a few particular facets of religious practice, which ironically may interfere with other (often more important) aspects of observance. For example, one patient in our clinic described such an extreme fear of being punished for having "impure" thoughts when she entered a place of worship that it resulted in her missing worship services altogether. Greenberg, Witztum, and Pisante (1987) noted that excessive religious behaviors associated with scrupulosity negatively impact one's functioning in other areas of religious life. Healthy religious observance, on the other hand, is generally typified by more accommodating approaches to most areas of religious belief and practice, viewing perfect adherence as an ideal rather than an imperative to avoid severe punishment. Another potential marker of scrupulosity is the degree of distress associated with religious practice even if the individual does not exceed standards, per se. That is, healthy religious practice is usually associated with positive emotions, whereas religious compulsive rituals are usually associated with fear and anxiety (e.g., Greenberg & Shefler, 2002).

Religious obsessive–compulsive disorder symptoms: research and theory

Prevalence

Religious obsessions and compulsions are a fairly prevalent manifestation of OCD. In the DSM-IV field trial conducted in the United States, for example, 5.9% of 425 OCD patients reported religious obsessions, making this the fifth most common obsessional theme (Foa et al., 1995). In 5% of the field trial patients, religion was the *primary* obsessional theme (Tolin, Abramowitz, Kozak, & Foa, 2001). Higher estimates were later reported by Eisen, Phillips, and Rasmussen (1999) and Mataix-Cols, Marks, Greist, Kobak, and Baer (2002), who found that 10% and 33% (respectively) of their large patient samples experienced religious obsessions. Findings from less secular societies indicate even higher rates of scrupulosity, with as many as 50% and 60% of OCD patients in Saudi Arabia and Egypt (respectively) reporting religious obsessions (Mahgoub & Abdel-Hafeiz, 1991; Okasha, Saad, Khalil, Seif, & Yehia, 1994).

Relationships among religion, scrupulosity, and obsessive–compulsive disorder

Although it does not appear to indicate a more globally severe form of OCD (Siev, Baer, & Minichiello, 2011; Tek & Ulug, 2001), scrupulosity is associated with increased depressive and anxious symptoms (Nelson, Abramowitz, Whiteside, & Deacon, 2006), as well as obsessive–compulsive personality traits (Siev, Steketee, Fama, & Wilhelm, 2011). Independent of the severity of OCD symptoms, individuals with religious obsessions have poorer insight, more perceptual distortions, and more magical ideation than do those with other types of obsessions (Tolin et al., 2001). Considering that scrupulosity involves the perception of sin, worries about violating religious standards, and fear of punishment from God, it is not surprising that affected individuals experience a great deal of guilt, anxiety, and interference with their ability to practice their religion (Siev, Baer, et al., 2011), in addition to impaired social and occupational functioning.

Obsessive and compulsive symptoms that focus on religion have been associated with greater religiosity (Abramowitz, Huppert, Cohen, Tolin, & Cahill, 2002; Greenberg & Shefler, 2002; Greenberg & Witztum, 1994; Lewis & Maltby, 1995; Nelson et al., 2006; Okasha et al., 1994; Sica, Novara, & Sanavio, 2002; Siev & Cohen, 2007; Steketee, Quay, & White, 1991). Yet, this should not be taken to infer that the relationship between religiosity and scrupulosity is causal—indeed, the studies conducted to date are correlational and cross-sectional. Additionally, many of the measures assessing religious obsessions err on the side of pathologizing normative religious engagement. Evidence suggests that although religious individuals with OCD are more likely than nonreligious individuals with OCD to have symptoms related to religion, religious individuals are not more likely to have OCD overall (Siev, Huppert, & Zuckerman, 2017). Moreover, the majority of religious people do not suffer from OCD. In fact, scrupulosity is not associated with higher levels of religiosity among Jewish individuals (Abramowitz et al., 2002; Hermesh, Masser-Kavitzky, & Gross-Isseroff, 2003), American Protestants (Nelson et al., 2006), Turkish Moslems (Tek & Ulug, 2001), and Iranian school children (Assarian, Biqam, & Asqarnejad, 2006). Siev, Baer, et al. (2011) found that 18% of those with scrupulosity indicated having no religious affiliation, although some of those participants reported having been raised in a religious tradition that influenced their symptoms. The rise of individual spirituality, in comparison to organized communal religion, may also shift the relationship between religious practice and OCD (Loewenthal, 2018). This research indicates that the relationship between religiosity and scrupulosity is a complex one that requires further study, especially from a cross-cultural perspective. Importantly, although religious beliefs do not *cause* OCD, they may inform the specific manifestation of symptoms, the content of obsessive beliefs, and the nature of compulsive rituals.

Cognitive and behavioral aspects of religious obsessive–compulsive disorder symptoms

Misinterpretation of intrusions

Research indicates that unwanted and intrusive thoughts (i.e., thoughts, images, and doubts that encroach into consciousness), including those of a religious nature (e.g., "What if there is no God"), are normal occurrences for most everyone (e.g., Rachman & de Silva, 1978). Whereas most people (even most religious people) regard such intrusions as insignificant "mental noise," such intrusions may develop into clinical obsessions if the person believes strongly that such thoughts are personally significant or threatening. Consider a faithful Christian who experiences the unwanted thought, "Jesus is a bastard." If he or she treats such an intrusion as meaningless mental flotsam, the thought would not be given much importance and would sooner or later unceremoniously disappear from consciousness. However, if the person holds more rigid beliefs about the meaning of thoughts, such as "I must never think badly of Jesus," or "My thoughts tell the kind of person I am," he or she might appraise this *unwanted* thought as significant—perhaps as a sin—even if it goes against his or her typical thoughts, behavioral disposition, and sense of self (e.g., "It's a sign I am falling away from Christianity"). Avoidance and compulsive behaviors are performed to control or dismiss the thought, as we discuss further below.

Religion and the misinterpretation of thoughts

Although beliefs about the importance of intrusive thoughts probably result from multiple factors, some authors (e.g., Rachman, 1997; Salkovskis, Shafran, Rachman, & Freeston, 1999) have suggested that religious doctrine can foster such beliefs because it (1) imposes explicit moral standards for thinking and behaving, (2) is inculcated by influential authority figures (e.g., clergy), and (3) includes the possibility of severe punishment (e.g., eternal damnation). The 10th commandment from the Bible, for example, forbids *coveting* (i.e., wishing to have) another person's "property" (which includes his wife). Similarly, in his Sermon on the Mount, Jesus warns his followers, "You're familiar with the command to the ancients, 'Do not murder'. I tell you that anyone who is so much as angry with a brother or sister is guilty of murder" (Matthew 5: 21–22) and "I say to you that everyone who looks on a woman to lust for her has committed adultery already in his heart" (Matthew 5:27–28). These passages exemplify the position that thoughts and actions are morally equivalent (i.e., *thought-action fusion*; TAF; Shafran, Thordarson, & Rachman, 1996) and that control over thoughts is important to avoid sin and punishment.

Several studies have found that highly religious people, relative to non-religious or less devout individuals, perceive the presence and meaning of negative unwanted thoughts as more personally significant, influential, and immoral (Abramowitz, Deacon, Woods, & Tolin, 2004; Berman, Abramowitz, Pardue, & Wheaton, 2010; Cohen & Rozin, 2001; Inozu, Karanci, & Clark, 2012; Rassin & Koster, 2003; Sica et al., 2002; Yorulmaz, Gençöz, & Woody, 2009). This relationship appears to be more pronounced among Christians relative to other religious groups (e.g., Cohen & Rozin, 2001; Inozu et al., 2012; Rassin & Koster, 2003; Siev & Cohen, 2007; Williams, Lau, & Grisham, 2013), perhaps since religious valuation of such thoughts is consistent with Christian religious doctrine. Studies also show that religiosity can be associated with the extreme fear of God and with the fear of committing sin. Although not part of most mainstream religions, the view that God is angry and vengeful, waiting for people to commit sins so that he can punish them, is often observed in individuals with scrupulosity (Abramowitz et al., 2002; Nelson et al., 2006). Indeed, Siev, Baer, et al. (2011) and Siev, Steketee, et al. (2011) found that among individuals with OCD, severity of scrupulosity was associated with a more negative perception of God (as punishing, fearsome, jealous, terrifying, angry, vengeful). Pirutinsky, Rosmarin, Pargament, and Midlarsky (2011) examined explicit and implicit beliefs about God and found elevated levels of scrupulosity among individuals with high explicit negative beliefs and relatively negative implicit associations.

Influence of religious denomination

The themes of OCD symptoms appear to be (at least in part) determined by the matters that are most important in the person's value system and sense of self. Indeed, the types of unwanted intrusive thoughts that are most subject to misinterpretation are those that already have a particular significance to the person. An implication of this for scrupulosity is that given the substantial theological differences across religions, it is expected that the precise content of religious obsessions and compulsions will vary depending on the religious traditions, values, customs, and doctrines that the person holds as important. While an Orthodox Jewish individual, for example, might have obsessional doubts that he violated dietary laws that are important in Judaism (e.g., keeping milk and meat separate), a Muslim individual might have obsessions about his relationship with the Prophet Mohammed.

Some religions emphasize judgments about morality and the importance of thoughts more than others. Christianity, for example, places great importance on individual conscience and maintaining certain beliefs—one's relationship with God and salvation hinges more on *belief* rather than on *deeds*. Judaism, Hinduism, and Islam have behavioral traditions and customs that are central to religious practice. Thus, the associations between religiosity, interpretations of intrusive thoughts, and scrupulosity may not be equivalent across all religions. Judaism and Islam are more ritualistic religions, with behavioral commandments for adherents to follow (Okasha et al., 1994; Siev & Cohen, 2007). It is not surprising that Christians endorse higher TAF beliefs compared to Jews (Siev & Cohen, 2007) and Muslims (Inozu et al., 2012). Jews and Muslims with scrupulosity might be more prone to misinterpret intrusive doubts about having properly fulfilled religious customs and commandments. Hindus, on the other hand, might be most prone to obsessional doubts about dirt and impurity. Indeed, Buchholz et al. (2019) found that scrupulosity differed across religious affiliations. Specifically, individuals who identified as Catholic reported the greatest levels of scrupulosity relative to those who identified as Protestant, Jewish, or having no religion. Further, scrupulosity was differentially associated with OCD symptom dimensions across religious affiliations, suggesting that the manifestation of scrupulosity varies on the basis of religious doctrine.

Religious beliefs and practices may also affect the severity of OCD symptoms. For example, while there is a clear emphasis on avoiding sin in Judaism, the Torah also discusses the importance of living life in this world (Huppert, Siev, & Kushner, 2007). This perspective may help Jewish individuals with OCD shift their attention toward improving quality of life rather than performing excessive rituals. Religious beliefs may also exacerbate OCD symptoms. Siev, Baer, et al. (2011), for example, found that scrupulous individuals with a more negative concept of God experienced more severe OCD symptoms. Some religious beliefs that are consistent with evidence-based treatment, such as acceptance and mindfulness in Buddhism, may attenuate symptoms and/or buffer against the development of OCD.

Intolerance of uncertainty

If religiosity is associated with beliefs that unwanted thoughts are important, and such beliefs are associated with scrupulosity, why do most religious people *not* suffer with scrupulosity (or OCD in general)? Clinical observations (e.g., Abramowitz & Jacoby, 2014) suggest that people with scrupulosity appear to seek a *guarantee* or *proof* that they have not committed a sin and that they will not receive punishment from God. The problem, however, is that scrupulosity tends to focus on matters that are not subject to such proof or assurance (i.e., they cannot be guaranteed and must be taken on faith). Accordingly, people who engage in healthy religious devotion may be protected against scrupulosity by their belief that *faith*—defined as trust or confidence in the absence of iron-clad objective facts—is sufficient for knowledge when it comes to matters of religion and spirituality. Put another way, faith allows most religious individuals to comfortably engage with religious practices and beliefs in the absence of *proof*.

Indeed, faithful members of religious communities are generally satisfied that their healthy participation in standard religious behaviors (e.g., attending services) is sufficient to satisfy their spiritual, moral, or religious obligation, despite the impossibility of guarantees or certainty. Most religious individuals even experience and tolerate doubt-laden thoughts about their faith on occasion. On the other hand, scrupulosity is characterized by an *intolerance of uncertainty* (IU). That is, people with scrupulosity have trouble accepting the inherent uncertainty of particular religious beliefs and doctrines (e.g., "There is a God who loves me unconditionally"). They believe that they can (and must) obtain absolute proof and consequently experience a great deal of anxiety and distress when they realize that no such proof exists. Other members of their religion accept these beliefs and doctrines on faith, even in the face of intellectual debate and ever-present differences in beliefs across members of their same religion; but it is as if those with scrupulosity have *lost their faith in faith*. Although there have been no studies focused on the relationship between IU and scrupulosity in particular, numerous investigations demonstrate an association between IU and OCD symptoms in general (e.g., Boelen & Carleton, 2012; Calleo, Hart, Björgvinsson, & Stanley, 2010).

Behavioral features

Engaging in behaviors such as avoidance of stimuli that trigger religious obsessions, thought suppression, and compulsive rituals is counterproductive in several ways. First, because they sometimes temporarily provide a reduction in obsessional distress, such strategies are negatively reinforced and evolve into patterns that consume substantial time and effort and interfere with functioning. Second, because they sometimes reduce anxiety and uncertainty (albeit temporarily), these behaviors prevent the person from learning that they can cope with the temporary discomfort associated with the intrusive thought or doubt until it naturally subsides. Third, avoidance and rituals paradoxically lead to an increase in the frequency of obsessional thoughts, possibly because the distracters become reminders (retrieval cues) of the intrusions (Najmi, Riemann, & Wegner, 2009). This further amplifies doubt and uncertainty. Finally, given that absolute certainty about some of these matters can never truly be attained (e.g., "Am I going to Hell?"), the very act of repeated checking and reassurance seeking perpetuates the obsessional thinking and need for certainty, as well as misinterpretations of obsessional thoughts as significant (e.g., Rachman, 2002; Radomsky, Gilchrist, & Dussault, 2006).

A conceptual model

Synthesizing the cognitive and behavioral processes described above, religious OCD symptoms (i.e., scrupulosity) can be understood as a problem that emerges when commonly occurring intrusive thoughts are misinterpreted as significant based on exaggerated and maladaptive beliefs about the importance of thoughts. Although the development of these beliefs might have its roots in the person's religious doctrine, scrupulosity represents rigid and exaggerated adherence ideals that deviate from norms of religious practice. Misinterpretation of normal intrusive thoughts as highly meaningful leads to obsessional preoccupation and doubt specific to the individual's particular religious beliefs. In the context of an IU, the mere *possibility* that one has sinned (and could be punished) provokes high levels of anxiety and distress. The person then engages in various compulsive, avoidance, and neutralizing strategies to reduce the distress, achieve certainty, banish the unwanted thought or doubt, and elude feared negative consequences; yet these strategies only intensify the sense of uncertainty, lead to more unwanted intrusions, and promote greater obsessional preoccupation. Moreover, they are negatively reinforced by the brief reduction in distress that they occasionally engender; thus they are repeated "compulsively." The result is a self-sustaining vicious cycle.

Clinical implications

The concepts and integrative model discussed in the previous section have implications for a cognitive behavior approach to clinical intervention. In the present section, we outline specific procedures that may be useful for helping scrupulous individuals weaken maladaptive beliefs that are inconsistent with the person's religion (e.g., rigid beliefs about the importance of intrusive thoughts), increase tolerance for uncertainty, and reduce the reliance on compulsive rituals and avoidance. We conceptualize treatment as helping scrupulous individuals follow their religion in a healthier and more *faithful* way.

Psychoeducation and treatment planning

It is often beneficial to begin treatment by helping the patient identify their own rigidly held beliefs about God, sin, and uncertainty. They might view God as petulant, easily angered, and vengeful, which is in contrast to the doctrine of most mainstream religions that God loves all people unconditionally. A related contrast may be between the definition of *faith*, which is a central part of religious adherence, and the client's IU and doubt. Thus, an important take-home message is that the client has, in a sense, created his or her own religion where faith is not enough—rather he or she requires a *guarantee* about things that cannot be guaranteed and about which most practitioners of the same religion accept based on faith. The therapist can discuss how treatment will help the patient become a more faithful follower of his or her religion since it will help them to *trust* God, rather than being fearful. Clinicians can also integrate religious coping with evidence-based OCD treatment to promote hope, meaning, and purpose. It is important to note, however, that coping focuses on the connecting and strengthening aspects of religion. Pirutinsky et al. (2011) found that negative religious coping (e.g., anger at God and religious disengagement) is associated with more severe depression among Orthodox Jews.

Exposure therapy

Exposure therapy is a set of procedures for extinguishing inappropriate fear (Abramowitz, Deacon, & Whiteside, 2011; Craske et al., 2008). Extinction is a cognitive process in which the individual learns new safety-based information to inhibit previously learned fear-based associations (i.e., inhibitory learning). In the present context, where there is no possibility of "proof" of sin, salvation, or other spiritual outcomes, the aim of exposure is to promote learning that intrusive thoughts, uncertainty, and anxiety are safe and manageable. One way to promote tolerance of anxiety and uncertainty is to elaborate on the uncertainty of feared consequences using imaginal exposure (e.g., "you can't be sure if God is upset with you"). For example, in vivo exposures to external stimuli that trigger doubts could be combined with imaginal exposures to help the person learn that they can manage such normal doubts, as opposed to trying to analyze, suppress, or gain reassurance about them (which maintains the problem).

The method of *expectancy tracking* can be used to this end. In this technique, the therapist tracks the client's expectancies of tolerating uncertainty, with the goal of continuing the exposure until expectancy violation is achieved (Jacoby & Abramowitz, 2016). For example, the therapist could assess how long the client believes she could tolerate feeling uncertain over whether she has committed "an unpardonable sin" and what activities she believes she could not accomplish while feeling this way. Exposures that provoke uncertainty over sin would then be used to induce doubt, and the patient would practice remaining uncertain for longer than she predicted would be possible and engaging in activities that she believed would be too challenging. The goal would be for the client to repeatedly learn that she can tolerate uncertainty and accomplish daily tasks without a guarantee (i.e., she can manage on faith alone).

Selection of particular stimuli for in vivo and imaginal exposure with religious clients should be consistent with the goal of helping the person learn and practice tolerating uncertainty (i.e., developing greater faith). Exposure situations that flagrantly violate religious laws are neither appropriate nor consistent with this goal. Individuals with religious obsessions and compulsions fear they *might* have sinned; thus exposure should entail situations that evoke doubts and uncertainty about sin, *but that do not involve committing blatantly sinful behavior itself.* As an analogous situation, consider someone with the obsession that he has mistakenly hit a pedestrian with his car. His fear involves uncertainty over whether or not such a mishap has occurred, not what to do in the event that one actually hits a pedestrian. Accordingly, rather than actually hitting individuals with his car, exposure would involve learning to manage acceptable risks such as driving through parking lots and streets with many pedestrians. Still, the nature of exposures that will evoke uncertainty over outcomes that require faith necessitates that the client be familiar with, and accept, the rationale for exposure. If the reason for engaging in such exposures is not clear to the patient, he or she may view cognitive-behavioral therapy as an assault on his or her religion. Abramowitz et al. (2011) provide an in-depth discussion of the use of exposure for religious obsessions and compulsions.

Response prevention

Response prevention, which entails resisting urges to perform compulsive rituals, also fosters faith through learning that uncertainty is tolerable. That is, it helps the client discover that compulsive rituals (e.g., prayer, confession, etc.), clarifications, and assurances are not necessary to resolve obsessional concerns or escape from anxiety and uncertainty. It is not only overt compulsive rituals that must be resisted, but any behavior performed in attempt to acquire reassurance. In addition, cues such as the presence of a therapist, loved one, or religious authority are important response prevention targets since such people might implicitly or explicitly serve as safety signals or provide reassurance, thus preventing tolerance of uncertainty. This highlights the importance of having clients practice exposures on their own, in the absence of the therapist (or anyone else), in addition to practicing in session. It further underscores the importance of getting any family members or clergy on board with refraining from providing religious or spiritual reassurance to clients during treatment. For clients who persistently ask questions about the possibility of sin, salvation, and the like, refraining from providing reassuring answers, and instead explaining the importance of remaining uncertain and using faith, is an important skill to teach those close to the patient.

For similar reasons we generally prefer that clients not visit with clergy members to discuss the lawfulness of treatment (or anything else). Indeed, most clients will have already discussed similar matters with their clergy (often repeatedly) and thus are likely to already have a sense of what the clergy member's response would be. In such cases, such a visit could equate to reassurance seeking. In line with the aims of treatment, we suggest first engaging clients in a discussion of what (based on previous visits) the clergy member is *likely* to tell them (even though they don't know for sure) and then foster faith that this answer would probably not have changed. That said, there may be situations in which avoiding consultation with clergy prevents the client from learning how to consult with clergy effectively and nonritualistically; these may be important skills for use after treatment. Huppert and Siev (2010), for example, have noted that careful consultation with clergy can motivate the individual to engage in exposure and response prevention because the clergy member can help distinguish intentional unacceptable thoughts that are inconsistent with doctrine (e.g., fantasies about elicit acts) from unintentional intrusive thoughts that cause distress and conflict with the client's values. Clergy members can also help determine exposure exercises that pose "acceptable risks" but still provoke obsessional fears and cause anxiety.

Finally, in planning which behaviors to target in response prevention, clients often require assistance differentiating between healthy religious behaviors and compulsive rituals (i.e., religious behaviors performed in response to obsessional fear and doubt). Allowing him or her to take the lead in sorting this out can be helpful. Religious behavior motivated by obsessional thoughts is "fear-based" rather than "faith-based." Here, the assistance of family members and religious authorities who can reinforce this distinction can be helpful. In general, religious rituals that are performed as meaningful expressions of faith and religious identity (even those that bring about solace in a general sense) do not need to be curtailed during treatment. On the other hand, rituals performed as a means of assuaging obsessional anxiety, guilt, or shame should be targeted. To illustrate, whereas seeking general support from a religious authority or one's community is healthy religious behavior, seeking reassurance regarding particular obsessional fears would be considered a compulsive ritual. Similarly, praying for the courage to engage in treatment would be considered appropriate, whereas praying for forgiveness regarding obsessional fears would be considered a violation of response prevention. It is important to assess the intent, proportion, and occasion of particular behaviors (as opposed to their topography) when determining whether a seemingly religious behavior should be targeted in response prevention.

Cognitive therapy

Therapists working with scrupulous individuals occasionally fall into the trap of trying to convince their clients that his or her obsessions are illogical, unlikely to come true, or otherwise senseless. Some therapists use cognitive therapy techniques based on the work of Beck (1976) or Ellis (1962) to try to demonstrate to the client that an obsessional fear is irrational or nonsensical (e.g., "Where's the evidence that your soul is possessed by the devil?"). Although the obsession intuitively seems like a good target for this sort of rational discussion, this approach overemphasizes short-term anxiety reduction (and reassurance) and will have a transient effect at best. As previously mentioned, there is no way to achieve certainty about the sorts of spiritual or enigmatic concerns that scrupulous individuals experience (e.g., whether or not one's soul is possessed by the devil). Rationality-based debates will, therefore, prove futile. It is likely that many have already tried (and failed) using such approaches to talk the scrupulous person out of their fears.

We suggest that if cognitive restructuring is used at all with individuals with religious OCD symptoms, it is used to challenge the client's catastrophic beliefs about the *intolerance* of anxiety, uncertainty, and distressing intrusive thoughts. Verbal cognitive techniques, for example, can be used to foster discussions to challenge the need for absolute certainty over matters that other followers of their religion accept on faith. Therapists can help clients generate lists of the pros and cons of continuing to try to gain certainty versus learning to live with normal everyday uncertainty and accept such enigmatic things on faith. Through such techniques, patients might come to realize that they already accept uncertainty in most other areas of her life (e.g., driving in a car to the treatment session!), and so have ample evidence that they can function sufficiently even in a state of uncertainty. The use of cognitive techniques in this way could set the table for the sorts of exposure and response prevention assignments described previously to diminish the significance of obsessional thoughts and uncertainty.

Discussion

Religious obsessions and compulsions (i.e., scrupulosity) can be conceptualized as a presentation of OCD focused on spiritual and moral themes that are exaggerated and distinct from normal religious practice. The relationship between scrupulosity, one's degree of religiosity, and his or her religious affiliation is complex, yet a growing body of research (almost entirely cross-sectional thus far) and clinical observations lead to a cognitive-behavioral model of the problem that assumes that to some degree, one's religious beliefs and values influence the misinterpretation of normally occurring unwanted thoughts as potentially sinful or foreboding of divine punishment. Because many religious matters are not subject to either confirmation or disconfirmation, but only to faith, clients' IU can lead to intense anxiety and urges to reduce this anxiety using strategies that end up having the opposite effects. This model has implications for how cognitive-behavioral interventions, such as exposure, response prevention, and cognitive therapy, can be applied in the treatment of religious OCD symptoms. Helping clients recognize that their need for certainty has resulted in a rejection of their religious faith can be a potent rationale for engaging in treatment. Treatment can be viewed as helping clients feel more comfortable with their own religious beliefs and practice their religion more faithfully, as opposed to making fear-based choices. Because the stakes are subjectively very high for the scrupulous individual—he or she might believe that their immortal soul or relationship with God is in danger—it is important for clinicians to hold an empathic position, develop the client's trust, and obtain the clarity needed to negotiate and address the intricacies of this presentation of OCD.

References

Abramowitz, J. S., Deacon, B. J., & Whiteside, S. P. H. (2011). *Exposure therapy for anxiety: Principles and practice*. New York: Guilford Press.

Abramowitz, J. S., Deacon, B. J., Woods, C. M., & Tolin, D. F. (2004). Association between protestant religiosity and obsessive-compulsive symptoms and cognitions. *Depression and Anxiety*, *20*(2), 70–76. Available from https://doi.org/10.1002/da.20021.

Abramowitz, J. S., Huppert, J. D., Cohen, A. B., Tolin, D. F., & Cahill, S. P. (2002). Religious obsessions and compulsions in a non-clinical sample: The Penn Inventory of Scrupulosity (PIOS). *Behaviour Research and Therapy*, *40*(7), 824–838. Available from https://doi.org/10.1016/S0005-7967(01)00070-5.

Abramowitz, J. S., & Jacoby, R. J. (2014). Scrupulosity: A cognitive–behavioral analysis and implications for treatment. *Journal of Obsessive-Compulsive and Related Disorders*, *3* (2), 140–149. Available from https://doi.org/10.1016/j.jocrd.2013.12.007.

American Psychiatric Association. (2013). *Diagnostic and statistical manual of mental disorders* (5th ed.). Arlington, VA: American Psychiatric Publishing.

Assarian, F., Biqam, H., & Asqarnejad, A. (2006). An epidemiological study of obsessive-com pulsive disorder among high school students and its relationship with religious attitudes. *Archives of Iranian Medicine*, *9*(2), 104–107.

Beck, A. T. (1976). *Cognitive therapy and the emotional disorders*. International Universities Press.

Berman, N. C., Abramowitz, J. S., Pardue, C. M., & Wheaton, M. G. (2010). The relationship between religion and thought–action fusion: Use of an in vivo paradigm. *Behaviour Research and Therapy*, *48*(7), 670–674. Available from https://doi.org/10.1016/j.brat.2010.03.021.

Boelen, P. A., & Carleton, R. N. (2012). Intolerance of uncertainty, hypochondriacal concerns, obsessive-compulsive symptoms, and worry. *Journal of Nervous and Mental Disease*, *200*(3), 208–213. Available from https://doi.org/10.1097/NMD.0b013e318247cb17.

Buchholz, J., Abramowitz, J. S., Riemann, B. C., Reuman, L., Blakely, S. M., Leonard, R. C., & Thompson, K. A. (2019). Scrupulosity, religious affiliation and symptom presentation in obsessive compulsive disorder. *Behavioural and Cognitive Psychotherapy*, *47*, 478–492.

Calleo, J. S., Hart, J., Björgvinsson, T., & Stanley, M. A. (2010). Obsessions and worry beliefs in an inpatient OCD population. *Journal of Anxiety Disorders*, *24*(8), 903–908.

Cohen, A. B., & Rozin, P. (2001). Religion and the morality of mentality. *Journal of personality and social psychology*, *81*(4), 697.

Craske, M. G., Kircanski, K., Zelikowsky, M., Mystkowski, J., Chowdhury, N., & Baker, A. (2008). Optimizing inhibitory learning during exposure therapy. *Behaviour Research and Therapy*, *46*(1), 5–27. Available from https://doi.org/10.1016/j.brat.2007.10.003.

Eisen, J. L., Phillips, K. A., & Rasmussen, S. A. (1999). Obsessions and delusions: The relationship between obsessive-compulsive disorder and the psychotic disorders. *Psychiatric Annals*, *29*(9), 515–522. Available from https://doi.org/10.3928/0048-5713-19990901-08.

Ellis, A. (1962). *Reason and emotion in psychotherapy*. Oxford, England: Lyle Stuart.

Foa, E. B., Kozak, M. J., Goodman, W. K., Hollander, E., Jenike, M. A., & Rasmussen, S. A. (1995). DSM-IV field trial: Obsessive-compulsive disorder. *The American Journal of Psychiatry*, *152*(1), 90–96.

Greenberg, D., & Shefler, G. (2002). Obsessive compulsive disorder in ultra-orthodox Jewish patients: A comparison of religious and non-religious symptoms. *Psychology and Psychotherapy: Theory, Research and Practice*, *75*(2), 123–130. Available from https://doi.org/10.1348/147608302169599.

Greenberg, D., & Witztum, E. (1994). The influence of cultural factors on obsessive compulsive disorder: Religious symptoms in a religious society. *Israel Journal of Psychiatry and Related Sciences*, *31*(3), 211–220.

Greenberg, D., Witztum, E., & Pisante, J. (1987). Scrupulosity: Religious attitudes and clinical presentations. *British Journal of Medical Psychology*, *60*(1), 29–37.

Hermesh, H., Masser-Kavitzky, R., & Gross-Isseroff, R. (2003). obsessive-compulsive disorder and Jewish religiosity. *The Journal of Nervous and Mental Disease*, *191*(3), 201. Available from https://doi.org/10.1097/01.NMD.0000055083.60919.09.

Huppert, J. D., & Siev, J. (2010). Treating scrupulosity in religious individuals using cognitive-behavioral therapy. *Cognitive and Behavioral Practice*, *17*(4), 382–392. Available from https://doi.org/10.1016/j.cbpra.2009.07.003.

Huppert, J. D., Siev, J., & Kushner, E. S. (2007). When religion and obsessive–compulsive disorder collide: Treating scrupulosity in ultra-orthodox Jews. *Journal of Clinical Psychology*, *63*(10), 925–941.

Inozu, M., Karanci, A. N., & Clark, D. A. (2012). Why are religious individuals more obsessional? The role of mental control beliefs and guilt in Muslims and Christians. *Journal of Behavior Therapy and Experimental Psychiatry*, *43*(3), 959–966. Available from https://doi.org/10.1016/j.jbtep.2012.02.004.

Jacoby, R. J., & Abramowitz, J. S. (2016). Inhibitory learning approaches to exposure therapy: A critical review and translation to obsessive-compulsive disorder. *Clinical Psychology Review*, *49*, 28–40. Available from https://doi.org/10.1016/j.cpr.2016.07.001.

Lewis, C. A., & Maltby, J. (1995). Religiosity and personality among U.S. adults. *Personality and Individual Differences*, *18*(2), 293–295. Available from https://doi.org/10.1016/0191-8869(94)00159-P.

Loewenthal, K. M. (2018). The OCD—religion package: Might it relate to the rise of spirituality? *Mental Health, Religion & Culture*, *21*(2), 123–130. Available from https://doi.org/10.1080/13674676.2018.1447554.

Mahgoub, O. M., & Abdel-Hafeiz, H. B. (1991). Pattern of obsessive-compulsive disorder in eastern Saudi Arabia. *The British Journal of Psychiatry*, *158*(6), 840–842. Available from https://doi.org/10.1192/bjp.158.6.840.

Mataix-Cols, D., Marks, I. M., Greist, J. H., Kobak, K. A., & Baer, L. (2002). Obsessive-compulsive symptom dimensions as predictors of compliance with and response to behaviour therapy: Results from a controlled trial. *Psychotherapy and Psychosomatics*, *71*(5), 255–262. Available from https://doi.org/10.1159/000064812.

McKay, D., Abramowitz, J. S., Calamari, J. E., Kyrios, M., Radomsky, A. S., Sookman, D., . . . Wilhelm, S. (2004). A critical evaluation of obsessive-compulsive disorder subtypes: Symptoms versus mechanisms. *Clinical Psychology Review*, *24*(3), 283–313. Available from https://doi.org/10.1016/j.cpr.2004.04.003.

Najmi, S., Riemann, B. C., & Wegner, D. M. (2009). Managing unwanted intrusive thoughts in obsessive–compulsive disorder: Relative effectiveness of suppression, focused distraction, and acceptance. *Behaviour Research and Therapy*, *47*(6), 494–503. Available from https://doi.org/10.1016/j.brat.2009.02.015.

Nelson, E. A., Abramowitz, J. S., Whiteside, S. P., & Deacon, B. J. (2006). Scrupulosity in patients with obsessive-compulsive disorder: Relationship to clinical and cognitive phenomena. *Journal of Anxiety Disorders*, *20*(8), 1071–1086. Available from https://doi.org/10.1016/j.janxdis.2006.02.001.

Okasha, A., Saad, A., Khalil, A., Seif, A., & Yehia, N. (1994). Phenomenology of obsessive-compulsive disorder: A transcultural study. *Comprehensive Psychiatry*, *35*(3), 191–197.

Pirutinsky, S., Rosmarin, D. H., Pargament, K. I., & Midlarsky, E. (2011). Does negative religious coping accompany, precede, or follow depression among Orthodox Jews? *Journal of Affective Disorders*, *132*(3), 401–405.

Rachman, S. J. (1997). A cognitive theory of obsessions. *Behaviour Research and Therapy*, *35*(9), 793–802.

Rachman, S. J. (2002). A cognitive theory of compulsive checking. *Behaviour Research and Therapy*, *40*(6), 624–639.

Rachman, S. J., & de Silva, P. (1978). Abnormal and normal obsessions. *Behaviour Research and Therapy*, *16*(4), 233–248.

Radomsky, A. S., Gilchrist, P. T., & Dussault, D. (2006). Repeated checking really does cause memory distrust. *Behaviour Research and Therapy*, *44*(2), 305–316. Available from https://doi.org/10.1016/j.brat.2005.02.005.

Ruscio, A. M., Stein, D. J., Chiu, W. T., & Kessler, R. C. (2010). The epidemiology of obsessive-compulsive disorder in the National Comorbidity Survey Replication. *Molecular Psychiatry*, *15*(1), 53–63. Available from https://doi.org/10.1038/mp.2008.94.

Salkovskis, P. M., Shafran, R., Rachman, S., & Freeston, M. H. (1999). Multiple pathways to inflated responsibility beliefs in obsessional problems: Possible origins and implications for therapy and research. *Behaviour Research and Therapy*, *37*(11), 1055–1072. Available from https://doi.org/10.1016/S0005-7967(99)00063-7.

Shafran, R., Thordarson, D. S., & Rachman, S. (1996). Thought-action fusion in obsessive compulsive disorder. *Journal of Anxiety Disorders*, *10*(5), 379–391. Available from https://doi.org/10.1016/0887-6185(96)00018-7.

Sica, C., Novara, C., & Sanavio, E. (2002). Religiousness and obsessive–compulsive cognitions and symptoms in an Italian population. *Behaviour Research and Therapy*, *40*(7), 813–823. Available from https://doi.org/10.1016/S0005-7967(01)00120-6.

Siev, J., Baer, L., & Minichiello, W. E. (2011). Obsessive-compulsive disorder with predominantly scrupulous symptoms: Clinical and religious characteristics. *Journal of Clinical Psychology*, *67*(12), 1188–1196. Available from https://doi.org/10.1002/jclp.20843.

Siev, J., & Cohen, A. B. (2007). Is thought-action fusion related to religiosity? Differences between Christians and Jews. *Behaviour Research and Therapy*, *45*(4), 829–837. Available from https://doi.org/10.1016/j.brat.2006.05.001.

Siev, J., Huppert, J. D., & Zuckerman, S. E. (2017). *Understanding and treating scrupulosity. The Wiley handbook of obsessive compulsive disorders* (pp. 527–546). New York: Wiley-Blackwell. Available from https://doi.org/10.1002/9781118890233.ch29.

Siev, J., Steketee, G., Fama, J., & Wilhelm, S. (2011). Sexual, religious, and contamination obsessions are associated with different obsessional beliefs and personality traits. In *45th annual convention of the association for behavioral and cognitive therapies*. Retrieved from <https://nsuworks.nova.edu/cps_facpresentations/1568>.

Steketee, G., Quay, S., & White, K. (1991). Religion and guilt in OCD patients. *Journal of Anxiety Disorders*, *5*(4), 359–367. Available from https://doi.org/10.1016/0887-6185(91)90035-R.

Tek, C., & Ulug, B. (2001). Religiosity and religious obsessions in obsessive–compulsive disorder. *Psychiatry Research, 104*(2), 99–108. Available from https://doi.org/10.1016/S0165-1781(01)00310-9.

Tolin, D. F., Abramowitz, J. S., Kozak, M. J., & Foa, E. B. (2001). Fixity of belief, perceptual aberration, and magical ideation in obsessive-compulsive disorder. *Journal of Anxiety Disorders, 15*(6), 501–510. Available from https://doi.org/10.1016/S0887-6185(01)00078-0.

Williams, A. D., Lau, G., & Grisham, J. R. (2013). Thought–action fusion as a mediator of religiosity and obsessive-compulsive symptoms. *Journal of Behavior Therapy and Experimental Psychiatry, 44*(2), 207–212.

Yorulmaz, O., Gençöz, T., & Woody, S. (2009). OCD cognitions and symptoms in different religious contexts. *Journal of anxiety disorders, 23*(3), 401–406.

CHAPTER 5

Spirituality, religion, and psychotic disorders

Philippe Huguelet
Department of Psychiatry, University Hospital of Geneva and University of Geneva, Geneva, Switzerland

Contents

Introduction

Considering spirituality/religion (S/R) in patients with psychotic disorders is difficult, since S/R can be a resource or a source of strain and can also sometimes be entangled with the disorders' symptoms. Some patients may display symptoms involving religious content; others (and sometimes the very same patients) may consider religion as one of the most important ways that they cope with symptoms of psychosis.

Indeed, patients experience major spiritual/existential difficulties as a consequence of having psychotic disorders that evolve in the long term.

Handbook of Spirituality, Religion, and Mental Health
DOI: https://doi.org/10.1016/B978-0-12-816766-3.00005-7

Such struggles may foster a search for the soothing effects that religion may provide. Thus, many questions arise concerning the role of S/R among individuals with psychotic disorders:

Does S/R affect the occurrence of psychosis?

Are there situations in which S/R may be harmful to patients?

Are patients more prone to engage in S/R activities?

Can religious coping help them?

Does S/R influence patients' outcomes?

How can we understand delusions with S/R content?

How can clinicians deal with the S/R issues that patients bring up? This chapter seeks to help clinicians find answers to these questions.

In early Christian churches, mental illnesses were thought to be caused by possession by demons, and sacramental healings and exorcisms were practiced. Overall, Christian views of mental illness oscillated between the biological and the spiritual (Koenig, 2005). In Islam, mental illness was considered to be a medical condition. Islamic hospitals were built during the 9th and 10th centuries (Cloarec, 1998) and encouraged prayers and incantations as a choice of treatment. Eastern traditions (Hinduism, Buddhism, Confucianism, and Taoism) provided different models of mental illness, with a focus on existential and transpersonal issues (Kinzie, 2000). Historical accounts of religious delusions go back to the first issues of the American Journal of Insanity, the precursor of the American Journal of Psychiatry (Farr & Howe, 1932; Workman, 1869). However, these early works failed to address the differences between functional and dysfunctional aspects of religion.

Over the last 30 years though, there has been an increasing body of literature trying to approach the topic of religious delusions in more scientific terms (e.g., Siddle, Haddock, Tarrier, & Faragher, 2002). The World Health Organization now considers spirituality, religion, and personal beliefs as an important area in the evaluation of quality of life (Culliford, 2002). Research has explored the influence of religion on psychosis with the concept of *coping* (Pargament & Brant, 1998), showing both positive and negative impacts.

Schizophrenia is generally understood through the stress-vulnerability model (Nuechterlein & Dawson, 1984). This model perceives schizophrenia as the result of a psychobiological vulnerability. The course of the disorder is determined by the interplay of biological and psychosocial factors. Protective factors improve psychosis' outcome, and stressors may unfavorably impact the course or severity of symptoms. From this view, S/R may represent either a protective factor or a stressor.

Over the past few years, *recovery* has been recognized as an organizing principle for the care for the mentally ill that can replace paternalistic, illness-oriented services (Sowers, 2005). Recovery focuses on personal fulfillment rather than on a complete restoration of a prior level of functioning (Andresen, Oades, & Caputi, 2003). It involves (1) finding hope, (2) reestablishing one's identity, (3) finding meaning-in-life, and (4) taking responsibility. Recovery-oriented care should include a variety of services that support consumer self-sufficiency, provide culturally sensitive treatments, and emphasize consumer choice.

S/R plays an important role in recovery-oriented care: first, it is often part of one's identity; second, religion can offer opportunities for patients, in terms of goals setting such as occupational activities; and overall, it can constitute a way of fulfilling one's aspirations, in terms of life goals, combining both social and self-accomplishing dimensions.

Spirituality/religion and psychotic disorders: research

Spirituality/religion and psychotic processes

Some studies report that increased religiosity may not be associated with better outcomes (Gearing et al., 2011). Abdelgawad, Chotalia, Parsaik, Pigott, and Allen (2017) showed that religious involvement was more likely among acutely psychotic inpatients. Also, there may be an association between religiosity and hallucinatory experiences (Steenhuis et al., 2016). Kovess-Masfety et al. (2018) examined associations between psychotic experiences (PEs) and religiosity in a total of 25,542 community-dwelling nonpsychotic adults. They found that among individuals with religious affiliations, those who reported more religiosity had increased odds of PEs. Hence, religion may be a risk factor for psychosis or psychotic-like symptoms, and/or PEs may lead to adopting religious beliefs. Yet, if S/R and PEs may seem similar, their phenomenology is quite different: altered states of perception or consciousness in a religious context have nothing to do with negative symptoms and cognitive disorganization (Rosmarin, Moreira-Almeida, & Koenig, 2018). Hence, this relationship still needs to be studied with better tools and methods (e.g., with qualitative research, prospective studies, and randomized controlled trials).

Religious coping in patients with psychosis

Pargament (1997) and Pargament and Brant (1998) indicated that a function of S/R is as a *coping behavior*. They described that religious coping can serve five purposes: spiritual (meaning, purpose, hope), self-development, resolve (self-efficacy), sharing (closeness, connectedness to a community), and restraint (help in keeping emotions and behaviors under control). Religious coping may be adaptive or not. In a study of 406 patients with psychosis, more than 80% indicated they used religion to cope (Tepper, Rogers, Coleman, & Malony, 2001). In a quantitative and qualitative study, Mohr, Brandt, Borras, Gillieron, and Huguelet (2006) studied the role of S/R as a coping mechanism among outpatients with schizophrenia. For 45% of the patients, religion was the most important element in their lives. Religion was used as a positive way of coping for 71% of subjects and as a negative way of coping for 14% of patients. These findings were replicated in Quebec, Canada, and in Durham, North Carolina, in a total of 276 outpatients (Mohr et al., 2012). Later, other studies confirmed the positive use of S/R as a coping mechanism (Das, Punnoose, Doval, & Nair, 2018; Grover, Davuluri, & Chakrabarti, 2014; Nolan et al., 2012; Rosmarin, Bigda-Peyton, Öngur, Pargament, & Björgvinsson, 2013; Triveni, Grover, & Chakrabarti, 2017).

Let us describe in greater detail how positive aspects of S/R coping work. At a *psychological level*, religion may enhance a positive sense of self (in terms of hope, comfort, meaning of life, love, compassion, self-respect, self-confidence, etc.). Religion provides meaning to illness, mainly through positive religious connotations (grace, a gift, God's test to induce spiritual growth, spiritual acceptance of suffering, etc.) and less frequently through negative connotations (the devil, demons, God's punishment, etc.). However, even if those meanings may be negative in religious terms, they can be positive by fostering an acceptance of the illness or a mobilization of resources to cope with the symptoms. Religious coping often has a *positive impact on symptoms* (e.g., by lessening the emotional or behavioral reactions to delusions and hallucinations and/or by reducing aggressive behavior). Religion can also help to reduce anxiety, depression, and negative symptoms. At the *social level*, religion provides guidelines for interpersonal behavior, which leads to reduced aggression and improved social relationships. However, and unfortunately, in spite of the subjective importance of religion, few psychotic patients actually receive social support from a religious community (Mohr et al., 2006).

Some patients report negative effects from religious coping. For these patients, religion is a source of despair and suffering. Patients may feel despair after the spiritual healing they have sought is unsuccessful. Others use religion to cope, but with negative outcomes (e.g., reading religious texts increases symptoms such as anxiety, delusions, depression, or suicide risk).

Effects of spirituality/religion on other aspects

Religion may protect patients with psychotic disorders against suicide. Only few research studies have addressed this important issue to date. Rosmarin et al. (2013) found an association between negative religious coping and increased frequency and intensity of suicidal ideation in psychotic patients. Concerning possible ways religion may play a role, a qualitative study by Huguelet et al. (2007) found that for 25% of all subjects religion played a protective role with regard to suicide, primarily through ethical condemnation of suicide, religious coping, and rediscovery of meaning-in-life through religion. However, 1 out of 10 patients reported negative aspects of religion: suicide attempts following a break with a religious community, suicide attempts involving religious delusions and hallucinations, wishing to die in order to be with God or to live another life after death, etc.

S/R may also provide guidelines that protect patients with schizophrenia from substance misuse (Huguelet, Borras, Gillieron, Brandt, & Mohr, 2009). Indeed, religious involvement has been significantly inversely correlated to substance misuse among those with psychotic disorders. In the latter study, content analysis showed that religion may play a protective role in patients by encouraging the cessation of substance misuse (42%), whereas it played a negative role in 3% of cases. Religion provides guidelines for living without substances, an alternative coping strategy replacing substance use, and a point of anchorage for a complete reorganization of life around spirituality.

Spirituality/religion delusions versus "normal faith"

The most effective way to assess the presence of a delusion is by following a list of criteria. For instance, the more a belief is implausible, unfounded, strongly held, not shared by others, distressing and preoccupying, the more likely it is to be a delusion (Freeman et al., 2007). The most common criteria are conviction, preoccupation, pervasiveness, negative emotionality, and action-inaction (Combs et al., 2006). Jones and Watson (1997) compared the characteristics of delusions in subjects with schizophrenia to beliefs about the existence of God in a control group of highly religious Christians. Their religious beliefs and delusions did not differ with regard to conviction, falsity, affect, or influence on behavior. They only differed in their degree of preoccupation and the role of perception in belief.

The prevalence of delusions with religious content varies across countries and cultures and in some studies has been associated with more severe hallucinations and bizarre delusions, poorer functioning, and longer duration of illness (Siddle et al., 2002). Delusions can be separated into three distinct categories: delusions of influence (e.g., delusions of being controlled, thought withdrawal, thought insertion, mind reading, etc.), self-significance delusions (delusions of grandeur, reference, religious delusions of guilt/sin), and persecutory delusions (Kimhi, Goetz, Yale, Corcoran, & Malaspina, 2005). Religious content can be found in each of these categories. Patients may have the conviction that they are being controlled by God or that their thoughts come from God; they may think that they are God; or they may be convinced that they are being persecuted by some religious figure. Delusions with religious content are unlikely to reflect a unitary phenomenon with a common neurocognitive or neurobiological underpinning. Rather, delusions with religious content may be related to former personal and social experiences and therefore must be understood in the context of a person's life and culture (Drinnan & Lavender, 2006). Rhodes and Jakes (2004) suggest that religious experience represents patients' attempts to interpret their anomalous experiences (e.g., a way to cope with distressing events such as hallucinations).

Interestingly, patients who have delusions with religious content may benefit from S/R coping *at the same time*. Mohr, Borras, Betrisey, et al. (2010) found in a study of 236 patients that delusions with religious content were not associated with a more severe clinical status compared to other kinds of delusions, except that religious delusions were associated with a lower treatment compliance. For almost half of the group with delusions with religious content (45%), S/R helped patients cope with their illness.

Spirituality/religion and acute psychosis

Religion sometimes represents a stressor likely to influence the course of psychotic disorders. To date, however, there is no evidence demonstrating that religious involvement a causal factor for either acute or chronic psychotic disorders. Some authors argue that religious conversion may play a role in precipitating psychosis in vulnerable individuals (Sedman & Hopkinson, 1966). Koenig (2005) has noted that some subjects experience episodes of psychosis following their religious conversions. Recently, Loch et al. (2019) found that among individuals at ultrahigh risk for psychosis, religion was mostly used to cope with positive symptoms, rather than serving as a stressor.

Spirituality as a source for meaning-in-life

Meaning involves at least two dimensions (Yalom, 1980): personal life meaning is concerned with one's goals in life, whereas cosmic meaning concerns the spiritual dimension of life (i.e., the manner in which human life is integrated into the universe). According to Park (2013), religion remains pervasive among humans because it provides a reliable system of meaning. S/R is often part of global meanings (beliefs, goals, and subjective sense of meaningfulness) and translates into daily meanings (interpretations, strivings and projects, life satisfaction and positive affect), which can be threatened and changed in stressful circumstances.

What are the determinants of meaning? S/R, self-esteem, and close relationships may help to gain meaning-inlife (Battista & Almond, 1973). Beyond this prerequisite, meaning is associated with phenomena that further orient individuals toward life goals. In particular, meaning depends on the fit between the values, goals, and needs of individuals and the values, goals, and needs of the social structure in which they live. Values can be defined as reinforcing factors, the benefits of which are often delayed (Wilson, Sandoz, & Kitchens, 2010). In a meta-analysis examining the relationship between religion and basic human values, it was shown that religious people tend to favor conservation (tradition, conformity, and security) and benevolence; they also tend to dislike openness to change (stimulation, self-direction, and hedonism), as well as self-enhancement through achievement and power (Saroglou, Delpierre, & Dernelle, 2004).

Huguelet, Guillaume, et al. (2016) found that the presence and enactment of values were associated with higher meaning-in-life among 176 psychiatric patients, 75 of whom were diagnosed with schizophrenia. For 26% of the patients, S/R was essential in providing meaning-in-life and was associated with better social functioning, self-esteem, quality of life, fewer negative symptoms, higher endorsement of values such as universalism, tradition (humility, devoutness), and benevolence (helpfulness), and a more meaningful perspective in life.

As religion and spirituality promote self-transcendence (benevolence and universalism) and conservation (conformity, tradition, and security) values, it is not surprising that S/R-based meaning-in-life is associated with higher levels of benevolence, tradition, and universalism. This result, keeping in mind the association of higher S/R with improved psychological health and benevolence (Huguelet, Mohr, et al., 2016), suggests that S/R may serve as a solace when severe mental illness hinders the achievement of social and vocational goals.

Spirituality/religion and the self-representation of the psychotic disorder

The different aspects of psychosis may influence patients' treatment choices. When becoming ill, many patients try to find *explanatory models* for their disorder related to conventional medicine, local traditions, or religion. To note, these explanations can be associated with each other (e.g., "God" may be the initiator of an illness by lowering one's immunity). Bhikha, Farooq, Chaudhry, and Husain (2012) found that in developing countries most patients with psychosis adopted supernatural/spiritual explanatory models, often combined with scientific ones. Pfeifer (1994) reported that in Switzerland, 38% of the patients related their psychological disorder to being possessed by an evil force. In Uganda, Teuton, Dowrick, and Bentall (2007) investigated the conceptualization of "madness" across indigenous healers, religious healers, and conventional physicians and nurses. For indigenous healers, "madness" was a sign of a deviation, a form of harm instigated by some jealous party. Religious healers attributed it to the evil influence of Satan. Pragmatically, these differences of explanations underline the necessity to improve the dialog between traditional healers and allopathic doctors in order to develop an integrative model of health care. Using educational interventions to identify and correct explanatory models may improve treatment adherence (Das et al., 2006).

Beyond explanation, research has been done on the way people cope with their illness by attributing *meaning-making* (i.e., both an explanatory model and a form of coping). Meaning-making coping is particularly relevant and adaptive for subjects living low control situations such as cancer (Park, 2010), other disorders, and possibly psychosis, conditions that are not amenable to direct repair. Pargament (1997) identified four spiritual meanings of illness: a benevolent religious reappraisal (i.e., redefining the illness through religion as benevolent and potentially beneficial); a punishing God reappraisal (redefining the illness as a punishment from God for the individual's sins); a demonic reappraisal (redefining the illness as the act of the Devil), and a reappraisal of God's powers (redefining God's power to influence the illness). These different spiritual meanings have been associated with positive and negative outcomes (Phillips & Stein, 2007). To note, the various contents of S/R interpretations of illness are not positive or negative, per se, in terms of coping. Rather, positive or negative value depends on the integration of the religious interpretation into the person's experience.

Spirituality/religion and attachment

Studies have found higher levels of *insecure religious attachment* in individuals with schizophrenia. As stated by Granqvist and Kirkpatrick (2008), "... the form of 'love' experienced in the context of the relationship with God resembles closely the prototypical attachment of a child to his or her mother." Two hypotheses have been derived from attachment theory concerning relations between religion and attachment style. The *correspondence hypothesis* suggests that there is a correspondence between early child–parent interactions and a person's ability to cope in relation to a spiritual figure. The *compensation hypothesis* suggests that an insecure attachment history would lead to a strong religiousness/spirituality and hence to a possible use of God as a surrogate attachment figure (Granqvist & Hagekull, 1990). Huguelet et al. (2015) reported that many patients with schizophrenia believed in a spiritual figure that functioned like an attachment figure. Among them, a compensation process was observed in some subjects (i.e., they showed a stable attachment to a spiritual figure in the context of a primary insecure attachment toward caregivers). Hence, the issue of attachment appears to be an important topic when considering the care of patients with psychosis.

Spirituality/religion and the neurobiology of psychosis

Howes and Murray (2014) reviewed how developmental alterations sensitize the dopamine system, increasing the likelihood of excessive presynaptic dopamine synthesis and release. Subsequent stress may also lead to dysregulated dopamine release, affecting cognitive processes. If positive symptoms of psychosis develop, these in turn cause further stress. In this model, religion when used as a coping factor to reduce stress is likely to have a positive impact on the emergence of dopamine dysregulation, particularly early in the illness (Du & Grace, 2013). Nevertheless, to our knowledge, no research has yet examined the way that religion may impact dopamine dysregulation when used to cope with stressors or symptoms, as seen in Loch et al.'s study (2019) of individuals at ultrahigh risk for psychosis.

Clinical implications

Spirituality/religion assessment in patients with psychosis

By conducting a spiritual assessment, clinicians should have a better picture of positive and/or negative religious coping, as well as a better understanding of other S/R issues discussed in this chapter (Mohr & Huguelet, 2014). Clinicians may fear that patients with psychosis might be destabilized when discussing religious issues. At least one study of psychiatric outpatients with psychosis found that spiritual assessment by clinicians was well tolerated (Huguelet et al., 2011). Moreover, patients' wish to discuss religious matters with their psychiatrist persisted following such assessments. This study suggested the possible usefulness of clinical interventions such as supporting positive religious coping; work on identity; values; fostering mobilization toward clergy, chaplain, or religious community; working on negative coping; and examining S/R perspectives on psychiatric disorder and treatment (Table 5.1).

Group therapy involving spirituality/religion

Kehoe (1999) has been a pioneer in the field of group therapy involving S/R. This activity consists of weekly sessions for up to 3 years. The group's aim is to foster tolerance, self-awareness, and nonpathological therapeutic exploration of a value system. Phillips, Lakin, and Pargament (2002) developed a psychoeducational group, where information is provided on specific topics such as spiritual resources, striving, and struggles, followed by discussions. Wong-McDonald (2007) described the effect of an S/R group rehabilitation program. This group consists of discussing spiritual concepts, encouraging forgiveness, listening to spiritual music, and encouraging spiritual and emotional support among members. Compared to usual treatment, this group intervention resulted in patients

Table 5.1 Religious and spiritual assessment (Mohr, Gillieron, Borras, Brandt, & Huguelet, 2007).

Religious/spiritual history
Family background
Religious education
Significant changes in religious beliefs or practices
Effect of the illness upon spirituality and/or religiousness
Current spiritual/religious beliefs and practices
Religious preference
Spiritual beliefs
Private religious practices
Organizational religious practices
Support from religious community
Subjective importance of religion
In day-to-day life
To give meaning to life
Subjective importance of religion to cope with the illness
To give meaning to the illness
To cope with symptoms
To get comfort
Coping style (self-directing, deferring, or collaborative)
Religion versus psychiatric care
Synergy
Antagonism

achieving their goals in 100% of cases compared to 57% of cases in the control group. Revheim, Greenberg, and Citrome (2010) developed a spirituality matters group (SMG) for hospitalized patients. SMG aims to offer comfort and hope through structured exercises focusing on S/R beliefs and coping. These exercises involve more specific activities such as reading from the book of Psalms or reciting and writing prayers in addition to cognitively oriented activities such as emotion-focused coping.

Domains of intervention related to spirituality/religion

We mentioned above how S/R could be integrated into recovery-oriented care. As explained by Yangarber-Hicks (2004), patients' reliance on S/R should not be dismissed as an aspect of psychotic symptomatology alone (e.g., a delusion). Given the above review of the literature, S/R can also serve as an empowering and recovery-promoting strategy that may be encouraged in some cases. Also, treatment could focus on religious coping styles when discussing problem-solving strategies.

Patients who engage in positive forms of S/R coping have better treatment outcomes, at least in the short term (Rosmarin et al., 2013). Mohr et al. (2011), in a 3-year follow-up, showed a positive effect of positive S/R coping at baseline on symptoms, social functioning, quality of life, and self-esteem. This suggests a causal role of religion in the outcome of schizophrenia. To note though, in the same cohort, the authors found that S/R coping was often labile over time, with changes being associated with reduced subjective quality of life and self-esteem. These changes are related to the S/R struggles of patients and suggest that there is a need to address such issues in clinical practice (Mohr, Borras, Rieben, et al., 2010).

At least in developed societies, domains of activities (e.g., volunteering, leisure, cultural investments, peer support, etc.) are not easy to find in the long term, particularly for psychotic patients suffering from residual symptoms. Research shows that many patients believe and pray alone but do not have social contacts related to their faith (Mohr et al., 2006). As in other areas of life, psychotic patients often have difficulties developing interpersonal and social networks. This is a point that can be a focus of treatment, which should emphasize the need to overcome such deficits by readaptation or individual counseling. Also, clinicians may support patients when they are rejected by their religious communities due to disturbing positive symptoms. Negative S/R coping should also be addressed, for instance in cases of inappropriate S/R fatalism leading to despair and/or social withdrawal.

Concerning addictions, positive or protective factors related to S/R should be discerned in order to reduce substance misuse. Relatedly, spiritual assessment should also be part of risk evaluation for suicide. Indeed, spiritual assessment may help clinicians may determine a patient's purpose in life and their desire to stay alive. Also, having a better idea of one's worldview may provide an understanding of what he/she considers is beyond death (i.e., a representation likely to play a role when considering suicide). Clinicians could support positive S/R coping, helping to fight despair and suicidal thoughts, restore hope, and find a reason to live. The incentive role of religion should also be considered, allowing one to work on situations such as a wish to die in order to live another life after death. Sometimes, anger with God or loss of faith (two forms of negative S/R coping) may warrant consultation with clergy or a chaplain. Suicidal risk may also be related to religious delusions and hallucinations requiring psychopharmacological management.

The complex relationships between delusions with religious content and religious coping can explain how confusing it can be for clinicians to manage this issue. Patients may be in a *spiritual crisis*. What is specific to the population of patients with psychosis is that such a crisis may be, to some extent, embedded to delusions or other "bizarre" thoughts. In such cases, clinicians cannot resolve the situation by sending the patient to a chaplain or clergy, who may not be trained to address these issues. A thorough assessment should help to disentangle "true" spiritual crisis from the expression of delusional thoughts. This can be helped by determining whether the patient is experiencing a relapse into psychosis? The situation can be even trickier considering that patients may be both symptomatic *and* in a spiritual crisis. Overall, clinicians should assess and address this issue before referring to a chaplain. In this latter case, such a discussion should help the chaplain by giving him/her the medical context of the patient (with patient authorization).

When examining the core themes of delusions with religious content, this may involve themes of good versus bad, life versus death (persecution, guilt/sin), the value of individual beings (grandiose delusion), free will (delusion of influence), and so forth. Even if these themes are expressed in a delusional way, they belong to the central preoccupations that people have had for centuries, variously elaborated by different religions.

In some cases, it may be difficult to disentangle religious conversion from an episode of acute psychosis. In a recent study, Kéri (2017) assessed 29 patients developing schizophrenia and 24 subjects experiencing religious conversion over 1 year. Both groups reported similar levels of perplexity and self-disorder (e.g., depersonalization). Diminished affectivity, disturbed contact, and perceptual/cognitive disorders were more pronounced in psychosis, whereas people with spiritual and religious problems reported more anxiety and depressive symptoms. Overall, individuals with religious conversion experienced deep subjective changes in their self. This is consistent with the view that religious conversion may be associated with profound and broad changes in core personal identity and with the reconstruction of beliefs and values (Paloutzian, 2014). These changes may involve spiritual and religious struggles accompanied by distress. Hence, even if the Kéri (2017) study gives support for the role of self-transformation in religious conversion, which might phenomenologically resemble PE, these experiences should not lead to unnecessary and harmful medicalization and stigmatization (Kéri, 2017).

Working on meaning appears to be important in patients with psychotic disorders, considering that it relies on values and that meaninglessness may alter well-being and foster symptoms (Huguelet, Mohr, et al., 2016). Corrie and Martin (2000) claimed that meaning could be a central framework that unites both existential and cognitive-behavioral techniques. Further work is needed to build a recovery-oriented form of care that addresses meaning (Lapierre, Dubé, Bouffard, & Alain, 2007). Yalom (1980) suggests that considering values may be an easier starting point when talking to patients who are not immediately comfortable with considering the lack of meaning. Assistance in finding a meaning should be provided to patients in the context of their psychiatric disorder, which often prevents them from fulfilling their goals. Overall, existentialists state that commitment may increase the possibility for building a coherent life scheme (Camus, 1985). Clinicians should work on the obstacles that prevent the patient from achieving it.

We described above how patients may find a meaning in their disorder, sometimes involving a religious component. Patients may be tormented by conflicts between S/R and psychiatric care. Some patients may be reluctant to take drugs, that being related to religious principles. Borras et al. (2007) found that S/R contributed to shaping understandings of their disease and attitudes toward medical treatment in some patients with schizophrenia. In this research, more than half of the patients had understandings of their illness and treatment directly influenced by their religious convictions. Also, there was a strong association between understandings of illness and treatment directly influenced S/R beliefs that affected nonadherence to treatment. Thirty-one percent of nonadherent patients indicated an incompatibility between their religious convictions and medication and supportive therapy, versus 8% of adherent patients. Marriott, Thompson, Cockshutt, and Rowse (2019) described how patients build insight through the process of meaning-making, "... in which the awareness of experiences is contextualized within the individual's worldview and therefore provides a more robust foundation to move forward in a positive (i.e., 'recovery') manner." This so-called "narrative insight" often includes religious aspects.

Treatments in other cultures

Triveni et al. (2017) found in India that a high proportion of patients with schizophrenia used positive religious coping, similar to healthy controls. Frequent use of religious coping was associated with lower levels of psychopathology and better quality of life. Spiritual explanatory models may be more frequent in developing countries (Bhikha et al., 2012), such models being associated with a longer time before receiving allopathic treatment. However, research has shown that mental illness may also be recognized as such in developing countries. For example, Younis (1978) reported in Sudan that schizophrenia was identified in 76% of cases. Nonetheless, spiritual healing has a place in developing countries, as shown by Campion and Bhugra (1997). In South India, almost half the patients seeking treatment in a psychiatric hospital had previously solicited help from religious healers. The highest rate was in the group diagnosed with schizophrenia (58%). Less than a third of patients reported improvement through these treatments, which consisted of chanting mantras, ingestion of holy water or ash, use of animal sacrifice, or other rituals. Overall, religious and "allopathic" care often coexists in the treatment of psychosis. There appear to be opportunities for dialog between "modern" psychiatry and religious healers (Teuton et al., 2007). As in western countries, this could be done while keeping in mind the principles of recovery. Both psychiatrists and religious healers should recognize that patients need good medication, psychosocial counseling, and something related to life goals but also to a sense of one's identity, which is sometimes strongly rooted in religion and culture.

Discussion

Research has found in various cultures that S/R does not trigger psychotic symptoms. Rather, it can assist in the treatment and recovery of those with psychosis, as with any mental disorder. The fear that some clinicians feel that prevents them from engaging in assessing and addressing S/R issues does not appear to be warranted. Even in situations such as those involving patients with both delusions with religious content and positive S/R coping, clinicians should seek to clarify the situation by performing an in-depth S/R assessment and by accepting S/R claims without challenging them (at least not immediately). In fact, it may be unethical for clinicians to ignore S/R issues given their prevalence and clear functional significance. In particular, positive S/R coping should be supported to help counteract the hopelessness and discouragement that are often present among those with chronic psychoses. Negative S/R coping (e.g., when the use of S/R worsens symptoms) must also be addressed by clinicians or by trained clergy when warranted.

References

Abdelgawad, N., Chotalia, J., Parsaik, A., Pigott, T., & Allen, M. (2017). Religiosity in acute psychiatric inpatients: Relationship with demographics, clinical features, and length of stay. *The Journal of Nervous and Mental Disease, 205*(6), 448–452.

Andresen, R., Oades, L., & Caputi, P. (2003). The experience of recovery from schizophrenia: Towards an empirically validated stage model. *Australian & New Zealand Journal of Psychiatry, 37*(5), 586–594.

Battista, J., & Almond, R. (1973). The development of meaning in life. *Psychiatry, 36*(4), 409–427.

Bhikha, A. G., Farooq, S., Chaudhry, N., & Husain, N. (2012). A systematic review of explanatory models of illness for psychosis in developing countries. *International Review of Psychiatry, 24*(5), 450–462.

Borras, L., Mohr, S., Brandt, P. Y., Gillieron, C., Eytan, A., & Huguelet, P. (2007). Religious beliefs in schizophrenia: Their relevance for adherence to treatment. *Schizophrenia Bulletin, 33*(5), 1238–1246.

Campion, J., & Bhugra, D. (1997). Experience of religious healing in psychiatric patients in South India. *Social Psychiatry and Psychiatric Epidemiology, 32*(4), 215–221.

Camus, A. (1985). *Le mythe de Sisyphe*. Paris: Gallimard "Folio". (in French).

Cloarec, F. (1998). *Bimarestans: Lieux de folie et de sagesse, la folie et ses traitements dans les hôpitaux médiévaux au Moyen-Orient*. Paris: L'Harmattan. (in French).

Combs, D., Adams, S., Michael, C., Penn, D., Basso, M., & Gouvier, W. (2006). The conviction of delusional beliefs scale: Reliability and validity. *Schizophrenia Research, 86* (1–3), 80–88.

Corrie, S., & Martin, M. (2000). The relationship between existential-phenomenological and cognitive-behaviour therapies. *European Journal of Psychotherapy, Counselling & Health, 3*(1), 7–24.

Culliford, L. (2002). Spirituality and clinical care. *British Medical Journal, 325*, 1434–1435.

Das, S., Punnoose, V. P., Doval, N., & Nair, V. Y. (2018). Spirituality, religiousness and coping in patients with schizophrenia: A cross sectional study in a tertiary care hospital. *Psychiatry Research, 265*, 238–243.

Das, S., Saravanan, B., Karunakaran, K., Manoranjitham, S., Ezhilarasu, P., & Jacob, K. (2006). Effect of a structured educational intervention on explanatory models of relatives of patients with schizophrenia: Randomised controlled trial. *British Journal of Psychiatry, 188*(3), 286–287.

Drinnan, A., & Lavender, T. (2006). Deconstructing delusions: A qualitative study examining the relationship between religious beliefs and religious delusions. *Mental Health, Religion & Culture, 9*(4), 317–333.

Du, Y., & Grace, A. A. (2013). Peripubertal diazepam administration prevents the emergence of dopamine system hyperresponsivity in the MAM developmental disruption model of schizophrenia. *Neuropsychopharmacology., 38*(10), 1881–1888.

Farr, C. B., & Howe, R. L. (1932). The influence of religious ideas on the etiology, symptomatology and prognosis of the psychoses: With special reference to social factors. *American Journal of Psychiatry, 88*, 845–865.

Freeman, D., Pugh, K., Green, C., Valmaggia, L., Dunn, G., & Garety, P. (2007). A measure of state persecutory ideation for experimental studies. *The Journal of Nervous and Mental Disease, 95*(9), 781–784.

Gearing, R. E., Alonzo, D., Smolak, A., McHugh, K., Harmon, S., & Baldwin, S. (2011). Association of religion with delusions and hallucinations in the context of schizophrenia: Implications for engagement and adherence. *Schizophrenia Research, 126*(1–3), 150–163.

Granqvist, P., & Hagekull, B. (1990). Religiousness and perceived childhood attachment: Profiling socialized correspondence and emotional compensation. *Journal for the Scientific Study of Religion, 38*(2), 254–273.

Granqvist, P., & Kirkpatrick, L. A. (2008). Attachment and religious representations and behaviour. In J. Cassidy, & P. R. Shaver (Eds.), *Handbook of attachment: Theory, research, and clinical applications* (pp. 906–933). New York: Guilford Press.

Grover, S., Davuluri, T., & Chakrabarti, S. (2014). Religion, spirituality, and schizophrenia: A review. *Indian Journal of Psychological Medicine, 36*(2), 119–124.

Howes, O. D., & Murray, R. M. (2014). Schizophrenia: An integrated sociodevelopmental-cognitive model. *Lancet, 383*(9929), 1677–1687.

Huguelet, P., Borras, L., Gillieron, C., Brandt, P. Y., & Mohr, S. (2009). Influence of spirituality and religiousness on substance misuse in patients with schizophrenia or schizo-affective disorder. *Substance Use and Misuse, 44*(4), 502–513.

Huguelet, P., Guillaume, S., Vidal, S., Mohr, S., Courtet, P., Villain, L., ... Perroud, N. (2016). Values as determinant of meaning among patients with psychiatric disorders in the perspective of recovery. *Scientific Reports, 6*, 27617.

Huguelet, P., Mohr, S., Betrisey, C., Borras, L., Gillieron, C., Marie, A. M., ... Brandt, P. Y. (2011). A randomized trial of spiritual assessment of outpatients with schizophrenia: Patients' and clinicians' experience. *Psychiatric Services, 62*(1), 79–86.

Huguelet, P., Mohr, S., Jung, V., Gillieron, C., Brandt, P. Y., & Borras, L. (2007). Effect of religion on suicide attempts in outpatients with schizophrenia or schizo-affective disorders compared with inpatients with non-psychotic disorders. *European Psychiatry, 22*(3), 188–194.

Huguelet, P., Mohr, S., Olié, E., Vidal, S., Hasler, R., Prada, P., ... Perroud, N. (2016). Spiritual meaning in life and values in patients with severe mental disorders. *The Journal of Nervous and Mental Disease, 204*(6), 409–414.

Huguelet, P., Mohr, S., Rieben, I., Hasler, R., Perroud, N., & Brandt, P. Y. (2015). Attachment and coping in psychosis in relation to spiritual figures. *BMC Psychiatry, 7* (15), 237.

Jones, E., & Watson, J. P. (1997). Delusion, the overvalued idea and religious beliefs: A comparative analysis of their characteristics. *British Journal of Psychiatry, 170*, 381–386.

Kehoe, N. C. (1999). A therapy group on spiritual issues for patients with chronic mental illness. *Psychiatric Services, 50*(8), 1081–1083.

Kéri, S. (2017). Self-transformation at the boundary of religious conversion and psychosis. *Journal of Religion and Health*. (Epub ahead of print).

Kimhi, D., Goetz, R., Yale, S., Corcoran, C., & Malaspina, D. (2005). Delusions in individuals with schizophrenia: Factor structure, clinical correlates, and putative neurobiology. *Psychopathology, 38*(6), 338–344.

Kinzie, J. D. (2000). The historical relationship between psychiatry and the major religions. In J. K. Boehnlein (Ed.), *Psychiatry and religion: The convergence of mind and spirit (issues in psychiatry)* (pp. 3–26). Washington, DC: American Psychiatric Publishing, Inc.

Koenig, H. G. (2005). *Faith and mental health*. Philadelphia, PA: Templeton Foundation Press.

Kovess-Masfety, V., Saha, S., Lim, C. C., Aguilar-Gaxiola, S., Al-Hamzawi, A., Alonso, J., et al. (2018). Psychotic experiences and religiosity: Data from the WHO World Mental Health Surveys. *Acta Psychiatrica Scandinavica, 137*(4), 306–315, 2018.

Lapierre, S., Dubé, M., Bouffard, L., & Alain, M. (2007). Addressing suicidal ideations through the realization of meaningful personal goals. *Crisis*, *28*(1), 16–25.

Loch, A. A., Freitas, E. L., Hortêncio, L., Chianca, C., Alves, T. M., Serpa, M. H., ... Rössler, W. (2019). Hearing spirits? Religiosity in individuals at risk for psychosis—Results from the Brazilian SSAPP cohort. *Schizophrenia Research.*, *204*, 353–359.

Marriott, M. R., Thompson, A. R., Cockshutt, G., & Rowse, G. (2019). Narrative insight in psychosis: The relationship with spiritual and religious explanatory frameworks. *Psychology and Psychotherapy*, *92*, 74–90.

Mohr, S., Borras, L., Betrisey, C., Brandt, P. Y., Gilliéron, C., & Huguelet, P. (2010). Delusions with religious content in patients with psychosis: How they interact with spiritual coping. *Psychiatry*, *73*(2), 158–172.

Mohr, S., Borras, L., Nolan, J., Gillieron, C., Brandt, P. Y., Eytan, A., et al. (2012). Spirituality and religion in outpatients with schizophrenia: A multi-site comparative study of Switzerland, Canada, and the United States. *International Journal of Psychiatry in Medicine*, *44*(1), 29–52.

Mohr, S., Borras, L., Rieben, I., Betrisey, C., Gillieron, C., Brandt, P. Y., et al. (2010). Evolution of spirituality and religiousness in chronic schizophrenia or schizo-affective disorders: A 3-years follow-up study. *Social Psychiatry and Psychiatric Epidemiology*, *45* (11), 1095–1103.

Mohr, S., Brandt, P. Y., Borras, L., Gillieron, C., & Huguelet, P. (2006). Toward an integration of spirituality and religiousness into the psychosocial dimension of schizophrenia. *American Journal of Psychiatry*, *163*(11), 1952–1959.

Mohr, S., Gillieron, C., Borras, L., Brandt, P. Y., & Huguelet, P. (2007). The assessment of spirituality and religiousness in schizophrenia. *The Journal of Nervous and Mental Disease*, *195*(3), 247–253.

Mohr, S., & Huguelet, P. (2014). The wishes of outpatients with severe mental disorders to discuss spiritual and religious issues in their psychiatric care. *International Journal of Psychiatry in Clinical Practice*, *18*(4), 304–307.

Mohr, S., Perroud, N., Gillieron, C., Pierre-Yves, B., Rieben, I., Borras, L., & Huguelet, P. (2011). Spirituality and religiousness as predictive factors of outcome in Schizophrenia and Schizoaffective disorders. *Psychiatry Research*, *186*(2–3), 177–182.

Nolan, J. A., McEvoy, J. P., Koenig, H. G., Hooten, E. G., Whetten, K., & Pieper, C. F. (2012). Religious coping and quality of life among individuals living with schizophrenia. *Psychiatric Services*, *63*(10), 1051–1054.

Nuechterlein, K. H., & Dawson, M. E. (1984). A heuristic vulnerability/stress model of schizophrenic episodes. *Schizophrenia Bulletin*, *10*(2), 300–312.

Paloutzian, R. F. (2014). Psychology of religious conversion and spiritual transformation. In L. R. Rambo, & C. E. Farhadian (Eds.), *The Oxford handbook of religious conversion* (pp. 209–239). Oxford: Oxford University Press.

Pargament, K. I. (1997). *The psychology of religion and coping*. New York: Guilford Press.

Pargament, K. I., & Brant, C. (1998). Religion and coping. In H. Koenig (Ed.), *Handbook of religion and mental health* (pp. 111–128). San Diego, CA: Academic Press.

Park, C. L. (2010). Making sense of the meaning literature: An integrative review of meaning-making and its effects on adjustment to stressful life events. *Psychological Bulletin*, *136*(2), 257–301.

Park, C. L. (2013). Why religion? Meaning as motivation. In K. I. Pargament (Ed.), *APA handbook of psychology, religion and spirituality: Vol. 1. Context, theory and research* (pp. 157–171). Washington, DC: American Psychological Association.

Pfeifer, S. (1994). Belief in demons and exorcism in psychiatric patients in Switzerland. *British Journal of Medical Psychology*, *67*(3), 247–258.

Phillips, R. E., Lakin, R., & Pargament, K. I. (2002). Development and implementation of a spiritual issues psycho educational group for those with serious mental illness. *Community Mental Health Journal, 38*(6), 487–495.

Phillips, R. E., 3rd, & Stein, C. H. (2007). God's will, God's punishment, or God's limitations? Religious coping strategies reported by young adults living with serious mental illness. *Journal of Clinical Psychology, 63*(6), 529–540.

Revheim, N., Greenberg, W. M., & Citrome, L. (2010). Spirituality, schizophrenia, and state hospitals: Program description and characteristics of self-selected attendees of a spirituality therapeutic group. *Psychiatric Quarterly, 81*(4), 285–292.

Rhodes, J. E., & Jakes, S. (2004). The contribution of metaphor and metonymy to delusions. *Psychology and Psychotherapy: Theory, Research and Practice*, 77(1), 1–17.

Rosmarin, D. H., Bigda-Peyton, J. S., Öngur, D., Pargament, K. I., & Björgvinsson, T. (2013). Religious coping among psychotic patients: Relevance to suicidality and treatment outcomes. *Psychiatry Research, 210*(1), 182–187.

Rosmarin, D. H., Moreira-Almeida, A., & Koenig, H. G. (2018). Religion and psychotic experiences. *Acta Psychiatrica Scandinavica, 138*(2), 173.

Saroglou, V., Delpierre, V., & Dernelle, R. (2004). Values and religiosity: A meta-analysis of studies using Schwartz's model. *Personality and Individual Differences, 37*, 721–734.

Sedman, G., & Hopkinson, G. (1966). The psychopathology of mystical and religious conversion experiences in psychiatric patients. *Confinia Psychiatrica, 9*(1), 1–19.

Siddle, R., Haddock, G., Tarrier, N., & Faragher, E. B. (2002). Religious delusions in patients admitted to hospital with schizophrenia. *Social Psychiatry and Psychiatric Epidemiology, 37*(3), 130–138.

Sowers, W. (2005). Transforming systems of care: The American Association of Community Psychiatrists guidelines for recovery oriented services. *Community Mental Health Journal, 41*(6), 757–774.

Steenhuis, L. A., Bartels-Velthuis, A. A., Jenner, J. A., Bruggeman, R., Nauta, M. H., & Pijnenborg, G. H. (2016). Religiosity in young adolescents with auditory vocal hallucinations. *Psychiatry Research, 236*, 158–164.

Tepper, L., Rogers, S. A., Coleman, E. M., & Malony, H. N. (2001). The prevalence of religious coping among persons with persistent mental illness. *Psychiatric Services, 52*(5), 660–665.

Teuton, J., Dowrick, C., & Bentall, R. P. (2007). How healers manage the pluralistic healing context: The perspective of indigenous, religious and allopathic healers in relation to psychosis in Uganda. *Social Science & Medicine, 65*, 1260–1273.

Triveni, D., Grover, S., & Chakrabarti, S. (2017). Religiosity among patients with schizophrenia: An exploratory study. *Indian Journal of Psychiatry, 59*(4), 420–428.

Wilson, K., Sandoz, E., & Kitchens, J. (2010). The Valued Living Questionnaire: Defining and measuring valued action within a behavioral framework. *The Psychological Record, 60*, 249–272.

Wong-McDonald, A. (2007). Spirituality and rehabilitation: Empowering persons with serious psychiatric disabilities at an inner-city community program. *Psychiatric Rehabilitation Journal, 30*(4), 295–300.

Workman, J. (1869). Insanity of the religious-emotional type, and its occasional physical relations. *American Journal of Insanity, 26*(1), 33–48.

Yalom, I. (1980). *Existential psychotherapy*. New York: Basic Books.

Yangarber-Hicks, N. (2004). Religious coping style and recovery from serious mental illness. *Journal of Psychology and Theology, 32*(4), 305–317.

Younis, Y. O. (1978). Attitudes of Sudanese urban and rural population to mental illness. *The Journal of Tropical Medicine and Hygiene, 81*(12), 248–251.

CHAPTER 6

Spirituality, religion, and eating disorders

P. Scott Richards[1], Sarah Weinberger-Litman[2], Michael E. Berrett[3] and Randy K. Hardman[4]
[1]Center for Change of Universal Health Services, Inc., Orem, UT, United States
[2]Marymount Manhattan College, Department of Psychology, New York, NY, United States
[3]Berrett and Company, LLC, Linden, UT, United States
[4]Counseling Center, Brigham Young University-Idaho, Rexburg, ID, United States

Contents

Introduction

Eating disorders (EDs) are among the most complex and multifaceted psychological disorders. Decades of research suggest biological components as well as sociocultural influences on the etiology and progression of ED pathology (Keski-Rahkonen, Raevuori, & Hoek, 2018; Treasure, Claudino, & Zucker, 2010). The role of spirituality/religion (S/R) in the development, maintenance, and treatment of EDs has recently emerged as a salient sociocultural factor worthy of exploration.

The DSM-V (American Psychiatric Association, 2013) currently recognizes four distinct categories of EDs, which share several overlapping characteristics. Anorexia nervosa (AN) is characterized by an extreme restriction of energy intake leading to a significantly low body weight in the context of age, sex, developmental stage, and overall physical health. In addition, those with a diagnosis of AN exhibit an extreme fear of gaining weight and usually place undue value on weight and shape for

Handbook of Spirituality, Religion, and Mental Health
DOI: https://doi.org/10.1016/B978-0-12-816766-3.00006-9

self-evaluation. Further, they may have a difficult time identifying the seriousness or extremity of their level of thinness. Bulimia nervosa (BN) is characterized by recurrent episodes of binge eating (i.e., eating objectively larger than normal amounts of food in a discrete period of time while experiencing a sense of loss of control and/or shame around eating), followed by the use of compensatory behaviors (i.e., purging, laxative use, excessive exercise) to counteract the binge episode(s). In addition, individuals with BN place undue emphasis on weight and shape for self-evaluation. Binge ED was added as a separate diagnostic category in the newest revision of the DSM and includes recurrent episodes of binge eating without the use of compensatory behaviors seen in BN. Remaining EDs that do not fit specifically into the above category are labeled as other specified feeding or ED. It is important to note that this diagnosis does not imply disorders of lesser clinical severity but rather diagnostic ambiguity or a transition period from one ED to another (American Psychiatric Association, 2013).

In addition to the full-blown EDs mentioned above, there exists a continuum of related behaviors or symptomatology that can collectively be referred to as disordered eating pathology (DEP), which can refer to both cognitive aspects of ED symptoms (i.e., high levels of body dissatisfaction, guilt or shame around food, weight and shape overvaluation) or the behavioral aspects of EDs (i.e., restricting total or specific food intake, bingeing and/or purging, or other compensatory behaviors, etc.). All of these can be considered core features of EDs (Fairburn, Cooper, & Shafran, 2003) and risk factors for their development even in the absence of a formal diagnosis. Therefore, much of the empirical research conducted on nonclinical samples focuses on DEP. While individuals that do go on to develop full-blown EDs may have some qualitative differences to those that remain in a subclinical category, high levels of DEP are the most proximal risk factors for the development of EDs and the research in nonclinical samples has made significant contributions to understanding S/R mechanisms and underpinning of these conditions.

Research connecting spirituality/religion to eating disorder behaviors

Historically, many religious and spiritual traditions have elaborate symbolism and rituals related to food. It has long been noted that asceticism and transcendence of the physical are a part of many religious traditions and food denial or fasting is often used as a form of religious devotion (Brumberg, 2000; Vandereycken & Van Deth, 1994). In addition, feminist scholars have argued that particularly for women, the use of their bodies as a vessel for religious expression has been culturally sanctioned and often is/was the only means women had of expressing their suffering (Lelwica, 2010). This is evidenced in case studies of fasting saints and modern-day ascetics (Brumberg, 2000; Lelwica, 2010). However, only more recently has empirical research focused on not only the association between S/R and DEP, but more specifically the psychological mechanisms through which S/R forces manifest themselves as relevant influences in the development of ED-related psychopathology.

Similar to the literature related to overall mental health, components of S/R have been found to have both a positive and negative impact on DEP and EDs (Akrawi, Bartrop, Potter, & Touyz, 2015; Berrett, Crowton, & Richards, 2018; Homan & Lemmon, 2016). It is possible that S/R exerts a direct positive effect on the reduction of ED symptomatology through a general reduction in overall levels of distress (Henderson & Ellison, 2015). Conversely, it may have a direct negative impact as related to a need for self-control in the case of restricting behaviors, or feelings of failure to self-regulate in the case of bingeing and an attempt to correct for this through the use of compensatory behaviors (Exline, Homolka, & Harriott, 2016). However, there is greater empirical support to suggest that S/R mitigates or exacerbates EDs and DEP specifically through the mediating/moderating role it exerts on psychological variables known to be associated with these symptoms (including but not limited to depression, anxiety, self-esteem, and body dissatisfaction) (Exline et al., 2016; Homan & Lemmon, 2016; Weinberger-Litman, Latzer, Litman, & Ozick, 2018; Weinberger-Litman, Rabin, Fogel, Mensinger, & Litman, 2016).

Some elements of S/R have been shown to prevent or lessen the development of ED symptoms in nonclinical samples, (Akrawi et al., 2015; Hall & Boyatzis, 2016; Richards, Weinberger-Litman, Susov, & Berrett, 2013; Weinberger-Litman et al., 2016) and among clinical samples, have been shown to be useful in recovery from EDs, which will be discussed in detail later in this chapter (Berrett et al., 2018; Richards et al., 2018; Richards, Hardman, & Berrett, 2007). S/R factors have specifically been shown to reduce body image—related distress, a proximal risk factor for ED development.

In a study of college women with high levels of body dissatisfaction, women who rated S/R as being highly important were more likely to use prayer or meditation to cope with body image—related distress (Jacobs-Pilipski, Winzelberg, Wilfley, Bryson, & Taylor, 2005). Reading theistically centered positive body affirmations reduced the established negative psychological effects of exposure to ultrathin models relative to a control group (Boyatzis, Kline, & Backof, 2007). Additionally, women who exhibit a secure nonanxious attachment to God have been shown to have lower levels of body dissatisfaction after viewing media images than those women with an anxious attachment style (Homan, 2012). Further, this reduction in body dissatisfaction was shown to be mediated by a reduction in social comparison which has been shown to be associated with DEP (Homan & Lemmon, 2014). Finally, this relationship was also illustrated with regard to body appreciation, which refers to positive feelings toward one's body, and has been shown to be associated with reduced DEP (Homan & Lemmon, 2016). Body appreciation should be considered an important factor in prevention and treatment of DEP as increased positive feelings toward one's body can mitigate the negative impact of cooccurring body dissatisfaction. The impact on social comparison was moderated by a secure attachment to God whereby those women who were more securely attached were more likely to maintain favorable levels of body appreciation despite engaging in social comparison processes or viewing images previously associated with a decrease in body appreciation (Homan & Lemmon, 2016).

However, S/R can also have negative effects on ED symptoms. In some research, individuals have been shown to use religious motivation to justify symptoms (Joughin, Crisp, Halek, & Humphrey, 1992; Marsden, Karagianni, & Morgan, 2007; Morgan, Marsden, & Lacey, 2000) or feelings of unworthiness (Richards et al., 2018). In clinical samples, individuals with EDs report feeling a sense of spiritual estrangement and alienation (Richards et al., 2018). Many ED patients perceive God negatively as being wrathful, vindictive, impersonal, or uncaring (Richards et al., 2018). This is consistent with the concept of divine struggle, or having negative thoughts and feelings about God, which predicts distress over time and is associated with both restrictive and dysregulated symptoms of EDs (Exline et al., 2016). Divine struggle is associated with greater levels of neuroticism, trait anger, and lower self-esteem, all of which are associated with the development of DEP and EDs and may be representative of these underlying psychological mechanisms

(Exline et al., 2016). Greater levels of negative religious coping (often characterized by feeling abandoned or punished by God), which may also represent religious struggle, have also been shown to be associated with higher levels of DEP (Latzer et al., 2015). High levels of divine struggle, feelings of unworthiness, and a punitive view of God and S/R in general may be related to the observation that many women with EDs report that the ED has replaced previous S/R elements in their lives and the disorder itself begins to take on an almost spiritual identity (Lelwica, 2010; Richards et al., 2018; Richards et al., 2007).

In addition, attention has been paid to underlying motivation for religious practice and research has consistently demonstrated that an extrinsic religious orientation (i.e., a focus on the external or social aspects of religious experience) has been shown to be associated with higher levels of ED symptoms in clinical samples (Smith, Richards, & Maglio, 2004) and higher levels of DEP and body dissatisfaction in nonclinical samples (Weinberger-Litman, Rabin, Fogel, & Mensinger, 2008). For example, among inpatients being treated for bulimia and college students who had scored within the clinical range on a measure of DEP, there was a positive association between an extrinsic religious orientation and disordered eating and body dissatisfaction (Smith et al., 2004). Consistent with these results, in a large nonclinical sample of women determined to be at increased familial risk for the development of disordered eating (based on family dysfunction and parental history of and ED), an extrinsic religious orientation was predictive of greater levels of disordered eating and strengthened the relationship between family dysfunction and ED symptoms (Forthun, Pidcock, & Fischer, 2003).

It has been suggested that religious orientation represents a particular cognitive or motivational style (Kirkpatrick & Hood, 1990) that engenders specific patterns of psychological and behavioral responses. In fact, an extrinsic religious orientation is consistently associated with greater levels of depression, anxiety, and low self-esteem in studies examining DEP, as well as general mental health (Weinberger-Litman et al., 2016), suggesting that an extrinsic orientation may be a proxy for additional psychological processes shown to contribute to EDs and DEP. It is therefore also likely that religious orientation is associated with specific psychosocial experiences that in turn are related to DEP. In recent studies, the association between an extrinsic orientation and DEP was found to be largely mediated by greater vulnerability to the internalization of negative sociocultural ideals and harmful media messages (e.g., ideas related to thinness and beauty) in both US and international samples (Weinberger-Litman et al., 2016, 2018). An extrinsic religious tendency was therefore associated with a greater vulnerability to external messaging in general, suggesting that this paradigm taps into one of the potential ways in which S/R factors represent complex cognitive and psychological mechanisms that may be linked to mental health outcomes.

Recent decades have seen significant advances in understanding the biological basis of EDs. Structural and functional neuroimaging studies have begun to elucidate the brain regions and the neurochemical disruptions associated with different variants of EDs (Favaro, Monteleone, Santonastaso, & Maj, 2018). Further, these studies help to understand how dysregulation of certain reward circuitry contributes to overlapping and disparate symptomatology across the EDs (Frank, 2015). In addition, significant research has focused on genetic variations in the systems that may contribute to ED symptoms (Culbert, Slane, & Klump, 2018). To date, there have not been any published studies that explore how the psychobiology of EDs may relate to elements of S/R. However, consistent research demonstrates a neurological basis for and response to spiritual experiences (Rim et al., 2019). Further, functional imaging studies are able to differentiate types of spiritual experiences based on activation in various brain regions (Miller et al., 2019). Therefore, it would be of particular interest to understand whether individuals with EDs or at high risk for their development exhibit differential neural responses to S/R imagery or tasks. In addition, the neurobiological impact of integrating S/R factors into psychological and behavioral treatment could elucidate the underlying mechanisms associated with the influence of S/R elements.

Taken together, the positive and negative aspects of S/R with regard to ED development suggest that internalized religious beliefs (Weinberger-Litman et al., 2016) and lower levels of divine struggle (Exline et al., 2016) may lead to a greater sense of solid identity formation and meaning in life. Particularly for adolescents, this can have a powerful salutary effect when it comes to the ability to withstand constant bombardment by media images and unrealistic expectation of beauty and thinness. Beyond this, it suggests that tapping into the elements of S/R beliefs that reduce negative affect, promote the formation of values, and encourage individuals to view the body as worthy of love and care (Strenger, Schnitker, & Felke, 2016) may reduce risk for the development of EDs in high-risk women. Conversely, religious experiences that induce feelings of guilt, shame, or failure may increase the impact of religious mechanisms that enhance deleterious psychological processes. Below, we integrate these findings and discuss the utilization of empirically supported strategies for incorporating elements of S/R into treatment.

Clinical issues and recommendations

Many practitioners and scholars have published books and articles that provide insights into how to integrate spiritual perspectives into ED treatment. Table 6.1 summarizes some of the contributions in this domain, including feminist, integrative-medical, metaphorical, narrative, Protestant Christian, and 12-step approaches (e.g., Berrett, Hardman, & Richards, 2010; Emmett, 2009; Johnson & Sansone, 1993; Johnston, 1996; Lelwica, 1999, 2010; Maine & Kelly, 2005; Manley & Leichner, 2003; Richards et al., 2007; Ross, 2007). These writers have also described a variety of spiritual therapeutic techniques that can be used for treating those with EDs.

We believe that there is value in all of these approaches depending on the treatment context and patients' cultures and religious backgrounds and encourage practitioners and researchers to familiarize themselves with the approaches that seem most relevant for them. Because of space limitations, the clinical recommendations offered in the remainder of this chapter will be based primarily on the treatment approaches developed during the past two decades by Berrett, Hardman, and Richards and their collaborators (e.g., Berrett et al., 2010, 2018; Hardman, Berrett, & Richards, 2003; Lea, Richards, Sanders, McBride, & Allen, 2015; Richards et al., 2007, 2013, 2018).

A spiritually integrative treatment model for eating disorders

Fig. 6.1 presents a conceptual model for a spiritually integrative treatment approach to EDs. This model, which has been adapted and expanded upon from Richards et al. (2018), represents the relationship between spirituality and ED treatment and recovery. On the left side of the figure, ED development and pathology are influenced by decreases in spiritual connection—and vice versa. The core clinical issue when patients are entrenched in their ED is that their locus of identity and worth is grounded in external criteria and values. Their true identity and worth have been lost in the worship and false promises of the ED (Hardman et al., 2003). What is meant by worship in this context is that in the natural development of the ED illness, patients unknowingly begin putting

Table 6.1 Spiritual approaches for treating eating disorder patients.

Author(s)	Conceptual framework	Role of spirituality in recovery	Spiritual interventions
Berrett, Hardman, and Richards	Theistic, integrative, multidisciplinary	Reclaiming one's sense of spirituality and placing faith in a Higher Power and the love of significant others rather than in the false promises of the ED can empower patients with a sense of hope, purpose, and spiritual worth, which motivates and facilitates physical and emotional healing and growth	Learn to "listen to one's heart;" solo times for contemplation, prayer, and spiritual journaling; reading sacred writings; spirituality and 12-step groups; service; forgiveness; art therapies; spiritual mindedness; giving and receiving gifts of love; living in a principled manner; spiritual assessments
Johnston	Feminist, metaphorical	Reclaiming one's feminine, intuitive capacities facilitates recovery	Connecting to one's heart; cultivating a state of receptivity; being still; focusing on being instead of doing; mindfulness; honoring one's emotions; keeping a journal of hunches and insights; testing and following one's intuitions
Manley and Leichner	Narrative, feminist, cognitive, spiritual	Spirituality can empower adolescents to discover and implement values of personal significance	Spirituality group; motivational work
Maine	Feminist, integrative	Spirituality is one part of a healthy, more complete and balance approach to living that can help women clarify their values and nurture their faith	Quiet time for reflection; mindfulness meditation; seeking balance; pondering the legacy one wishes to leave; clarifying one's values and priorities; learning to breath fully; learning to love one's body
Lelwica	Feminist, spiritual	Spirituality can help women reject the dogma that having a perfect body will give them health, happiness, and well-being and instead find meaning and purpose through a connection to the sacred	Mindfulness; cultural criticism; developing an embodied ethics of eating; building nourishing relationships; accepting one's self and body; experiencing and accepting pain and suffering; extending compassion to self and others

Ross and Wingate	Integrative-medical, (body–mind–spirit)	Getting in touch with the deeper urges of the soul or spirit and with their spiritual longings can help patients find their passion in life and bring renewed vigor for and purpose in life	Buddhist prayer; guided imagery; hypnosis, mindfulness meditation; progressive relaxation; yoga; bodywork therapies; practicing gratitude; forgiveness; nurturing inspiration and awe; enjoying art; serving others; going to church; relationships with pets; supplements and herbs
Emmett	Psychospiritual, existential	Spirituality can help patients reclaim the self and restore a healing sense of wholeness and holiness	Facilitating psychospiritual literacy; conducting a spiritual assessment; psychospiritual restructuring; encouraging authenticity; affirming spiritual worthiness; sowing seeds of faith, hope, and love
Cumella, Eberly, and Wall	Protestant Christian	Spiritual healing and growth are necessary for physical, psychological, and social recovery and growth	Spiritual assessment; classes to explore spiritual issues; daily attendance at chapel; songs of praise and worship; Celebrate Recovery groups; Christian 12-step groups
Johnson, Sansone, and Yeary	12-Step, theistic	Faith in and reliance on a Higher Power rather than self is essential for overcoming addictive eating-disordered behaviors	Group support; confession; restitution; seeking forgiveness from God and others; prayers of petition and invocation; meditation; service to others

Source: Adapted from Richards, P. S., Weinberger-Litman, S. L., Susov, S., & Berrett, M. E. (2013). Religiousness and spirituality in the etiology and treatment of eating disorders (pp. 319–333). In K. I. Pargament, J. Exline, J. Jones, A. Mahoney, & E. Shafranske (Eds.), *APA handbook of psychology, religion, and spirituality* (Vol. 2). Washington, DC: American Psychological Association.

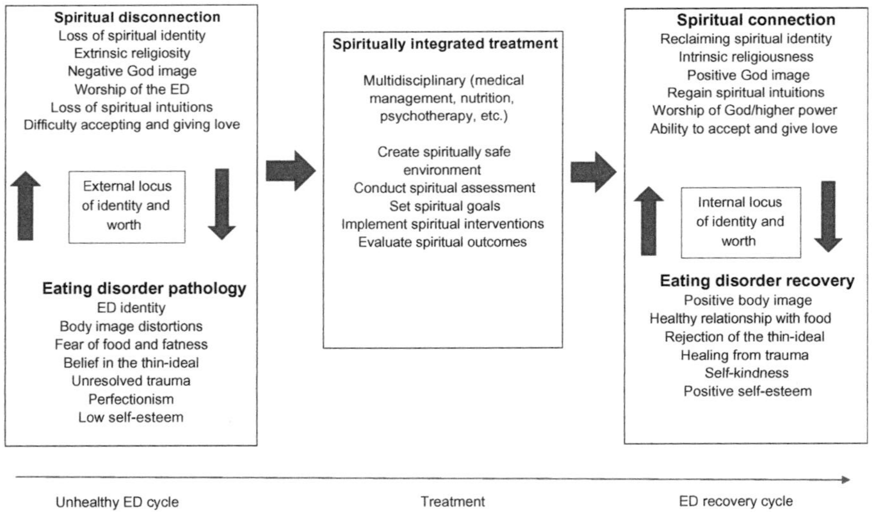

Figure 6.1 Role of spirituality in eating disorder (ED) treatment and recovery. *Adapted from Richards, P. S., Caoili, C. L., Crowton, S. A., Berrett, M. E., Hardman, R. K., Jackson, R. N., & Sanders, P. W. (2018). An exploration of the role of religion and spirituality in the treatment and recovery of patients with eating disorders.* Spirituality in Clinical Practice, 5, *88–103.*

more faith in illness as the solution or answer to their suffering. The middle of Fig. 6.1 is intended to illustrate that spiritually integrated treatment helps break the unhealthy ED cycle. Spiritually integrated treatment helps patients reconnect with religious and spiritual resources in their lives (Richards et al., 2007). This enables them to begin the healthy cycle of ED recovery. On the right side of Fig. 6.1, it can be seen that ED recovery is influenced by spiritual connections—and vice versa. During spiritually integrated treatment, shifting attention from disordered eating to healthy living allows patients to rediscover areas of their lives that have been neglected during their disorder. A renewed spiritual connection shifts patient's locus of identity and worth from external to internal criteria and values, which facilitates healing and ED recovery. We elaborate further on this model below.

Loss of spiritual connection

Spiritual connection refers to the quality of patients' relationship with their spirituality, which they may define as their God or Higher Power; those who love them; their own hearts; their sense of purpose, meaning, and deepest desires; their own best self; their connection with nature; or any other spiritual source. Spiritual connection is often lost in the drive to maintain disordered eating. For many women, as their ED becomes more severe, their connection to God or their Higher Power decreases. The ED becomes the focus of the woman's attention and worship and replaces God and spiritual sources of identity and coping. Furthermore, as women disconnect from spiritual sources of meaning and support, they rely more fully on the ED and thinness as their source of meaning and as an escape from their emotional pain. This creates a vicious cycle where spiritual disconnection and ED pathology mutually and destructively influence each other (Richards et al., 2007, 2018). In our clinical work, we have noticed that the loss of spiritual connection in patients' lives is manifested in numerous ways, including (1) loss of spiritual identity, (2) focus on extrinsic versus intrinsic religious motivations, (3) negative images of God or spirituality, (4) worshiping or placing faith in the ED as an answer or solution to their suffering, (5) loss of spiritual intuitions, and (6) difficulty in accepting and giving love. Due to space limitations, we can only briefly describe each of these spiritual problems here, but we have described them and other spiritual problems in more detail in previous publications (e.g., Berrett et al., 2010, 2018; Richards et al., 2007).

Loss of spiritual identity

Nearly all women who struggle with an ED lose touch with their sense of identity and worth. For those who are religiously and spiritually inclined, this includes the loss of their spiritual identity (Berrett et al., 2018; Richards et al., 2007). According to Berrett et al. (2018), "Spiritual identity is the very core of personhood ... [and] represents a full and complete identity. It is the recognition, awareness, and embodiment of the whole self – the integration and acceptance of self in various sectors of life: physical, mental, emotional, relational, and spiritual" (p. 339). For many patients, the loss of their spiritual sense of identity is extremely painful because they feel that they have lost God or that God has abandoned them. They no longer feel worthy of God's love. They lose their sense of identity as a woman and as a valued creation or daughter of God and come to "see themselves exclusively as an eating disorder, or as the expression of an eating disorder" (Richards et al., 2007, p. 44).

Extrinsic religious motivations

As discussed earlier, research provides some support for the idea that those who are involved in religious communities and activities for perceived social and personal gain (i.e., extrinsic religious motivations) may be more vulnerable to EDs (Smith et al., 2004; Weinberger-Litman et al., 2008, 2016). In our clinical work, we have noticed that a major feature of ED psychopathology is an external locus of identity and worth. Religious women who are suffering with an ED may rely too heavily upon perceived approval from their religious community for their sense of identity and self-esteem.

Negative images of God

Some theistic patients feel that God abandoned them during the most difficult and traumatic times of their lives. Many patients feel that God is unreachable or capricious. Patients can also have painful beliefs that God views them as sinful, unworthy, and defective—and they feel alienated and disconnected, undeserving of God's help (Richards et al., 2007).

Worshiping or placing faith in the eating disorder

Many women suffering with EDs report that the ED becomes their God (Richards et al., 2007, 2018). Rather than placing their faith and hopes for success and happiness in God or their spiritual source, they come to believe that it is the ED—and thinness—that will give them success, love, and happiness and solutions to their suffering (Hardman et al., 2003). Thinness becomes their object of worship. This unintentional shifting toward placing faith in the ED illness is not a conscious choice, but rather, a natural progression of the development of the illness.

Loss of spiritual intuitions

As EDs worsen, those suffering lose the ability to recognize the impressions and intuitions of their hearts because these feelings are lost in internal conflict and turmoil—and in the many negative messages of the ED mind (Berrett et al., 2010; Johnston, 1996; Richards et al., 2007). As a result, women do not trust themselves to have valid impressions or intuitions. They lose this source of emotional and spiritual guidance, which undermines their ability to make healthy choices. Rather than looking inward and trusting their own thoughts, feelings, and spiritual intuitions when making choices, they rely on excessive overthinking, the negative pressures of perfectionistic thoughts, and external criteria for success and worth provided by peers, media, and other sources of social influence and pressure.

Difficulty accepting and giving love

One of the consequences of an ED is that those suffering ED experience a diminished ability to accept and give love, which undermines their ability to deepen loving relationships (Richards et al., 2007). This inability stems in part from their feelings of shame, worthlessness, unlovability, and fear of vulnerability (Berrett et al., 2010; Richards et al., 2018). Many patients resist or refuse love from others on the grounds that they believe they are the exception to love. They believe everyone else is deserving of love, but they are not. The loss of these deeper connections of love with others often leaves patients feeling alone and lost. Their obsessive preoccupation with food, body image, and illness becomes an obstacle to love and connection with God, spirituality, and close interpersonal relationships (Berrett et al., 2010).

Guidelines for spiritually integrated treatment of eating disorders

The model described above has a corresponding set of clinical guidelines, which are consistent with the general approach of the American Psychiatric Association (2010), which recommends a multidisciplinary approach to treatment of EDs. Medical doctors, nurses, psychiatrists, psychologists, family therapists, and dietitians are part of the treatment team.

Medical management; nutrition and weight stabilization; medication; and individual, group, and family psychotherapies are all necessary interventions with those who have severe EDs. Within this context, spiritual perspectives and interventions are combined with evidence-based, best-practice medical and psychological treatment methods in a treatment-tailoring manner depending on patients' preferences and needs (Richards et al., 2007).

In order to implement spiritual approaches and interventions in a sensitive and effective manner, it is crucial to establish a spiritually safe therapeutic environment (Richards et al., 2007). Many patients are uncertain whether it is acceptable to talk about religious and spiritual issues during psychotherapy (Richards & Bergin, 2005), perhaps out of the misconception that the separation of church and state in government also applies to mental health treatment. This is not the case, and letting patients know that they have the right to discuss spiritual issues during treatment can help allay fears they may have about doing so. There are several things treatment providers can do to help establish a spiritually safe and open therapeutic environment. Including questions about patients' religious background, affiliation, and beliefs on intake questionnaires and other assessment measures sends the message and gives permission to talk about religious issues—and it can provide valuable information for helping therapists understand their patients' worldviews and values (Berrett et al., 2010; Richards et al., 2007).

During informed consent procedures, therapists should also explicitly tell patients that it is okay to talk about religious and spiritual issues during treatment, if the patient wishes. As treatment proceeds, if patients bring up religious or spiritual issues for discussion, therapists should, of course, listen carefully and communicate interest in learning about this area of patients' lives (Richards & Bergin, 2005). Therapists should also take a client-centered approach and seek to work within their patients' religious or spiritual framework and values. They should similarly seek to learn and use the language of patients' spirituality rather than imposing their own spiritual language or values on patients (Berrett et al., 2010). If patients seem uncomfortable or unwilling to discuss spiritual issues, treatment providers should respect their preference and treatment should proceed without a spiritual focus. Helping patients understand what spirituality is and how it may be beneficial to address in treatment can help establish a spiritually safe and open environment. We recommend that treatment providers define spirituality broadly and to seek to understand patients' beliefs about what spirituality means to them. If spirituality is defined broadly to include things such as love, kindness, forgiveness, compassion, and hope, this can help patients more fully recognize how spiritually is evident in their lives (Berrett et al., 2010). While patients may be religious or nonreligious, we believe that all patients are spiritual in nature and that finding and embracing their spirituality can assist them in reclaiming a positive sense of identity (Berrett et al., 2018).

For patients who desire a spiritually integrated approach, assessing patients' S/R background is essential. A thorough assessment of patients' functioning should be conducted at the beginning of treatment, including their physical, nutritional, psychological, social, and spiritual functioning. A careful religious and spiritual assessment can help the treatment staff work within the patient's belief system in a respectful manner. Patients' spirituality can be assessed through written intake questionnaires, clinical interviews, and standardized measures of religious orientation and spirituality (Richards et al., 2007). Due to space limitations, we will not say more about conducting a religious and spiritual assessment here, but this information is available in other publications (e.g., Berrett et al., 2010, 2018; Richards & Bergin, 2005; Richards et al., 2007). Activities as simple as asking patients to talk about their spiritual hero, and why they chose that hero, can provide much insight into patients' spiritual beliefs and values (Berrett et al., 2018).

Spiritual interventions in treatment should not begin until after a careful assessment of the patients' psychological functioning, spiritual background and beliefs, and attitudes about exploring spiritual issues during treatment. Berrett et al. (2010) described six pathways to spiritual reconnection and recovery: listening to the heart, learning a language of spirituality, mindfulness and spiritual mindedness, principled living, receiving and giving the good gifts of love, and holding up the therapeutic mirror which reflects spiritual identity. They also described a variety of spiritual interventions that can help patients progress along these spiritual pathways toward spiritual reconnection and recovery from illness.

Interventions that can be useful during individual therapy include spiritual discussions, reading sacred writings, writings of the heart, prayer, spiritual imagery, listening to sacred music, honesty without self-judgment, repentance, meditation, time in nature, forgiveness, letter writing, letter to the ED, solo time, and spiritual journaling (Richards et al., 2007). Group and family therapy interventions can include many activities that are designed to promote openness, honesty, vulnerability, and connections with self and others (Richards et al., 2007). Effective interventions help to make the implicit and unspoken seen and shared in a safe environment. Patients and families have opportunities to face fears, take risks, and begin practicing new perspectives, approaches, and choices for their lives and relationships. They can begin to experience the power of love, compassion, and acceptance from others, while at the same time, sharing their own good hearts and love with the people in their lives. They can confront pain, see the truths and negative costs of the ED, and open their spiritual eyes and see themselves for who they really are without the ED (Berrett et al., 2010, 2018; Richards et al., 2007).

Ethical considerations

In keeping with evidence-based practice, we recommend that treatment providers who integrate spirituality into ED practice monitor the outcomes of treatment on a routine basis (Lea et al., 2015; Richards et al., 2007). This recommendation is based on research that shows that continuous assessment of ED patients' progress leads to treatment course correction and improved outcomes (Simon et al., 2013). Many types of research designs can contribute to the evidence base (APA, 2006), but we recommend, at a minimum, that treatment facilities use a practice-based evidence research design where treatment processes and outcomes are monitored from session to session (Barkham, Hardy, & Mellor-Clark, 2010). Computerized and online outcome assessment systems make it feasible for practitioners and treatment facilities to conduct such research. This is a worthy goal to work toward for all therapists and their patients.

Beyond remaining within an evidence-based framework, there are a variety of potential ethical pitfalls treatment providers should be alert to when integrating spirituality into treatment. These include the dual relationships (religious and professional), displacing or usurping religious authority, imposing religious values on patients, violating work setting (church-state) boundaries, and practicing outside of the boundaries of professional competence (Richards & Bergin, 2005). Due to space limitations, we refer readers to other books and articles that have discussed these concerns (e.g., Richards & Bergin, 2005; Richards et al., 2007).

Therapists should also assess whether patients wish to include discussions about their spiritual beliefs in treatment before implementing spiritual interventions. There are several situations where spiritual interventions may be contraindicated, including when patients say they would prefer not to participate in them, when patients are delusional or psychotic, when spiritual issues are not relevant to the patient's clinical issues, and with children and adolescents whose parents have not given consent to include the discussion of spiritual issues in treatment (Richards & Bergin, 2005). Patients who are antireligious or nonreligious may be offended and feel excluded if there is too much focus on religious or spiritual issues. Therapists should always work within the belief systems of their patients and not use interventions that conflict with patients' spiritual beliefs. Patients should be encouraged to take the lead in their own spiritual journey (Berrett et al., 2010).

Discussion

Historical and more recent empirical research has led to a better understanding of the mechanisms through which S/R may be relevant to EDs. Recent research has been aimed at understanding the development and treatment of these issues in religiously and spiritually diverse communities (Akrawi et al., 2015; Hall & Boyatzis, 2016). As S/R has become more widely recognized as an important contributor to the sociocultural milieu of risk factors for EDs and related symptoms, treatment approaches addressing ED patients' S/R beliefs and concerns have been developed.

Successful treatment for EDs requires a multidisciplinary assessment and treatment approach (Brownell & Walsh, 2017). When patients reconnect with spiritual resources, they discover a source of strength and support that can sustain and motivate them during and after treatment (Berrett et al., 2018; Richards et al., 2007, 2018). When they reconnect to love of and from others, this also is a healing process. When they reconnect to themselves—who they really are—and strengthen their sense of spiritual identity and goodness, they are building a foundation for treatment, recovery, and lifelong peace. To include spiritual resources for recovery requires sensitivity and competency and in-depth emotional and spiritual work (Richards et al., 2007). We hope that treatment providers who work with ED patients will make greater efforts to include religious and spiritual resources in their work, in order to more fully facilitate and support their patients' healing and recovery.

References

Akrawi, D., Bartrop, R., Potter, U., & Touyz, S. (2015). Religiosity, spirituality in relation to disordered eating and body image concerns: A systematic review. *Journal of Eating Disorders*, *3*(1), 29.

American Psychiatric Association. (2010). *Practice guideline for the treatment of patients with eating disorders* (4th ed.). Arlington, VA: Author.

American Psychiatric Association. (2013). *Diagnostic and statistical manual of mental disorders* (5th ed.). Washington, DC: Author.

American Psychological Association. (2006). Evidence-based practice in psychology. *American Psychologist, 61*, 271–285.

Barkham, M., Hardy, G. E., & Mellor-Clark, J. (Eds.), (2010). *Developing and delivering practice-based evidence: A guide for the psychological therapies*. Chichester: Wiley.

Berrett, M. E., Crowton, S. A., & Richards, P. S. (2018). Finding self again: The dismantling of eating disorder and trauma identity. In A. Seubert, & P. Virdi (Eds.), *Trauma-informed approaches to eating disorders*. New York: Springer Publishing Company.

Berrett, M. E., Hardman, R. K., & Richards, P. S. (2010). The role of spirituality in eating disorder treatment and recovery. In M. Maine, B. H. McGilley, & D. W. Bunnell (Eds.), *Special issues in the treatment of eating disorders: Bridging the gaps* (pp. 367–385). Maryland Heights, MO: Elsevier.

Boyatzis, C. J., Kline, S., & Backof, S. (2007). Experimental evidence that theistic-religious body affirmations improve women's body image. *Journal for the Scientific Study of Religion, 46*(4), 553–564.

Brownell, K. D., & Walsh, B. T. (Eds.), (2017). *Eating disorders and obesity: A comprehensive handbook*. Guilford Publications.

Brumberg, J. J. (2000). *Fasting girls: The history of anorexia nervosa*. New York: Vintage Books.

Culbert, K. M., Slane, J. D., & Klump, K. L. (2018). *Genetics of eating disorders. Annual review of eating disorders* (pp. 35–50). CRC Press.

Emmett, S. (2009). Wholeness and holiness: A psychospiritual perspective. In M. Maine, W. N. Davis, & J. Shure (Eds.), *Effective clinical practice in the treatment of eating disorders: The heart of the matter* (pp. 19–33). New York: Routledge. (2009).

Exline, J. J., Homolka, S. J., & Harriott, V. A. (2016). Divine struggles: Links with body image concerns, binging, and compensatory behaviours around eating. *Mental Health, Religion & Culture, 19*(1), 8–22. Available from https://doi.org/10.1080/13674676.2015.1087977.

Fairburn, C. G., Cooper, Z., & Shafran, R. (2003). Cognitive behaviour therapy for eating disorders: A "transdiagnostic" theory and treatment. *Behaviour Research and Therapy, 41*(5), 509–528.

Favaro, A., Monteleone, P., Santonastaso, P., & Maj, M. (2018). *Psychobiology of eating disorders. Annual review of eating disorders* (pp. 9–34). CRC Press.

Forthun, L. F., Pidcock, B. W., & Fischer, J. L. (2003). Religiousness and disordered eating: Does religiousness modify family risk? *Eating Behaviors, 4*, 7–26.

Frank, G. K. (2015). Recent advances in neuroimaging to model eating disorder neurobiology. *Current Psychiatry Reports, 17*(4), 22.

Hall, M. E. L., & Boyatzis, C. J. (2016). God in the bod: Charting the course of research on religiosity and the body. *Mental Health, Religion, & Culture, 19*, 1–7. Available from https://doi.org/10.1080/13674676.2015.1130467.

Hardman, R. K., Berrett, M. E., & Richards, P. S. (2003). Spirituality and ten false pursuits of eating disorders: Implications for counselors. *Counseling and Values, 48*, 67–78.

Henderson, A. K., & Ellison, C. G. (2015). My body is a temple: Eating disturbances, religious involvement, and mental health among young adult women. *Journal of Religion and Health, 54*(3), 954–976.

Homan, K. J. (2012). Attachment to God mitigates negative effect of media exposure onwomen's body image. *Psychology of Religion and Spirituality, 4*(4), 324.

Homan, K. J., & Lemmon, V. A. (2014). Attachment to God and eating disorder tendencies: The mediating role of social comparison. *Psychology of Religion and Spirituality*, *6*(4), 349.

Homan, K. J., & Lemmon, V. A. (2016). Perceived relationship with God moderates the relationship between social comparison and body appreciation. *Mental Health, Religion, & Culture*, *18*(6), 425–439.

Jacobs-Pilipski, M. J., Winzelberg, A., Wilfley, D. E., Bryson, S. W., & Taylor, C. B. (2005). Spirituality among young women at risk for eating disorders. *Eating Behaviors*, *6*(4), 293–300.

Johnson, C. L., & Sansone, R. A. (1993). Integrating the twelve-step approach with traditional psychotherapy for the treatment of eating disorders. *International Journal of Eating Disorders*, *14*, 121–134.

Johnston, A. (1996). *Eating in the light of the moon: How women can transform their relationships with food through myths, metaphors and storytelling*. Carlsbad, CA: Gurze Books.

Joughin, N., Crisp, A. H., Halek, C., & Humphrey, H. (1992). Religious belief and anorexia nervosa. *International Journal of Eating Disorders*, *12*, 397–406.

Keski-Rahkonen, A., Raevuori, A., & Hoek, H. W. (2018). *Epidemiology of eating disorders: An update. Annual review of eating disorders* (pp. 66–76). CRC Press.

Kirkpatrick, L. A., & Hood, R. W. (1990). Intrinsic extrinsic religious orientation: The boon or bane of contemporary psychology of religion? *Journal for the Scientific Study of Religion*, *29*(4), 442–462. Available from https://doi.org/10.2307/1387311.

Lea, T., Richards, P. S., Sanders, P. W., McBride, J. A., & Allen, G. E. (2015). Spiritual pathways to healing and recovery: An intensive single-N study of an eating disorder patient. *Spirituality in Clinical Practice*, *2*, 191–201.

Lelwica, M. M. (1999). *Starving for salvation*. New York: Oxford University Press.

Lelwica, M. M. (2010). *The religion of thinness*. Carlsbad, CA: Gurze Books.

Latzer, Y., Weinberger-Litman, S. L., Gerson, B., Rosch, A., Mischel, R., Hinden, T., ...& Silver, J. (2015). Negative religious coping predicts disordered eating pathology among Orthodox Jewish adolescent girls. *Journal of Religion and Health* *54*(5), 1760–1771.

Maine, M., & Kelly, J. (2005). *The body myth: Adult women and the pressure to be perfect*. Hoboken, NJ: Wiley.

Marsden, P., Karagianni, E., & Morgan, J. F. (2007). Spirituality and clinical care in eating disorders: A qualitative study. *International Journal of Eating Disorders*, *40*(1), 7–12.

Manley, R. S., & Leichner, P. (2003). Anguish and despair in adolescents with eating disorders: Helping to manage suicidal ideation and impulses. *Crisis*, *24*, 31–36.

Miller, L., Balodis, I. M., McClintock, C. H., Xu, J., Lacadie, C. M., Sinha, R., & Potenza, M. N. (2019). Neural correlates of personalized spiritual experiences. *Cerebral Cortex*, *29*(6), 2331–2338.

Morgan, J. F., Marsden, P., & Lacey, J. H. (2000). "Spiritual starvation?": A case series concerning Christianity and eating disorders. *International Journal of Eating Disorders*, *28*(4), 476–480.

Richards, P. S., & Bergin, A. E. (2005). *A spiritual strategy for counseling and psychotherapy* (2nd ed.). Washington, DC: American Psychological Association.

Richards, P. S., Caoili, C. L., Crowton, S. A., Berrett, M. E., Hardman, R. K., Jackson, R. N., & Sanders, P. W. (2018). An exploration of the role of religion and spirituality in the treatment and recovery of patients with eating disorders. *Spirituality in Clinical Practice*, *5*, 88–103.

Richards, P. S., Hardman, R. K., & Berrett, M. E. (2007). *Spiritual approaches in the treatment of women with eating disorders*. Washington, DC: American Psychological Association.

Richards, P. S., Weinberger-Litman, S. L., Susov, S., & Berrett, M. E. (2013). Religiousness and spirituality in the etiology and treatment of eating disorders. In K. I. Pargament, A. Mahoney, & E. P. Shafranske (Eds.), *APA handbook of psychological, religion, and spirituality: Vol. 2. An applied psychology of religion and spirituality* (pp. 319–333). Washington, DC: American Psychological Association.

Rim, J. I., Ojeda, J. C., Svob, C., Kayser, J., Drews, E., Kim, Y., … Weissman, M. M. (2019). Current understanding of religion, spirituality, and their neurobiological correlates. *Harvard Review of Psychiatry*, *27*(5), 303–316.

Ross, C. C. (2007). *Healing body, mind and spirit: An integrative medicine approach to the treatment of eating disorders*. Denver, CO: Outskirts Press.

Simon, W., Lambert, M. J., Busath, G., Vazquez, A., Berkeljon, A., Hyer, K., … Berrett, M. (2013). Effects of providing patient progress feedback and clinical support tools to psychotherapists in an inpatient eating disorders treatment program: A randomized controlled study. *Psychotherapy Research*, *23*, 287–300.

Smith, M. H., Richards, P. S., & Maglio, C. J. (2004). Examining the relationship between religious orientation and eating disturbances. *Eating Behaviors*, *5*, 171–180.

Strenger, A. M., Schnitker, S. A., & Felke, T. J. (2016). Attachment to God moderates the relation between sociocultural pressure and eating disorder symptoms as mediated by emotional eating. *Mental Health, Religion & Culture*, *19*(1), 23–36.

Treasure, J., Claudino, A. M., & Zucker, N. (2010). Eating disorders. *The Lancet*, *375*, 583–593. Available from https://doi.org/10.1016/S0140-6736(09)61748-7.

Vandereycken, W., & Van Deth, R. (1994). *From fasting saints to anorexic girls*. New York: New York University Press.

Weinberger-Litman, S. L., Latzer, Y., Litman, L., & Ozick, R. (2018). Extrinsic religious orientation and disordered eating pathology among modern orthodox Israeli adolescents: The mediating role of adherence to the superwoman ideal and body dissatisfaction. *Journal of Religion and Health*, *57*(1), 209–222.

Weinberger-Litman, S. L., Rabin, L. A., Fogel, J., & Mensinger, J. L. (2008). The influence of religious orientation and spiritual well-being on body dissatisfaction and disordered eating in a sample of Jewish women. *International Journal of Child and Adolescent Health*, *1*(4), 373–387.

Weinberger-Litman, S. L., Rabin, L. A., Fogel, J., Mensinger, J. L., & Litman, L. (2016). Psychosocial mediators of the relationship between religious orientation and eating disorder risk factors in young Jewish women. *Psychology of Religion and Spirituality*, *8*(4), 265.

CHAPTER 7

Spirituality/religion and substance use disorders

Hilary S. Connery[1,2] and Jeff Devido[3,4]
[1]Division of Alcohol, Drugs, and Addiction, McLean Hospital, Belmont, MA, United States
[2]Department of Psychiatry, Harvard Medical School, Boston, MA, United States
[3]Department Health and Human Services, Behavioral Health and Recovery Services, Marin County, CA, United States
[4]UCSF Weill Institute for Neurosciences, School of Medicine, University of California, San Francisco, CA, United States

Contents

Introduction

Substance use disorders (SUD) comprise a category of mental health disorders organized around behavioral dysregulation and compulsive substance use patterns. SUD are characterized by (1) loss of control during substance use (e.g., using greater amounts or for longer durations than one planned or using inappropriately in circumstances in which it would involve known physical or social risk to do so, such as while driving, during employment, or engaged in sole responsibility for the care of dependents), (2) substance craving and/or preoccupation with desire to use substances during abstinent periods, and (3) negative personal and societal consequences resulting from substance use, such as relational conflict, negative health consequences, and loss of income or productivity. SUD are dimensional—ranging from mild to severe—and may develop in multiple ways.

Handbook of Spirituality, Religion, and Mental Health
DOI: https://doi.org/10.1016/B978-0-12-816766-3.00007-0

For instance, those with a strong family history of SUD may have genetic vulnerability upon substance exposure, early exposure due to environmental vulnerability, or both. Regardless of heritable vulnerability, SUD cannot develop without substance exposure and frequent access to substances increases the probability of developing SUD over time.

Once established, SUD is a neurobehavioral syndrome that manifests in predictable behaviors and involves well-established changes in neurobiological circuitry governing executive functioning, mood, substance craving, reward states, stress reactivity, and motivated behaviors (Volkow, Koob, & McLellan, 2016). Heterogeneity in persistence versus remission of SUD is extensive for some substances, such as alcohol (McCabe, West, Strobbe, & Boyd, 2018; Moss, Chen, & Yi, 2010), and less so for drugs such as opioids, which generally require medications (i.e., the mu-opioid antagonist naltrexone and the mu-opioid agonists buprenorphine and methadone), to stabilize the underlying neurobiological dysregulation in order to achieve remission (Connery, 2015).

The development of SUD involves learning and neuroadaptation within motivational or "reward" circuitry of the brain, including the ventral tegmental area, nucleus accumbens, amygdala, hippocampus, extended striatum, insula, and the prefrontal cortex (Koob & Volkow, 2010; Volkow et al., 2016). These brain regions facilitate reinforcement learning for survival processes such as eating and sexual reproduction. Substances with liability for addiction all have in common the capacity to activate dopamine release in the nucleus accumbens at greater levels than natural rewards (e.g., food and sexual intimacy). Dopamine release in the accumbens first signals that a stimulus is "good" and thereby begins an associative learning response that pairs the stimulus with information about its source (e.g., environmental and internal cues concurrent with the stimulus). This learning assists with being able to experience the stimulus again by establishing its importance, or "salience," mediated by the amygdala, and also by identifying environmental cues predictive of the stimulus so that one can orient behavior toward reexperiencing the stimulus, mediated by hippocampal and corticostriatal pathways. After taking a pleasurable substance repeatedly, learning occurs rapidly and can be established without conscious awareness that both attention and motivated behaviors are now preferentially oriented toward substance-seeking and substance-taking. As these initial phases progress, dopamine release becomes a marker of anticipated substance pleasure and thus is involved in craving for the substance even prior to taking of the substance. Internal, physiological cues (such as physiological arousal) detected in the insula also become associated with substance-seeking and reinforcement. Whereas repeated administration of natural rewards will desensitize dopamine release and thereby signal satiation, repeated administration of addictive substances does not produce dopamine desensitization early on (satiety feedback is greatly diminished, which is further associated with a person taking more substance than intended).

As SUD progresses to moderate and severe stages, dopamine release is diminished and stress circuitry within the extended amygdala and basal forebrain is enhanced, leading to loss of intrinsic motivation, sensitivity to negative emotional arousal, and to physiological stressors, and an increasingly aversive substance withdrawal syndrome marked by intense craving, anxious and depressed mood, catastrophic thinking, and physiological hyperarousal and irritability. This creates an entrapping vicious cycle for those with SUD: the taking of the substance is no longer pleasurable in its original sense and the absence of substance-taking is intolerable, so one is compulsively taking the drug just to feel more "normal" and the rest of existence is miserable and exhausting. This trapped existence is commonly associated with despair and elevated suicidal thoughts and behaviors.

In a small study ($n = 19$ devout, young adult Mormons used as their own case controls in repeated stimulation sessions) using functional magnetic resonance imaging, researchers reported that peak religious experiences were associated with replicable and consistent brain activation, seconds prior to peak experience, within bilateral nucleus accumbens, frontal attentional, and ventromedial prefrontal cortical loci (Ferguson et al., 2018). Such preliminary data suggest an intriguing possibility that positive spiritual and religious experiences may evoke healthy functional responses within reward circuitry and thus may provide a novel intervention for ameliorating the dysregulated reward circuitry responses evidenced in moderate to severe SUD. Replication of this report in larger samples, other faith communities, and testing among those with SUD may tell us more about the future potential for using spiritual and religious interventions as therapeutic neurointerventional strategies for SUD.

The heterogeneity in both the development and persistence of SUD is an aspect of the illness that is perhaps most confusing to both the individuals with SUD and to family members and society. Why does one person develop an addiction, while another does not? What allows one person with SUD to achieve stable remission and recovery, while another experiences continuous relapsing episodes in spite of repeated attempts to stop? For as long as substance use problems have existed, society has puzzled over the presentation of SUD: how can an individual with a normal capacity of thought and behavior express a distinct *incapacity* that appears to be confined to control over substance use? Even with current scientific knowledge of these brain processes, it is a frequent and natural human response to contemplate whether or not SUD represents a failure of moral conviction or personal determination, and this perspective has greatly influenced policy, treatment, and widespread discrimination and stigma against those living with SUD. In fact, the experiences of social isolation, shame and guilt, and despair over persistent SUD are often internalized by those living with SUD as evidence of their own character defect or moral failing. It may be self-evident that such internalized beliefs would, in most cases, pose barriers to recovery from SUD, and it is this aspect of SUD treatment in which integrated spiritual mental health interventions may be most promising.

12-Step programs and substance use disorder treatment

Against the stigma associated with persistent SUD as a moral failure, and the historical limitations of medical treatments for chronic SUD, 12-step programs based on the original model of Alcoholics Anonymous (AA) emerged at the community level to organize and address the important aspect of treatment involving a "spiritual awakening" and proposed a personal need to rely on help from a Higher Power, facilitated through the principles and support of the AA fellowship, in order to heal fully from SUD (Alcoholics-Anonymous, 1939). With over two million members estimated worldwide in 2017, AA (and similar 12-step mutual-help programs for substances other than alcohol) remains active and highly visible in SUD treatment and community recovery supports today.

There is consistent evidence in clinical trials, particularly robust for alcohol use disorder, that adjunctive participation in 12-step programs improves short-term and long-term outcomes for treatment-seeking individuals with SUD alone, as well as for SUD combined with other co-occurring mental health disorders, such as depression and anxiety (Humphreys, Blodgett, & Wagner, 2014; Kelly, 2017; Tonigan, Pearson, Magill, & Hagler, 2018). It is more difficult to name spirituality/religion (S/R) as solely responsible for this effectiveness in practice, however, since the AA model not only activates S/R enhancement (through encouraging prayer, spiritual gratitude, seeking intervention from a sacred Higher

Power), but also nurtures positive/protective social networks and cognitive reappraisals aimed at maintaining abstinence (Dermatis & Galanter, 2016; Kelly, 2017). The 12-step aphorisms reflect this multimodal approach: "Let go and let God" (explicitly positive religious coping, see section below), "one day at a time" (behavioral activation focusing on the moment rather than becoming overwhelmed with long-term projections), "stinkin' thinkin'" (identification of negative cognitions typically associated with a desire to use substances), and "if you hang around a barber shop, you're likely to get a haircut" (acknowledging and enhancing awareness of high-risk social situations that increase the probability of relapse behavior).

A recent meta analysis of randomized controlled trials (RCTs) of S/R intervention efficacy within treatment-seeking SUD populations (Hai, Franklin, Park, DiNitto, & Aurelio, 2019) highlights both the moderate efficacy of current S/R therapeutics for SUD patients, as well as substantial methodological problems associated with studies to date on this important topic. For instance, only 20 of thousands of published studies on the topic meet threshold criteria for an RCT from which one may interpret causal impact of the S/R intervention on treatment outcomes. Among these, the only studies employing active control groups were studies delivering interventions that support 12-step program engagement. Only 5 of the 20 studies included used clear methods for assessing fidelity adherence to the delivered intervention. None of the studies were double-blinded (which may not be possible in such studies), and 17 of 20 studies used only self-report measures as the primary outcome. These pose significant limitations to interpretation of results; however, this meta analysis supported a slightly superior relative efficacy of 12-step program facilitation over other SUD interventions, including cognitive behavioral therapy for relapse prevention, motivational enhancement, and family therapy. Although this adds to the literature supporting S/R interventions in SUD treatment as delivered within the 12-step recovery model, it must be noted that the 12-step program model incorporates aspects of cognitive behavioral therapy, motivational enhancement, and family "guidance" (not therapy), and therefore may be the only model in these studies that is inclusive of components of all evidence-based treatments for SUD to date. This hampers the interpretation of relative efficacy and supports the modern "eclectic" approach of combining evidence-based therapies within SUD treatment programs. More well-designed studies that clearly delineate intervention components and fidelity to manualized protocols are needed, along with studies of S/R interventions that are not delivered as 12-step program facilitation. It is also important to highlight that the majority of those with SUD are *not* treatment-seeking, and therefore more studies of all evidence-based interventions for SUD are needed among populations not seeking SUD recovery. It is possible that S/R interventions may be most relevant to such populations, since often their aims are not limited to direct substance reduction outcomes, and they may serve a critical treatment engagement role.

Positive religious coping

Positive religious coping (PRC) is a construct measuring how an individual may experience God within a benevolent or supportive relationship (Pargament, Koenig, & Perez, 2000). It is measurable using the psychometrically validated religious coping questionnaire scale, which measures both PRC and negative religious coping (NRC, i.e., holding punitive views of relationship with God). PRC has been measured in SUD populations that are and are not participating in 12-step programs of recovery. In clinical practice, it may be best to begin an exploratory analysis of an individual's specific patterns or propensities toward positive and negative religious coping, in order to collaboratively identify specific thoughts and beliefs that may be recovery-enhancing or recovery-interfering.

PRC has a protective effect in adolescents and youths for reducing alcohol (Knight et al., 2007) and stimulant misuse (Gallucci, Hackman, & Wilkerson, 2018). In adults with SUD, PRC is most robustly associated with improved outcomes for alcohol use disorder (Martin, Ellingsen, Tzilos, & Rohsenow, 2015), but may also be associated with positive outcomes in drug use disorders (Medlock et al., 2017; Puffer, Skalski, & Meade, 2012) and in those with combined alcohol and drug use disorders (Montgomery, Stewart, Bryant, & Ounpraseuth, 2014).

More research is needed to clarify the unique role(s) PRC may play in achieving positive outcomes. One study in alcohol use disorder patients found no distinct benefit for PRC on 6-month outcomes (Martin et al., 2015). Although drinking outcomes were significantly improved, PRC occurred among those with positive *general coping*, and PRC did not confer additional unique benefit beyond general coping. This raises an unanswered question regarding a specific role for PRC in mediating positive outcomes for substance-using patients. The majority of studies on PRC in substance-using individuals are cross-sectional in design and have not examined longitudinal increases in PRC as a unique mediator of positive outcomes. A small study in treatment-seeking opioid use disorder patients ($n = 45$) found that increases in PRC during treatment significantly correlated with enhanced frequency of 12-step participation during the first 2 weeks following discharge from detoxification treatment, but was not associated with postdischarge opioid use (Puffer et al., 2012). A larger study in treatment-seeking alcohol use disorder patients ($n = 364$) followed prospectively over 6–30 months likewise showed significant association of greater PRC with greater 12-step participation (Krentzman, Strobbe, Harris, Jester, & Robinson, 2017), controlling for drinking outcomes. There was no clear relationship between increases in 12-step participation influencing change in PRC over time and, in this study, levels of PRC within individuals remained relatively stable over time. It may be that enhancing PRC during treatment could significantly facilitate recovery-oriented behaviors, such as 12-step participation, and more research targeting PRC enhancement is warranted.

Negative religious coping

Clinicians generally first encounter SUD patients during an active use or relapse episode that causes them to seek clinical care. During these episodes, spiritual struggles are commonly observed across several themes that negatively reflect self-identity, despair, anger, shame and guilt, and loneliness. For those experiencing NRC, studies in those living with opioid use disorder suggest that NRC may represent a modifiable risk factor associated with greater opioid craving and poorer self-efficacy for achieving opioid abstinence and that corrective interventions may provide a novel clinical target to improve opioid use outcomes (Medlock et al., 2017; Puffer et al., 2012). Larger studies of NRC in those with alcohol use disorder report gender differences observed longitudinally in treatment, with men more likely than women to engage in NRC (Krentzman, 2017). In transitional age youth, NRC is associated with substance use in men, but not women (Parenteau, 2017). NRC appears to be much less common than PRC in women with SUD and is associated with trauma and mental health severity rather than with substance use (Fallot & Heckman, 2005). Although more research is needed to fully understand the implications of NRC for clinical care of SUD, Table 7.1 provides examples of commonly observed spiritual struggles in patients with active SUD that may be addressed during treatment with either secular or S/R cognitive

Table 7.1 Common spiritual struggles occurring during episodes of active substance use and a hypothetical patient worksheet for completing therapeutic cognitive reappraisals, using secular or S/R content, or both. The term "God" may be personalized to the individual's religious or spiritual beliefs.

Spiritual struggle: themes	Maladaptive thought or belief	Secular cognitive reappraisal	S/R cognitive reappraisal
Personal failure	I'm an addict who has failed myself and others.	I am living with substance use disorder, which is treatable. This is an illness from which I will recover.	I am living with substance use disorder, and I trust that God will help me in my efforts to heal.
Hopelessness	I've ruined my life and I can't stop using alcohol/drugs.	Things can change for the better; I can make effective choices now.	Although things seem hopeless, nothing is impossible with God on my side.
Isolation/disconnection	I am so alone.	I have others that care about me even though I feel alone.	God's love is with me always, I can seek His Presence.
Loss of self-identity and self-respect	I must be a weak person to have my life ruined by alcohol/drugs.	I am a valuable person with both strengths and vulnerabilities.	Alone I am weak, but with the grace of God I am strong.
Loss of connection with personal/life goals	My life is pointless.	My life has meaning in spite of alcohol/drug use. Now is a good time to reassess my goals.	I trust that God will lead me on a path of recovery, and I will find a better life.
Guilt and shame	My substance use is evidence that I don't care enough about myself or others.	I need my substance use disorder treated in order to take good care of myself and others.	Nothing I have done is bigger than the mercy of God. As I achieve recovery, I will become better at taking care of myself and others.
Anger	I hate my life and having this disease.	Recovery is possible and will restore meaning to my life.	If I am patient with myself and others, God will restore my peace.

reappraisals, displayed in a hypothetical patient. Other discussions of incorporating spirituality into cognitive behavioral therapy of SUD may be found in the literature (Hodge & Lietz, 2014).

Incorporating spirituality/religion into clinical care

Screening, Brief Intervention, and Referral to Treatment (SBIRT) is a commonly used evidence-based model that systematically identifies and targets interventions to reduce or prevent problematic alcohol or illicit drug use. SBIRT has been validated across multiple healthcare settings (primary care, emergency care, and specialty care settings) and may be delivered effectively by trained nonspecialists (Babor, Del Boca, & Bray, 2017; Madras et al., 2009). In practice, SBIRT involves the use of evidence-based SUD screening tools, such as the Drug Abuse Screening Test (DAST; Skinner, 1982) or the Alcohol Use Disorders Identification Test (AUDIT; Bohn, Babor, & Kranzler, 1995), paired with a simple algorithm for providing impactful brief interventions (BIs, e.g., a motivational conversation about changing substance use, and/or nonjudgmental provision of education and medical recommendations), followed by facilitated connection of the patient with appropriate SUD treatment services as needed. Although S/R is not commonly provided in routine SBIRT practice, this framework may also conveniently support S/R interventions as part of a comprehensive menu of options for care in all clinical settings. This is outlined in the following sections.

The first step in SBIRT for SUD is to systematically screen all patients for the presence of problematic substance use. One cannot hope to impact a patient's substance use without first identifying either its presence or the presence of factors that may increase the patient's risk of problematic use. Similarly, in an "S/R-enhanced" SBIRT model, the first step would be identification of an individual's S/R beliefs and/or values. While SUD screening is designed to identify the presence of *disorders* or at-risk factors that may lead to disorders, S/R screening can identify both S/R sources of potential strength or support (e.g., active practice of religious faith, sense of belonging and meaning in life) and S/R beliefs that may be neutral (e.g., absence of placing personal value on S/R) or negative (e.g., belief that one has ruptured a relationship with a spiritual community).

Similar to the DAST and AUDIT mentioned earlier, validated screening tools are available to standardize the process of identifying S/R

Table 7.2 Psychometrically validated S/R assessments studied in substance-using populations.

Assessment	Functional domains[a]	Number of items
Spirituality Self-Rating Scale (Galanter et al., 2007)	CBA	6
The Brief Multidimensional Measure of Religiousness/Spirituality (Stewart & Koeske, 2006)	CBA	30
The Index of Core Spiritual experience INSPIRIT-R (Heinz et al., 2007)	CBA	7
The Spiritual Transcendence Scale (Piedmont, 2004)	CA	24
The Spiritual Well-being Scale (Ellison, 1983; Paloutzian et al., 1982)	CA	20

[a]Assessments incorporate items reflecting content in: C = cognitive domain; B = behavioral domain; A = affective domain [as per Monod et al. (2011)].

strengths and liabilities. As with all sensitive screening content, it is advisable to begin with seeking permission to inquire about S/R: "Would you like your spiritual or religious beliefs to be included as part of your treatment?" This creates an atmosphere of respect for the person's level of comfort in discussing personal aspects of S/R and may also provide the opportunity to reinforce confidentiality in the clinical encounter.

With permission granted, clinicians may choose from multiple validated screening and assessment tools to assess aspects of S/R, albeit the majority of assessments are not specifically relevant to SUD populations. S/R screening and assessment in clinical practice has been reviewed in two comprehensive papers on the subject (Balboni et al., 2017; Monod et al., 2011). Much of the available literature on S/R screening and assessment is specific to individuals in palliative care or other primary medical settings, rather than to individuals with SUD or in SUD treatment settings; notable exceptions that have studied SUD populations are summarized in Table 7.2 and briefly described below.

Spiritual assessment measures

Spirituality Self-Rating Scale (SSRS; Galanter et al., 2007): This six-item assessment, designed to capture a global assessment of "spiritual orientation toward life," was developed by Galanter and colleagues using cross-sectional surveys of individuals in a variety of different SUD treatment settings, as well as in non-SUD treatment settings. The SSRS consists of the following questions, each of which is answered on a Likert-type scale from 0 (least agreement) to 5 (most agreement):

1. It is important for me to spend time in private spiritual thought and meditation.
2. I try hard to live my life according to my religious beliefs.
3. The prayers or spiritual thoughts that I say when I am alone are as important to me as those said by me during services or spiritual gatherings.
4. I enjoy reading about my spirituality and/or my religion.
5. Spirituality helps to keep my life balanced and steady in the same ways as my citizenship, friendships, and other memberships do.
6. My whole approach to life is based on my spirituality.

In validating this screening tool, the authors found that individuals in SUD treatment settings considered an S/R orientation to recovery to be relatively important. Furthermore, the authors posit that use of the SSRS could be helpful in not only identifying the relative importance an individual may place on S/R in their recovery from SUD, but also in helping to guide treatment referrals. For example, scoring higher on the SSRS may reflect the unique role that S/R may play in an individual's readiness to engage in programs having a strong 12-step philosophy. Conversely, scoring lower on the SSRS may guide a clinician toward treatment recommendations that are less overtly S/R-oriented, such as Self-Management and Recovery Training (SMART), a mutual-help organization that utilizes primarily cognitive behavioral approaches to reducing substance use (Beck et al., 2017).

Brief Multidimensional Measure of Religiousness/Spirituality (BMMRS; Stewart & Koeske, 2006): An abbreviated version (30 items) of the original 81 items compiled by the Fetzer Institute and the National Institute on Aging has been validated within SUD populations and accurately reflects measurements of three primary factors within the BMMRS (Fetzer, 1999): (1) assessment of *meaning* or purpose in daily life; (2) *private religious and spiritual practices*, reflecting intentional personal involvement in S/R beliefs and values; and (3) *organized religiousness*, reflecting personal alignment with a given religious institution as observed in attitudes and behavior. These factors collectively capture S/R self-identity and identification with others sharing S/R daily practices and values.

Index of Core Spiritual Experience INSPIRIT-R (Heinz, Epstein, & Preston, 2007): The INSPIRIT-R assessment contains seven items designed to capture normative religious experiences (i.e., not those experienced during traumatizing or extraordinary circumstances) and relationship with God. It was originally developed within medical settings (Kass, Friedman, Leserman, Zuttermeister, & Benson, 1991) and was found to correlate positively with favorable health outcomes. Heinz and colleagues tested the utility of this measure in a drug-using cohort and found that religious experiences are common in this population, particularly among women and African Americans, and there were trends indicating that greater S/R experience correlated with improved substance outcomes.

Spiritual Transcendence Scale (STS; Piedmont, 2004): Originally developed by Piedmont in 1999, the 24-item STS grew out of research proposing that spiritual transcendence, the perception of spiritual unity, and relatedness in the world may be uniquely measured as a dimension of personality providing motivational influence on an individual's thoughts and behaviors (Piedmont, 1999). STS also offered a "nonreligious," pro-social conceptualization of this dimension, with three domains: *universality*, reflecting beliefs that life is organized around a purposeful meaning; *prayer fulfillment*, the subjective appreciation of being in communion during prayer; and *connectedness*, reflecting personal values associated with acknowledgment that one's life is positively intertwined with others in an orderly manner. A small study among SUD outpatients suggested that universality and connectedness domains may be particularly relevant to good SUD treatment outcomes, as would be expected for populations needing to create new safe and positive social networks to support recovery.

Spiritual Well-Being Scale (SWBS; Ellison, 1983; Paloutzian, Ellison, Peplau, & Perlman, 1982): The SWBS is a 20-item scale developed for the purpose of capturing S/R constructs in quality of life measures and includes assessments of both spiritual well-being (i.e., a sense of one's life having coherent meaning and/or purpose), as well as religious well-being (i.e., coherent faith and relationship with God) (Ellison, 1983; Paloutzian et al., 1982). Studies have shown scoring positively on the SWBS to be protective against drug use (Staton-Tindall, Duvall, Stevens-Watkins, & Oser, 2013) and scoring low on SWBS to be correlated with drug use (Jalali, Shabrandi, Jalali, & Salari, 2019).

There is little evidence to support the use of any given S/R assessment over another in an individual with SUD. Further research is therefore needed to determine whether any particular S/R screening tool captures important SUD state-specific factors that others do not. Monod and colleagues reviewed categories of psychometrically validated S/R assessments used in healthcare research (Monod et al., 2011) that may help to guide use within SUD populations according to functional domains assessed within assessments [*examples below are taken from* Monod et al. (2011)]:

1. *Cognitive* expressions of spirituality that capture beliefs or attitudes about spirituality (e.g., "Do you believe meditation has value?").
2. *Behavioral* expressions of spirituality that reflect either (or both) public or private active behaviors related to spirituality (e.g., "How often do you go to church?").
3. *Affective* expressions of spirituality that provide a snapshot of the individual's dynamic spiritual state (e.g., "Do you feel peaceful?").

Table 7.2 lists the assessments above along with their functional domains. The cognitive functional domain represents an assessment of relatively stable-in-time beliefs around S/R (i.e., does one believe that S/R has value). The behavioral functional domain, on the other hand, reflects actions or behaviors undertaken in accordance with their S/R orientation (i.e., what does one *do* in relation to their S/R). If not impelled by some outside force, this domain is also largely stable-in-time; however, in SUD populations, this functional domain may become a key target of treatment. The affective functional domain more specifically assesses one's S/R state at a moment in time and is therefore a dynamic domain. Assessment of one's affective functional domain can provide a snapshot of where an individual currently resides in relation to where they would like to be in terms of their S/R (i.e., is one in a state of S/R distress or peace?).

Spirituality/religion brief intervention

In the SBIRT model for systematically addressing SUD, BIs can take many forms. In some instances, a BI can be as simple as the provision of educational materials about one's risk status in relation to SUD and/or treatment options. BI can also take the form of more complex, nuanced conversations regarding motivations and behaviors, such as motivational interviewing or motivational enhancement therapy, directed toward ambivalent motivational states (Miller & Rose, 2015). In any of its forms, the goal of BI is to pivot the results of the screening into a nonjudgmental, patient-centered collaborative conversation or exchange of information informed by the screening responses. Using the S/R functional domain construct outlined above, one could envision a clinical conversation such as follows:

> I appreciate that you took the time to talk with me about your spiritual background, current state in relation to your spiritual life, and your current

spiritual needs and desires. From what we discussed, you described a strong belief that spirituality is real and very important to you *[cognitive domain]*. I also understand that you identify with Buddhist spiritual practices and there was a time when you were very connected to a local *sangha* and regularly meditated *[behavioral domain]*. Yet since your heroin use escalated you've lost connection with that community and those practices, and would really like to get back to that, but can't seem to figure out how to do it and right now it feels hopeless *[affective domain]*.

Following a conversation summarizing findings such as this (organized around the S/R functional domains), a provider might then explore with the patient any ambivalence they are experiencing about living with SUD and simultaneously holding positive S/R beliefs and values. While it is not within the scope of this chapter to comprehensively review motivational interviewing strategies and tactics, we will provide here a brief mention of some core principles as they might be applied within an S/R-enhanced SBIRT model.

The fundamental target of motivational interviewing is to elicit *change talk* from a client (i.e., verbalization of a patient's own reasons and motivations to change a particular behavior). Simply put, people are more likely to change if they decide to change, and they are more likely to decide to change if they talk about possibilities for change. Tactically, motivational interviewing uses a combination of open-ended questions (i.e., those questions that are not answered simply with "yes" or "no" responses), along with reflective listening (i.e., presenting back to the client what they have communicated, which may be more than what they actually said, such as indirectly alluding to core values or emotions) to elicit and evoke talk about change possibility and/or commitment to changing. Here is an example applied to S/R:

Provider: You're concerned that with your current heroin use you'll never be welcomed back to your meditation community.
Patient: Yeah. I've burned that bridge. They'll just see me as a "junkie."
Provider: The community will judge you negatively and see you as a burden.
Patient: I worry about that, but I've also seen them welcome back people who had fallen away from the community.
Provider: It's possible they will help you instead of judging you.
Patient: I dunno. I feel that I let them down by relapsing.
Provider: In the past your community provided you with support and encouragement, and now you're feeling ashamed because you're worried you let them down.

Patient: I guess it is more about me feeling badly than them judging me. Maybe I just need to call one of them up and see if they can give me a ride to a meeting.

Provider: Your own shame has held you back from reaching out, which might turn things around for you. Would it be OK to think out loud with me now about what it might be like to reach out in spite of how badly you're feeling about yourself? Maybe there is someone you could imagine being able to re-connect with.

In this exchange, the provider had already explored through screening that this patient identified S/R as important and something that would be valuable to incorporate into recovery from heroin use disorder. The provider listened reflectively to elicit the patient's own thoughts about the desire and meaning of returning to their S/R community. The exchange ends with a powerful declaration of not only change, but *action*—calling someone. Although the provider could have just said from the outset, "Why don't you just call one of your old friends from the community?" motivational interviewing highlights the importance of an individual arriving at change options independently in order to experience self-agency in change.

Spirituality/religion referral to treatment

In the SBIRT model for systematically addressing SUD, referral to treatment is the final step, which involves providing concrete suggestions about treatment options tailored to the needs and motivations of the individual as determined through the screening and BI process. For example, an individual assessed to have risky alcohol use who expresses some interest in learning more about available treatment options may be provided with information about access to various medications for reducing alcohol use as well as information on local mutual-help meetings and professional counseling.

Similarly, a provider undertaking S/R-enhanced SBIRT may utilize the screening and BI to guide S/R referral options. This requires providers to become familiar with S/R referral options in the community or to be able to effectively refer the individual to someone who is more familiar with these options. In these latter instances, partnership with a chaplain or local faith leader, or with a peer counselor or recovery coach who is more knowledgeable about S/R resources in the community, is important. Overall, the goal is to provide the patient with a clear menu of options and next steps to foster S/R community connections. Having one's healthcare provider acknowledge the importance of S/R as part of an individual's recovery and treatment planning, and then assist with facilitation of reconnection or new connections to S/R resources, provides a clinically appropriate and possibly life-saving treatment intervention, particularly during this era of increasing substance poisoning deaths associated with SUD and despair.

Discussion

SUD are neurobehavioral syndromes characterized by behavioral dysregulation and compulsive substance use patterns, with varying severity of functional and health consequences and varying trajectories of progression or remission. Vulnerability to the development of SUD is determined by a complex interplay between a host of internal (e.g., genetic predispositions, cooccurring medical or other psychiatric disorders) and external (e.g., exposure to substances, trauma history, social environment) factors. Upon repeated exposure to addictive substances, the development of SUD reflects changes in neurocircuitry involved in the experience of pleasure (e.g., mesolimbic "reward circuits"), mood and emotion, stress reactivity, and learning and memory. These neuroadaptive changes drive the continued use of substance(s), despite negative consequences normally associated with adaptive learning, and result in a predictable set of behavioral expressions that include loss of control over substance use, substance craving, and negative personal, health, and societal consequences that are substance-related. SUD may be effectively treated with evidence-based medical and psychosocial therapies and seem to also be responsive to S/R interventions, particularly those associated with 12-step programs. In some cases, severe SUD may progress in severity such that consequences (i.e., loss of significant relational supports, loss of employment or vocation, exposure to infectious disease and resulting medical disability, homelessness, and incarceration for illegal activities associated with SUD) pose enormous challenges to recovery.

Historically, many treatment approaches to SUD have called upon S/R themes and directive behavioral changes as a means of counteracting the neurobehavioral manifestations of SUD. For example, 12-step programs such as AA emphasize the need for personal S/R enhancement through prayer, spiritual gratitude, and surrender to a Higher Power in order to loosen the cognitive preoccupation with desire to use substances and also to foster healthier social networks that emphasize pleasure in natural rewards over substance-related rewards. To date, the scientific evidence base supports a modestly positive impact of S/R engagement on measurable SUD treatment outcomes, although the literature is fraught with methodological limitations that need to be addressed in future research.

Clinical applications of S/R interventions during treatment of SUD remain poorly articulated in evidence-based care, with the exception of manualized approaches to facilitating 12-step program engagement, for example, Twelve Step Facilitation (Nowinski, Baker, & Carroll, 1995). More research is needed to consider client-centered applications of S/R that may support both treatment-seeking and the large majority of nontreatment-seeking persons living with SUD. We propose the exploration of facilitated S/R engagement incorporated into the "SBIRT" model commonly employed by SUD healthcare providers and systems in identifying, providing support and motivational enhancement, and referrals to specialty consultation/treatment as needed for SUD. In such a model, validated S/R screening tools may facilitate identification of interest in S/R engagement and support BIs and referrals when appropriate, regardless of whether these specifically target reduced substance use as an outcome, or more generally address the challenges and losses associated with moderate to severe SUD that pose substantial barriers to engagement with treatment.

S/R is a significant dimension of many people's self-understanding and can be a source of meaning and resilience under challenging circumstances. Systematically addressing clinical opportunities to foster S/R engagement may benefit both SUD populations and the communities that serve them.

References

Alcoholics-Anonymous. (1939). *Alcoholics Anonymous: The story of how many thousands of men and women have recovered from alcoholism*. New York: Alcoholics Anonymous World Services.

Babor, T. F., Del Boca, F., & Bray, J. W. (2017). Screening, brief intervention and referral to treatment: Implications of SAMHSA's SBIRT initiative for substance abuse policy and practice. *Addiction*, *112*(Suppl. 2), 110–117. Available from https://doi.org/10.1111/add.13675.

Balboni, T. A., Fitchett, G., Handzo, G. F., Johnson, K. S., Koenig, H. G., Pargament, K. I., ... Steinhauser, K. E. (2017). State of the science of spirituality and palliative care research part II: Screening, assessment, and interventions. *Journal of Pain and Symptom Management*, *54*(3), 441–453. Available from https://doi.org/10.1016/j.jpainsymman.2017.07.029.

Beck, A. K., Forbes, E., Baker, A. L., Kelly, P. J., Deane, F. P., Shakeshaft, A., ... Kelly, J. F. (2017). Systematic review of SMART Recovery: Outcomes, process variables, and implications for research. *Psychology of Addictive Behaviors*, *31*(1), 1–20. Available from https://doi.org/10.1037/adb0000237.

Bohn, M. J., Babor, T. F., & Kranzler, H. R. (1995). The Alcohol Use Disorders Identification Test (AUDIT): Validation of a screening instrument for use in medical settings. *Journal of Studies on Alcohol*, *56*(4), 423–432.

Connery, H. S. (2015). Medication-assisted treatment of opioid use disorder: Review of the evidence and future directions. *Harvard Review of Psychiatry*, *23*(2), 63–75. Available from https://doi.org/10.1097/hrp.0000000000000075.

Dermatis, H., & Galanter, M. (2016). The role of twelve-step-related spirituality in addiction recovery. *Journal of Religion & Health*, *55*(2), 510–521. Available from https://doi.org/10.1007/s10943-015-0019-4.

Ellison, C. W. (1983). Spiritual well-being: Conceptualization and measurement. *Journal of Psychology and Theology*, *11*(4), 330–340. Available from https://doi.org/10.1177/009164718301100406.

Fallot, R. D., & Heckman, J. P. (2005). Religious/spiritual coping among women trauma survivors with mental health and substance use disorders. *The Journal of Behavioral Health Services & Research*, *32*(2), 215–226.

Ferguson, M. A., Nielsen, J. A., King, J. B., Dai, L., Giangrasso, D. M., Holman, R., ... Anderson, J. S. (2018). Reward, salience, and attentional networks are activated by religious experience in devout Mormons. *Society for Neuroscience*, *13*(1), 104–116. Available from https://doi.org/10.1080/17470919.2016.1257437.

Fetzer. (1999). *Multidimensional measurement of religiousness, spirituality for use in health research*. Kalamazoo, MI: Fetzer Institute., A Report of a National Working Group.

Galanter, M., Dermatis, H., Bunt, G., Williams, C., Trujillo, M., & Steinke, P. (2007). Assessment of spirituality and its relevance to addiction treatment. *Journal of Substance Abuse Treatment*, *33*(3), 257–264. Available from https://doi.org/10.1016/j.jsat.2006.06.014.

Gallucci, A. R., Hackman, C., & Wilkerson, A. (2018). Examining the relationship between religious coping and the misuse of prescription stimulants among a sample of undergraduate students. *Substance Use & Misuse*, *53*(9), 1571–1579. Available from https://doi.org/10.1080/10826084.2017.1416405.

Hai, A. H., Franklin, C., Park, S., DiNitto, D. M., & Aurelio, N. (2019). The efficacy of spiritual/religious interventions for substance use problems: A systematic review and meta-analysis of randomized controlled trials. *Drug and Alcohol Dependence*, *202*, 134–148. Available from https://doi.org/10.1016/j.drugalcdep.2019.04.045.

Heinz, A., Epstein, D. H., & Preston, K. L. (2007). Spiritual/religious experiences and in-treatment outcome in an inner-city program for heroin and cocaine dependence. *The Journal of Psychoactive Drugs*, *39*(1), 41–49. Available from https://doi.org/10.1080/02791072.2007.10399863.

Hodge, D. R., & Lietz, C. A. (2014). Using spiritually modified cognitive-behavioral therapy in substance dependence treatment: Therapists' and clients' perceptions of the presumed benefits and limitations. *Health & Social Work*, *39*(4), 200–210. Available from https://doi.org/10.1093/hsw/hlu022.

Humphreys, K., Blodgett, J. C., & Wagner, T. H. (2014). Estimating the efficacy of alcoholics anonymous without self-selection bias: An instrumental variables re-analysis of randomized clinical trials. *Alcoholism: Clinical and Experimental Research*, *38*(11), 2688–2694. Available from https://doi.org/10.1111/acer.12557.

Jalali, A., Shabrandi, B., Jalali, R., & Salari, N. (2019). Methamphetamine abusers' personality traits and its relational with spiritual well-being and perceived social support.

Current Drug Research Reviews, *11*(1), 44–50. Available from https://doi.org/10.2174/1874473711666181017121256.

Kass, J. D., Friedman, R., Leserman, J., Zuttermeister, P. C., & Benson, H. (1991). Health outcomes and a new index of spiritual experience. *Journal for the Scientific Study of Religion*, *30*(2), 203–211. Available from https://doi.org/10.2307/1387214.

Kelly, J. F. (2017). Is alcoholics anonymous religious, spiritual, neither? Findings from 25 years of mechanisms of behavior change research. *Addiction*, *112*(6), 929–936. Available from https://doi.org/10.1111/add.13590.

Knight, J. R., Sherritt, L., Harris, S. K., Holder, D. W., Kulig, J., Shrier, L. A., … Chang, G. (2007). Alcohol use and religiousness/spirituality among adolescents. *Southern Medical Journal*, *100*(4), 349–355. Available from https://doi.org/10.1097/SMJ.0b013e3180316a32.

Koob, G. F., & Volkow, N. D. (2010). Neurocircuitry of addiction. *Neuropsychopharmacology*, *35*(1), 217–238. Available from https://doi.org/10.1038/npp.2009.110.

Krentzman, A. R. (2017). Longitudinal differences in spirituality and religiousness between men and women in treatment for alcohol use disorders. *Psychology of Religion and Spirituality*, *9*(Suppl. 1), S11–S21. Available from https://doi.org/10.1037/rel0000096.

Krentzman, A. R., Strobbe, S., Harris, J. I., Jester, J. M., & Robinson, E. A. R. (2017). Decreased drinking and alcoholics anonymous are associated with different dimensions of spirituality. *Psychology of Religion and Spirituality*, *9*(Suppl 1), S40–S48. Available from https://doi.org/10.1037/rel0000121.

Madras, B. K., Compton, W. M., Avula, D., Stegbauer, T., Stein, J. B., & Clark, H. W. (2009). Screening, brief interventions, referral to treatment (SBIRT) for illicit drug and alcohol use at multiple healthcare sites: Comparison at intake and 6 months later. *Drug and Alcohol Dependence*, *99*(1–3), 280–295. Available from https://doi.org/10.1016/j.drugalcdep.2008.08.003.

Martin, R. A., Ellingsen, V. J., Tzilos, G. K., & Rohsenow, D. J. (2015). General and religious coping predict drinking outcomes for alcohol dependent adults in treatment. *The American Journal on Addictions*, *24*(3), 240–245. Available from https://doi.org/10.1111/ajad.12181.

McCabe, S. E., West, B. T., Strobbe, S., & Boyd, C. J. (2018). Persistence/recurrence of and remission from DSM-5 substance use disorders in the United States: Substance-specific and substance-aggregated correlates. *Journal of Substance Abuse Treatment*, *93*, 38–48. Available from https://doi.org/10.1016/j.jsat.2018.07.012.

Medlock, M. M., Rosmarin, D. H., Connery, H. S., Griffin, M. L., Weiss, R. D., Karakula, S. L., & McHugh, R. K. (2017). Religious coping in patients with severe substance use disorders receiving acute inpatient detoxification. *The American Journal on Addictions*, *26*(7), 744–750.

Miller, W. R., & Rose, G. S. (2015). Motivational interviewing and decisional balance: Contrasting responses to client ambivalence. *Behavioural and Cognitive Psychotherapy*, *43*(2), 129–141. Available from https://doi.org/10.1017/s1352465813000878.

Monod, S., Brennan, M., Rochat, E., Martin, E., Rochat, S., & Bula, C. J. (2011). Instruments measuring spirituality in clinical research: A systematic review. *Journal of General Internal Medicine*, *26*(11), 1345–1357. Available from https://doi.org/10.1007/s11606-011-1769-7.

Montgomery, B. E., Stewart, K. E., Bryant, K. J., & Ounpraseuth, S. T. (2014). Dimensions of religion, depression symptomatology, and substance use among rural African American cocaine users. *Journal of Ethnicity in Substance Abuse*, *13*(1), 72–90. Available from https://doi.org/10.1080/15332640.2014.873605.

Moss, H. B., Chen, C. M., & Yi, H. Y. (2010). Prospective follow-up of empirically derived Alcohol Dependence subtypes in wave 2 of the National Epidemiologic Survey on Alcohol And Related Conditions (NESARC): Recovery status, alcohol use disorders and diagnostic criteria, alcohol consumption behavior, health status, and treatment seeking. *Alcoholism: Clinical and Experimental Research*, *34*(6), 1073–1083. Available from https://doi.org/10.1111/j.1530-0277.2010.01183.x.

Nowinski, J., Baker, S., & Carroll, K. (1995). *NIAAA project MATCH monograph series*. National Institute on Alcohol Abuse and Alcoholism.

Paloutzian, R., Ellison, C., Peplau, L., & Perlman, D. (1982). *Loneliness: A sourcebook of current theory, research and therapy*. New York: Wiley.

Parenteau, S. C. (2017). Religious coping and substance use: The moderating role of sex. *Journal of Religion & Health*, *56*(2), 380–387. Available from https://doi.org/10.1007/s10943-015-0166-7.

Pargament, K. I., Koenig, H. G., & Perez, L. M. (2000). The many methods of religious coping: Development and initial validation of the RCOPE. *Journal of Clinical Psychology*, *56*(4), 519–543.

Piedmont, R. L. (1999). Does spirituality represent the sixth factor of personality? Spiritual transcendence and the five-factor model. *Journal of Personality*, *67*(6), 985–1013. Available from https://doi.org/10.1111/1467-6494.00080.

Piedmont, R. L. (2004). Spiritual transcendence as a predictor of psychosocial outcome from an outpatient substance abuse program. *Psychology of Addictive Behaviors*, *18*(3), 213–222. Available from https://doi.org/10.1037/0893-164x.18.3.213.

Puffer, E. S., Skalski, L. M., & Meade, C. S. (2012). Changes in religious coping and relapse to drug use among opioid-dependent patients following inpatient detoxification. *Journal of Religion & Health*, *51*(4), 1226–1238. Available from https://doi.org/10.1007/s10943-010-9418-8.

Skinner, H. A. (1982). The drug abuse screening test. *Addictive Behaviors*, 7(4), 363–371.

Staton-Tindall, M., Duvall, J., Stevens-Watkins, D., & Oser, C. B. (2013). The roles of spirituality in the relationship between traumatic life events, mental health, and drug use among African American women from one southern state. *Substance Use & Misuse*, *48*(12), 1246–1257. Available from https://doi.org/10.3109/10826084.2013.799023.

Stewart, C., & Koeske, G. F. (2006). Research: A preliminary construct validation of the multidimensional measurement of religiousness/spirituality instrument: A study of southern USA samples. *The International Journal for the Psychology of Religion*, *16*(3), 181–196. Available from https://doi.org/10.1207/s15327582ijpr1603_3.

Tonigan, J. S., Pearson, M. R., Magill, M., & Hagler, K. J. (2018). AA attendance and abstinence for dually diagnosed patients: A meta-analytic review. *Addiction*, *113*(11), 1970–1981. Available from https://doi.org/10.1111/add.14268.

Volkow, N. D., Koob, G. F., & McLellan, A. T. (2016). Neurobiologic advances from the brain disease model of addiction. *The New England Journal of Medicine*, *374*(4), 363–371. Available from https://doi.org/10.1056/NEJMra1511480.

CHAPTER 8

Spirituality/religion and behavioral addictions

Joshua Briggs Grubbs and Jennifer Tegan Grant
Department of Psychology, Bowling Green State University, Bowling Green, OH, United States

Contents

Introduction

Addiction and religion have a complicated and longstanding relationship. Even ancient religious texts offer guidance regarding adherents' engagement with potentially addictive behaviors. Not surprisingly then, there is a rich body of literature examining how religion and spirituality are associated with addictive behaviors, treatment for such behaviors, and various related outcomes (for a review see White, 1998). Historically, the vast majority of this research and writing has directly concerned substance use and abuse (see Chapter 7: Spirituality/religion and substance use disorders of this volume for an up to date review). However, in recent years—particularly in the past 20 years—mental health communities have increasingly recognized the prevalence and problems of so-called *behavioral addictions*. These disorders, though relatively novel in current diagnostic

Handbook of Spirituality, Religion, and Mental Health
DOI: https://doi.org/10.1016/B978-0-12-816766-3.00008-2

taxonomies and nosologies, are increasingly encountered in public life, academic research, and clinical work. This attention has included a burgeoning body of work examining how such disorders are related to religion and spirituality more broadly. What follows is a summary and synthesis of this research, with key recommendations for future research and current clinical practice.

Behavioral addictions

Substance addictions have been recognized as real and problematic behavior patterns for hundreds, if not thousands, of years. However, over the past half-century, there has been an increasing focus on the potential for some behavior patterns to become dysregulated, out of control, or addictive (Castellani, 2000). Although veritable laundry lists of such addictions have been posed in recent years (e.g., food addiction, cryptocurrency addiction, internet addiction), we have chosen herein to focus on those that have a defined evidence base and diagnostic recognition of some sort.

Gambling disorder

The first problematic behavior pattern to be recognized as potentially addictive in nature was Pathological Gambling. Historical accounts, including sacred texts from various religions, have pointed toward the capacity for gambling behaviors to become out of control or dysregulated. However, it was not until the late 20th century that excessive, compulsive, or addictive gambling was recognized by a major diagnostic system. In 1980, the *Diagnostic and Statistical Manual of Mental Disorders, Third Edition* included the diagnosis of "Pathological Gambling." At the time of its inclusion, this diagnosis was thought of as an impulse control disorder, rather than an addiction, and was entirely based on the clinical impressions of a few key researchers (Reilly & Smith, 2013). Over the years that followed, the definition for the disorder shifted slightly with each revision of the *DSM*, becoming more nuanced as more empirical, epidemiological, and etiological data were collected.

At present, with the most recent editions of the *DSM-5* and the *International Classification of Diseases-11* (*ICD-11*), Gambling Disorder is now recognized as an addictive disorder (Petry et al., 2014). Current conceptualizations of gambling disorder note that it is an addiction characterized by a loss of control over gambling activities (Reilly & Smith, 2013). Specifically, gambling disorder is manifested by the following:

repeated engagement in gambling behaviors, even when such behaviors are causing harm or distress in a person's life; patterns of hiding or concealing gambling behavior, often involving outright lies to loved ones and significant others; patterns of escalation in which an individual spends more time and money gambling than previously intended; and both cognitive and emotional obsessions with gambling, wherein gambling itself or thoughts about gambling consume most aspects of the individual's time and activities. In short, gambling disorder is characterized by a pathological engagement in gambling behaviors, despite severe and life-altering consequences.

Importantly, gambling disorder is the best understood of all nonsubstance-related addictive behavior patterns (Fauth-Bühler, Mann, & Potenza, 2017). There is an impressive body of literature now supporting its classification as an addictive disease and a large and expanding literature related to its treatment; there is similarly an impressive body of literature demonstrating that the neurobiology of gambling disorder is similar to the same neurobiology seen in chemical dependence (for reviews, see Grant, Brewer, & Potenza, 2006; Potenza, 2008, 2013). Moreover, even at subclinical levels—that is, at levels below diagnostic thresholds—it is known to cause problems and distress in peoples' lives (Grubbs, Chapman, Milner, Gutierrez, & Bradley, 2018; Grubbs, Chapman, & Shepherd, 2019; Weinstock, April, & Kallmi, 2017). Collectively, these works point toward an understanding of gambling disorder as a dimensional pathology, with a broad range of potentially problematic outcomes associated with various levels of severity.

Compulsive sexual behavior disorder

With the latest edition of the *ICD* (i.e., the *ICD-11*), the World Health Organization (WHO) elected to include a new diagnosis of compulsive sexual behavior disorder (CSBD; World Health Organization, 2018). Although this represents the first official diagnostic recognition of problematically excessive or dysregulated sexual behaviors, the notion of "sexual addiction" has been discussed in the academic and popular literature for decades. Moreover, the diagnosis of hypersexual behavior disorder was almost included in the *DSM-5*, though ultimately omitted for a variety of reasons (Kafka, 2010; Reid et al., 2012; Reid & Kafka, 2014). Although these previous explorations do not wholly match the current criteria for CSBD, they are similar in form and in function.

At present, CSBD is characterized by persistent patterns of failure to control sexual impulses, urges, and behaviors, resulting in clinically impairing levels of distress or consequences in daily life (World Health Organization, 2018). Moreover, the individual with CSBD is likely to have experienced obsessive rumination about sexual behavior, repeated failed attempts to control the behavior, continued engagement in the behavior despite life-altering consequences, and reduced satisfaction in sexual behaviors. Additionally—and particularly relevant for understanding this disorder's interactions with religion and spirituality—none of the symptoms of CSBD can be attributable to psychological or emotional distress stemming from moral or religious objections to one's own sexual behavior. That is, one cannot receive this diagnosis if he or she is only experiencing distress and impairment about sexual behaviors due to religious scrupulosity, moral incongruence, or a guilty conscience (Kraus & Sweeney, 2019). Despite being classified as an impulse control disorder, a growing body of current evidence suggests that both the key features of this disorder and the neurobiological mechanisms underlying the disorder are likely addictive in nature (Kowalewska et al., 2018; Kraus, Voon, & Potenza, 2016a, 2016b).

Gaming disorder

The *ICD*-11 also included gaming disorder as a diagnosis, which encompasses excessive or compulsive engagement in digital or video game environments (World Health Organization, 2018). According to current diagnostic criteria, the individual must be experiencing impairment and/or distress in daily life secondary to an inability to regulate or control gaming behaviors. Moreover, the gaming behavior must be an increasing priority to such an extent that it interferes with other priorities, activities, relationships, and responsibilities. Finally, the disorder must have been present for at least 12 months. Currently, this diagnosis is still controversial (Aarseth et al., 2016; Billieux et al., 2017), with a number of scholars calling for caution in its use. Even so, for the time being, the diagnosis of gaming disorder is supported by the WHO, and, as such, research is expanding rapidly on the topic. Importantly, in contrast with CSBD, gaming disorder has been included as a diagnosis under the category of "Disorders due to addictive behaviors" in the *ICD-11*. That is, much like gambling disorder, gaming disorder is considered a true addictive disorder.

Relation of spirituality/religion to behavioral addictions

Generally speaking, religion is often seen as a buffer or vanguard against addictive behavior patterns of diverse origins (Gomes, de Andrade, Izbicki, Almeida, & de Oliveira, 2013; Hodge, Andereck, & Montoya, 2007; Montgomery, Stewart, Bryant, & Ounpraseuth, 2014). That is, there is a considerable body of research suggesting that religious individuals are less likely to experience addictions such as alcoholism (Feigelman, Wallisch, & Lesieur, 1998) or polysubstance abuse (Acheampong, Lasopa, Striley, & Cottler, 2016). Moreover, there is also a large body of research examining how religiousness is related to the treatment and resolution of addictive disorders. Indeed, the very foundations of Alcoholics Anonymous—the most internationally prevalent treatment network for alcoholism—is founded on aspects of religion and spirituality (Kelly, Hoeppner, Stout, & Pagano, 2012). Not surprisingly then, a considerable body of literature now suggests that religion can be an important resource to individuals seeking to recover from a substance use disorder (Fallot & Heckman, 2005; Kendler et al., 2003). Even so, given the relative novelty of behavioral addictions, or at least the relative novelty of their recognition by psychiatric and mental health communities, research exploring the associations between religion and behavioral addictions is still burgeoning. Below, we review what is known about the influence of religion and spirituality on problematic gambling behaviors, on compulsive sexual behaviors (CSBs), and on compulsive gaming behaviors.

Gambling disorder and spirituality/religion

Broadly speaking, religion and spirituality are considered restrictive forces on gambling behaviors (Binde, 2007). This is not surprising, given that the majority of major world religions have prohibitions against or condemnations of gambling behavior. In some cases, these are unequivocal. For example, the United Methodist Church's Social Principles specifically refers to gambling as a "menace to society" that is "deadly to the best interests of ... spiritual life." Similarly, the Qur'an states that "... gambling ... and divining arrows are but defilement from the work of Satan" (Pickthall, 2001). In other cases, these condemnations are reserved for cases in which the gambling results in negative consequences. For example, the Catholic Catechism explicitly condemns "games of chance" when they "deprive someone of what is necessary," either for themselves or for the needs of others. Additionally, the Mishnah Sanhedrin 3:3 states:

"These are the invalid: dice-players . . . when they have no other trade; but when they have another trade, they are acceptable." Given these condemnations, it is not surprising to find that religiousness (in both the United States and internationally) seems to be associated with lower levels of gambling behaviors in general (Ellison & McFarland, 2011; Ghandour & El Sayed, 2012; Welte, Barnes, Tidwell, & Hoffman, 2008). Both in terms of lifetime frequency and past-year frequency, religious individuals report less gambling than the nonreligious do. This effect is particularly notable for Christianity and Islam (Ghandour & El Sayed, 2012), though it is observable across many other faiths as well.

Despite the buffering effect that religiousness seems to have on gambling behaviors, many religious individuals do still gamble (Welte et al., 2008) and, among those that do, religiousness might be seen as a risk factor for greater problems (Eitle, 2011). For example, national surveys in the United States have shown that religious individuals who do gamble (though a minority of religious individuals) are more likely to gamble frequently or excessively in comparison to nonreligious gamblers (Welte et al., 2008). That is, there seems to be a sort of selection effect with regards to religion and gambling, wherein religion generally leads to abstinence from gambling, but among those who do not abstain, there is a greater likelihood of problematic patterns. This has been more fully explored in other works that have noted that gambling behavior among conservative Protestant Christians (i.e., Evangelicals) is associated with greater risk for problematic gambling (Eitle, 2011). Moreover, very recent work has noted that religious individuals are more prone to cognitive distortions around gambling, which, in turn, predicts greater gambling severity (Kim, Shifrin, Sztainert, & Wohl, 2018). In two international studies of gambling individuals, religious individuals who did gamble were more likely to experience cognitive distortions around gambling (e.g., erroneous or factually wrong beliefs about gambling), which predicted greater levels of problem gambling. Again, such a finding suggests that religious individuals who do engage in gambling behaviors may be prone to particularly problematic outcomes. This may represent a selection effect, that is, that religious involvement prevents most of the milder forms of gambling, but the more severe forms are resistant to religious norms.

Given the body of literature demonstrating that religiousness is generally associated with negative attitudes toward and condemnations of gambling behavior, and that religious individuals who do gamble are prone to more problems with gambling, it is perhaps unsurprising to find that such behaviors are associated with negative religious and spiritual outcomes. Specifically, a nascent body of research now suggests that gambling behaviors—particularly problematic gambling behaviors—are associated with greater religious and spiritual struggles.

Religious and spiritual struggles are difficulties or tensions in an individual's religious and spiritual life (Exline, Pargament, Grubbs, & Yali, 2014). Generally speaking, these struggles fall into one of six categories dispersed among three domains: supernatural struggles (struggles with the divine or with demonic/evil forces), interpersonal struggles (struggles with other people about or due to religious or spiritual themes), and intrapersonal struggles (struggles of doubt, ultimate meaning, or feelings of moral shortcoming). Importantly, these struggles are distinct from both general religiousness and psychological distress (Grubbs, Wilt, Stauner, Exline, & Pargament, 2016; Stauner et al., 2016). Moreover, these struggles are generally associated with lower well-being (Wilt, Grubbs, Exline, & Pargament, 2016; Wilt, Grubbs, Pargament, & Exline, 2017) and tend to be associated with a number of addictive behavior patterns (Faigin, Pargament, & Abu-Raiya, 2014), including gambling.

One study, conducted by Grant and Grubbs (2019), showed that gambling problem severity may predict religious and spiritual struggles. Specifically, they found that divine, demonic, moral, and doubt struggles were predicted by gambling problem severity both cross-sectionally and at a 6-month follow-up. Moreover, interpersonal and ultimate meaning struggles were predicted by gambling problem severity cross-sectionally, but this did not continue at the follow-up time-point. These results suggest that engaging in problematic gambling behaviors may increase an individual's chance of experiencing religious and spiritual struggles. In particular, they may increasingly struggle with feelings of disconnect from their Higher Power, being attacked by evil spirits, conflicts with their moral values, and distressful doubts about their beliefs, regardless of whether they reach clinical levels of a gambling disorder or not.

Additionally, very recent work (Gutierrez, Chapman, Grant, & Grubbs, 2018) found that—among US Veterans seeking residential treatment for problematic gambling behaviors—religious and spiritual struggles were found to decrease over the course of treatment. Specifically, over the course of a 5-week residential treatment program, people who successfully finished the program experienced notable decreases in diverse spiritual struggles. This decrease corresponded to decreases in psychopathology overall. Although such findings do not necessarily indicate a causal pathway between these domains, they do indicate that there is at least a correlation between difficulties in spirituality/religion (S/R) and gambling.

Compulsive sexual behavior and spirituality/religion

Much like (and perhaps even more so than) gambling, religion is generally associated with more restrictive attitudes toward sexual activity. That is, religious belief systems, across the globe, are generally thought to be associated with greater limitations on when sexual activity is appropriate, more conservative sexual values, and more careful proscriptions about sexual behavior (Haidt & Hersh, 2001; Lefkowitz, Gillen, Shearer, & Boone, 2004; Rowatt & Schmitt, 2003; Scott, 1998). Almost all major world religions discuss issues of sexual purity and sexual cleanliness (Haidt & Hersh, 2001). All major monotheistic religions have, traditionally, discouraged a wide variety of sexual practices (van den Akker, van der Ploeg, & Scheepers, 2013). Finally, many current iterations of major world religions specifically prohibit high-risk promiscuous sexual behaviors (Jakobsen & Pellegrini, 2004).

Given the prohibitions of most major world religions on open or progressive sexual values, it is not surprising to find that religious individuals tend to have more conservative sexual values. Religious individuals tend to endorse monogamous values (Mark, Rosenkrantz, & Kerner, 2014), reject the use of sexual media, such as internet pornography (Boulton, 2008; Thomas, 2013, 2016), reject premarital or extramarital sexual behaviors (Burdette, Ellison, Sherkat, & Gore, 2007), report restrictive attitudes toward sexual fantasy (Ahrold & Meston, 2010), and report less use of pornography in general (Grubbs, Exline, Pargament, Hook, & Carlisle, 2015). As such, one might expect religiousness to be associated with lower levels of CSB. Such a supposition is premature.

Whereas religion and spirituality are typically associated with lower reported levels of gambling behaviors, the relationships between S/R and CSBs are a bit more complex. Generally speaking, religiousness is associated with less risky sexual behaviors and greater engagement in sexual chastity (Sinha, Cnaan, & Gelles, 2007). Moreover, in populations with diagnosed hypersexuality or CSBD, religiousness seems to be associated with lower levels of unsafe sexual practices or partnered sexual compulsivity (Reid, Carpenter, & Hook, 2016). Even so, there is now a compelling body of literature that shows that religiousness is associated with greater self-report of CSBs (Griffin et al., 2016).

A number of studies have now shown that, despite being associated with lower levels of pornography use in general, S/R are associated with greater self-reports of feeling addicted to pornography (Gola, Lewczuk, & Skorko, 2016; Grubbs, Exline, et al., 2015; Leonhardt & Willoughby, 2017; Volk, Thomas, Sosin, Jacob, & Moen, 2016). Moreover, these findings are not simply cross-sectional. Over time, feelings of addiction to internet pornography are often very well-predicted by a combination of religiousness and moral incongruence about pornography use (Grubbs, Wilt, Exline, Pargament, & Kraus, 2018). Collectively, these findings suggest—quite convincingly—that religiousness is likely a risk factor for greater reports of CSBs, particularly solitary sexual behaviors (for reviews, see Grubbs & Perry, 2019; Grubbs, Perry, Wilt, & Reid, 2019; Kwee, Dominguez, & Ferrell, 2007; Williams, 2017).

At present, the prevailing theoretical mechanism for understanding why religious individuals are more likely to report greater levels of CSB is moral incongruence (Grubbs & Perry, 2019; Grubbs, Perry, et al., 2019). That is, a body of research now shows that religiously based scruples (Borgogna & McDermott, 2018) around sexuality and pornography use are likely to lead people who engage in such behaviors to feel a great degree of incongruence between their beliefs and behaviors (Perry, 2018). This incongruence, in turn, seems to drive pathological interpretations of one's own behaviors (e.g., that they are addictive or compulsive), even when there is little objective evidence for such conclusions (Grubbs, Wilt, et al., 2018). This also holds true for self-reported CSB, more generally with greater incongruence between values and behaviors predicting greater experiences of self-perceived compulsive sexuality (Hook et al., 2015; Walton, 2019). Moreover, devoutly religious individuals also seem to experience greater difficulty in suppressing sexual urges and desires that they find incongruent with their sexual values, leading to symptoms of obsessiveness and self-perceived compulsivity (Efrati, 2019), though we would note that this research has been met with some controversy (Pirutinsky, 2018).

Importantly, identifying incongruence as a source of pathological interpretations of sexual behavior, particularly among the religious, does not minimize the clinical significance of such feelings or interpretations. That is, there is a considerable body of evidence to suggest that feeling as if your sexual behaviors are out of control is indeed associated with problems in overall functioning, regardless of how accurate such interpretations are (Grubbs, Stauner, Exline, Pargament, & Lindberg, 2015). Longitudinally, self-reported feelings of addiction to pornography predict greater psychological distress in general (Grubbs, Stauner, et al., 2015). Moreover, such self-reports are also associated, both cross-sectionally and longitudinally, with greater experiences of difficulties in religious and spiritual life (Grubbs, Exline, Pargament, Volk, & Lindberg, 2017). Such a body of work is consistent with other work finding that self-reported feelings of hypersexuality are associated with greater religious and spiritual struggles (Griffin et al., 2016) and negative religious coping (Giordano & Cecil, 2014). Additionally, research among undergraduates in the United States has also found that religious and spiritual struggles are robustly associated with self-reported feelings of addiction to sex, both cross-sectionally and over time (Faigin et al., 2014), arguably demonstrating a cyclical relationship between religious and spiritual struggles. These findings also extend to Jewish communities in some circumstances, with spiritual struggles being linked to CSB among men raised in Orthodox Jewish communities, but not among men raised in other Jewish affiliations (Rosmarin & Pirutinsky, 2019)

Gaming disorder and spirituality/religion

Whereas there is already a body of research examining the relationships between religion/spirituality and both gambling disorder and CSBD, there is a dearth of research examining how religion and spirituality relate to gaming disorder. This absence of research extends to gaming more generally, with relatively little research examining how religion and spirituality predict gaming behaviors at all. In the one study (as of 2018) to explicitly examine the role of religiousness in predicting gaming behavior (Braun, Kornhuber, Lenz, & Cohort Study on Substance Use Risk Factors, 2016), religiousness was found to predict lower levels of gaming in general and lower risk for addictive gaming tendencies. However, among studies that have looked at problematic gaming behavior and religious outcomes (e.g., religious and spiritual struggles), no statistically detectable links have been observed (Faigin et al., 2014). As such, the links between gaming disorder and religion/spirituality are much less clear than the links between religion/spirituality and other addictive behavior disorders. Accordingly, a great deal of future research in this domain is needed.

Implications for future research directions

As psychiatric and mental health research communities have increasingly recognized the potential for addictive behavior patterns, there has also been greater recognition of the role of religion and spirituality in influencing the experience, expression, and treatment of such conditions. Presently, there is a body of research suggesting that religion and spirituality have complex relationships with addictive behavior patterns. In some regards, religion and spirituality seem to be vanguards against the experience of such problems—with S/R people being generally less likely to experience gambling-related problems, compulsive sexuality, or compulsive gaming. In particular, this buffer seems to be a function of abstinence from the behaviors in question. Yet, in other regards, S/R seems to exacerbate such problems, with several studies indicating that religious individuals who do engage in behaviors that are potentially addictive are actually more likely to experience problems (or at least religion prohibitions are less effective in preventing more severe addictive behaviors).

Collectively these findings point to a need for more nuanced understandings of the complexities of how religion and spirituality influence addictive behavior patterns. Notably, despite significant advances in our understanding of the neurobiology of behavioral addictions over the past decade, there have been no published studies on the neurobiological correlates of spirituality/religion as they relate to behavioral addictions. Furthermore, as has been demonstrated over recent years (Exline et al., 2014; Exline, Park, Smyth, & Carey, 2011), religion and spirituality are not monolithic constructs associated with universally good or universally bad outcomes. Rather, they are complex dimensions of human identity that have the potential for both positive and negative influences. This is especially true in morally charged domains, such as controversial behaviors. Continued work—particularly longitudinal studies and treatment research—is needed to further understand how religion and spirituality are influencing and influenced by addictive behavior patterns. The relative absence of such research, particularly prospective studies, hampers causal and mechanistic inferences about the role of religion and spirituality in the etiology and experience of addictive behaviors.

We also note that the relationships between addictive behaviors and religion and spirituality should not be treated as unidirectional. A compelling body of research shows that addictive behaviors are likely to be related to greater religious and spiritual struggles. As such, clinical intervention should consider such possibilities when treating addictive behaviors. Moreover, given the links between religious and spiritual difficulties and other domains of well-being, such difficulties might be pertinent foci of treatment as well. That is, rather than conceptualizing treatment as exclusively limited to the presenting problem—the addictive behavior—treatment should also address religious and spiritual difficulties that might arise as a result of the addictive behavior.

Spirituality/religion and treatment of behavioral addictions

Clinically, the conclusions of the present work bear distinct implications. Primarily, clinical work with people struggling with addiction or addictive behaviors needs to assess religious and spiritual constructs as well. More to the point, clinicians that only assess for the presence or absence of religion and spirituality are not likely capturing the full nuance of how religion and spirituality are related to the problem at hand. Accordingly, when dealing with addictive behaviors, it is imperative that clinicians assess religiousness and spirituality broadly, as well as the specific ways in which religion and spirituality are entwined with the presenting problem.

Despite some of the negative outcomes associated with religion and gambling, there is some research suggesting that religion and spirituality are assets to the recovery process for people who are dealing with problematic gambling behavior. Specifically, Gamblers Anonymous (GA)—the largest community-based treatment modality or support group for gambling disorder recovery—relies heavily on aspects of religion and spirituality, particularly belief in a higher power (Ferentzy & Skinner, 2003). Interestingly, in controlled studies of which aspects of GA seem to predict relapse versus abstinence among gamblers in recovery, belief in a higher power did predict substantially lower rates of relapse (Oei & Gordon, 2008).

Collectively, the present findings point to a few clear conclusions with regards to the understanding of religion in the context of treating gambling disorder. Primarily, religion and spirituality often condemn engagement in gambling behaviors. Accordingly, religious individuals are less likely to engage with gambling, which serves as a protective factor. However, among those that do, religion and spirituality might actually serve as risk factors for greater problems with gambling and more cognitive distortions about gambling. These effects are compounded by the fact that problematic gambling seems to predict religious and spiritual difficulties as well, both cross-sectionally and over time. Even so, religion and spirituality—particularly when integrated as part of the recovery process—seem to predict better outcomes and greater abstinence from gambling.

With regards to treatment for CSBD, relatively little is currently known (Efrati & Gola, 2018b; Grubbs, Hook, Griffin, & Davis, 2015), particularly in comparison to longer established addictive disorders. A number of case studies have suggested that CSBD is treatable via a variety of methods (Gola & Potenza, 2016; Kraus, Meshberg-Cohen, Martino, Quinones, & Potenza, 2015) and that addressing religious/spiritual relevant constructs—particularly moral incongruence—might be necessary in treatment (Kraus & Sweeney, 2019). Moreover, burgeoning research in Sexaholics Anonymous—which is based on the same 12 steps as Alcoholics Anonymous—suggests that progression through various steps in the program is associated with diminished symptoms of compulsive sexuality (Efrati & Gola, 2018a). Although such findings are not directly indicative of the role of S/R in treating compulsive sexuality, they do suggest that a system that is based on spirituality and spiritual wholeness does have promise in treating CSBs. Even so, due to the burgeoning nature of the research in this domain, there is still a great deal that is unknown with regard to the role that religion and spirituality play in the treatment of CSBD.

We also note that, as has been highlighted with the literature regarding both gambling disorder and CSBD, religion may be a double-edged sword in the treatment of addiction. In both cases, religiousness and spirituality may be assets to recovery and buffers against relapse, but they may also be exacerbating reactions to and evaluations of one's own behaviors. As such, comprehensive assessments of religious and spiritual beliefs and practices are necessary.

Based on current research, it is wholly plausible that some clients' experiences of addiction are better accounted for by religiously or spiritually based scruples or guilt. In such cases, therapeutic intervention could have several targets. For an individual dealing with self-reported pornography addiction that is secondary to excessive guilt and shame resulting from moral incongruence, treatment might not simply focus on behavioral regulation or abstinence. Rather, it might focus on fostering attitudes of psychological flexibility, acceptance, and value-consistent actions. That is, for such an individual, addiction treatment involving standard abstinence strategies and 12-step group involvement may be of little use. However, strategies to enhance behaviors consistent with values, while ameliorating negative self-views or excessive shame, may be more successful.

Discussion

The serious consideration of behavioral addiction as a distinct mental health concern has only begun to gain mainstream acceptance. Research about disorders such as CSBD, gambling disorder, and gaming disorder has advanced considerably in recent years, but is still burgeoning. Alongside these growing bodies of research, there is increasing interest in the roles that religion and spirituality may play in the etiology, course, and treatment of these addictive disorders. Whereas religion and spirituality seem to be a buffer against problems with gambling disorder, they appear to be potential risk factors in other regards, such as negatively contributing to self-perceptions among individuals who struggle with these disorders. This latter and somewhat counterintuitive point is still being explored by various research groups, but may arise due, in part, to the complicated relationships between religion and addictive behavior more generally. Even so, there is evidence that religion and spirituality can be useful resources in the treatment of addictive behaviors, particularly when clients have concerns about how their addictive behaviors have influenced their religious and spiritual life.

References

Aarseth, E., Bean, A. M., Boonen, H., Colder Carras, M., Coulson, M., Das, D., . . . Van Rooij, A. J. (2016). Scholars' open debate paper on the World Health Organization ICD-11 Gaming Disorder proposal. *Journal of Behavioral Addictions*, *6*(3), 267–270. Available from https://doi.org/10.1556/2006.5.2016.088.

Acheampong, A. B., Lasopa, S., Striley, C. W., & Cottler, L. B. (2016). Gender differences in the association between religion/spirituality and simultaneous polysubstance use (SPU). *Journal of Religion and Health*, *55*(5), 1574–1584. Available from https://doi.org/10.1007/s10943-015-0168-5.

Ahrold, T. K., & Meston, C. M. (2010). Ethnic differences in sexual attitudes of U.S. college students: Gender, acculturation, and religiosity factors. *Archives of Sexual Behavior*, *39*(1), 190–202. Available from https://doi.org/10.1007/s10508-008-9406-1.

Billieux, J., King, D. L., Higuchi, S., Achab, S., Bowden-Jones, H., Hao, W., . . . Poznyak, V. (2017). Functional impairment matters in the screening and diagnosis of gaming disorder. *Journal of Behavioral Addictions*, *6*(3), 285–289. Available from https://doi.org/10.1556/2006.6.2017.036.

Binde, P. (2007). Gambling and religion: Histories of concord and conflict. *Journal of Gambling Issues* (20), 145. Available from https://doi.org/10.4309/jgi.2007.20.4.

Borgogna, N. C., & McDermott, R. C. (2018). The role of gender, experiential avoidance, and scrupulosity in problematic pornography viewing: A moderated-mediation model. *Sexual Addiction & Compulsivity*. Available from https://doi.org/10.1080/10720162.2018.1503123.

Boulton, C. (2008). Porn and me(n): Sexual morality, objectification, and religion at the wheelock anti-pornography conference. *The Communication Review*, *11*(3), 247–273. Available from https://doi.org/10.1080/10714420802306544.

Braun, B., Kornhuber, J., Lenz, B., & Cohort Study on Substance Use Risk Factors. (2016). Gaming and religion: The impact of spirituality and denomination. *Journal of Religion and Health*, *55*(4), 1464–1471. Available from https://doi.org/10.1007/s10943-015-0152-0.

Burdette, A. M., Ellison, C. G., Sherkat, D. E., & Gore, K. A. (2007). Are there religious variations in marital infidelity? *Journal of Family Issues*, *28*(12), 1553–1581. Available from https://doi.org/10.1177/0192513X07304269.

Castellani, B. (2000). *Pathological gambling: The making of a medical problem*. SUNY Press.

Efrati, Y. (2019). God, I can't stop thinking about sex! The rebound effect in unsuccessful suppression of sexual thoughts among religious adolescents. *Journal of Sex Research*, *56* (2), 146–155. Available from https://doi.org/10.1080/00224499.2018.1461796.

Efrati, Y., & Gola, M. (2018a). Compulsive sexual behavior: A twelve-step therapeutic approach. *Journal of Behavioral Addictions*, 7(2), 445–453. Available from https://doi.org/10.1556/2006.7.2018.26.

Efrati, Y., & Gola, M. (2018b). Treating compulsive sexual behavior. *Current Sexual Health Reports*, *10*(2), 57–64. Available from https://doi.org/10.1007/s11930-018-0143-8.

Eitle, D. (2011). Religion and gambling among young adults in the United States: Moral communities and the deterrence hypothesis. *Journal for the Scientific Study of Religion*, *50* (1), 61–81. Available from https://doi.org/10.1111/j.1468-5906.2010.01552.x.

Ellison, C. G., & McFarland, M. J. (2011). Religion and gambling among U.S. adults: Exploring the role of traditions, beliefs, practices, and networks. *Journal for the Scientific Study of Religion*, *50*(1), 82–102. Available from https://doi.org/10.1111/j.1468-5906.2010.01553.x.

Exline, J. J., Pargament, K. I., Grubbs, J. B., & Yali, A. M. (2014). The religious and spiritual struggles scale: Development and initial validation. *Psychology of Religion and Spirituality*, *6*(3), 208.

Exline, J. J., Park, C. L., Smyth, J. M., & Carey, M. P. (2011). Anger toward God: Social-cognitive predictors, prevalence, and links with adjustment to bereavement and cancer. *Journal of Personality and Social Psychology*, *100*(1), 129–148. Available from https://doi.org/10.1037/a0021716.

Faigin, C. A., Pargament, K. I., & Abu-Raiya, H. (2014). Spiritual struggles as a possible risk factor for addictive behaviors: An initial empirical investigation. *The International Journal for the Psychology of Religion*, *24*(3), 201–214. Available from https://doi.org/10.1080/10508619.2013.837661.

Fallot, R. D., & Heckman, J. P. (2005). Religious/spiritual coping among women trauma survivors with mental health and substance use disorders. *The Journal of Behavioral Health Services & Research*, *32*(2), 215–226. Available from https://doi.org/10.1007/BF02287268.

Fauth-Bühler, M., Mann, K., & Potenza, M. N. (2017). Pathological gambling: A review of the neurobiological evidence relevant for its classification as an addictive disorder. *Addiction Biology*, *22*(4), 885–897.

Feigelman, W., Wallisch, L. S., & Lesieur, H. R. (1998). Problem gamblers, problem substance users, and dual-problem individuals: An epidemiological study. *American Journal of Public Health*, *88*(3), 467–470. Available from https://doi.org/10.2105/AJPH.88.3.467.

Ferentzy, P., & Skinner, W. (2003). Gamblers Anonymous: A critical review of the literature. *Journal of Gambling Issues* (9). Available from https://doi.org/10.4309/jgi.2003.9.9.

Ghandour, L. A., & El Sayed, D. S. (2012). Gambling behaviors among university youth: Does one's religious affiliation and level of religiosity play a role? *Psychology of Addictive Behaviors*, *27*(1), 279. Available from https://doi.org/10.1037/a0030172.

Giordano, A. L., & Cecil, A. L. (2014). Religious coping, spirituality, and hypersexual behavior among college students. *Sexual Addiction & Compulsivity*, *21*(3), 225–239. Available from https://doi.org/10.1080/10720162.2014.936542.

Gola, M., Lewczuk, K., & Skorko, M. (2016). What matters: Quantity or quality of pornography use? Psychological and behavioral factors of seeking treatment for problematic pornography use. *The Journal of Sexual Medicine*, *13*(5), 815–824. Available from https://doi.org/10.1016/j.jsxm.2016.02.169.

Gola, M., & Potenza, M. N. (2016). Paroxetine treatment of problematic pornography use: A case series. *Journal of Behavioral Addictions*, *5*(3), 529–532. Available from https://doi.org/10.1556/2006.5.2016.046.

Gomes, F. C., de Andrade, A. G., Izbicki, R., Almeida, A. M., & de Oliveira, L. G. (2013). Religion as a protective factor against drug use among Brazilian university students: A national survey. *Revista Brasileira de Psiquiatria*, *35*(1), 29–37. Available from https://doi.org/10.1016/j.rbp.2012.05.010.

Grant, J. E., Brewer, J. A., & Potenza, M. N. (2006). The neurobiology of substance and behavioral addictions. *CNS Spectrums*, *11*(12), 924–930.

Grant, J. T., & Grubbs, J. B. (2019). *Gambling with God: The Effect of Gambling on Religious and Spiritual Struggles* [Preprint]. PsyArXiv. Available from https://doi.org/10.31234/osf.io/g7cr9.

Griffin, B. J., Worthington, E. L., Leach, J. D., Hook, J. N., Grubbs, J. B., Exline, J. J., & Davis, D. E. (2016). Sexual congruence moderates the associations of hypersexual behavior with spiritual struggle and sexual self-concept. *Sexual Addiction & Compulsivity*, *23*(2–3), 279–295. Available from https://doi.org/10.1080/10720162.2016.1150924.

Grubbs, J. B., Chapman, H., Milner, L., Gutierrez, I. A., & Bradley, D. F. (2018). Examining links between posttraumatic stress and gambling motives: The role of positive gambling expectancies. *Psychology of Addictive Behaviors*, *32*(7), 821–831. Available from https://doi.org/10.1037/adb0000399.

Grubbs, J. B., Chapman, H., & Shepherd, K. A. (2019). Post-traumatic stress and gambling related cognitions: Analyses in inpatient and online samples. *Addictive Behaviors*, *89*, 128–135. Available from https://doi.org/10.1016/j.addbeh.2018.09.035.

Grubbs, J. B., Exline, J. J., Pargament, K. I., Hook, J. N., & Carlisle, R. D. (2015). Transgression as addiction: Religiosity and moral disapproval as predictors of perceived addiction to pornography. *Archives of Sexual Behavior*, *44*(1), 125–136. Available from https://doi.org/10.1007/s10508-013-0257-z.

Grubbs, J. B., Exline, J. J., Pargament, K. I., Volk, F., & Lindberg, M. J. (2017). Internet pornography use, perceived addiction, and religious/spiritual struggles. *Archives of Sexual Behavior*, *46*(6), 1733–1745. Available from https://doi.org/10.1007/s10508-016-0772-9.

Grubbs, J. B., Hook, J. N., Griffin, B. J., & Davis, D. E. (2015). Evaluating outcome research for hypersexual behavior. *Current Addiction Reports*, *2*(3), 207–213.

Grubbs, J. B., & Perry, S. L. (2019). Moral incongruence and pornography use: A critical review and integration. *Journal of Sex Research*, *56*(1), 29–37. Available from https://doi.org/10.1080/00224499.2018.1427204.

Grubbs, J. B., Perry, S. L., Wilt, J. A., & Reid, R. C. (2019). Pornography problems due to moral incongruence: An integrative model with a systematic review and meta-analysis. *Archives of Sexual Behavior*, *48*(2), 397–415. Available from https://doi.org/10.1007/s10508-018-1248-x.

Grubbs, J. B., Stauner, N., Exline, J. J., Pargament, K. I., & Lindberg, M. J. (2015). Perceived addiction to Internet pornography and psychological distress: Examining relationships concurrently and over time. *Psychology of Addictive Behaviors: Journal of the Society of Psychologists in Addictive Behaviors*, *29*(4), 1056–1067. Available from https://doi.org/10.1037/adb0000114.

Grubbs, J. B., Wilt, J. A., Exline, J. J., Pargament, K. I., & Kraus, S. W. (2018). Moral disapproval and perceived addiction to internet pornography: A longitudinal examination. *Addiction (Abingdon, England)*, *113*(3), 496–506. Available from https://doi.org/10.1111/add.14007.

Grubbs, J. B., Wilt, J. A., Stauner, N., Exline, J. J., & Pargament, K. I. (2016). Self, struggle, and soul: Linking personality, self-concept, and religious/spiritual struggle. *Personality and Individual Differences*, *101*, 144–152.

Gutierrez, I. A., Chapman, H., Grubbs, J., & Grant, J. (2018). *The Prevalence and Impact of Religious and Spiritual Struggles among Veterans in a Residential Gambling Treatment Program (Pre-Print)* [Preprint]. PsyArXiv. Available from https://doi.org/10.31234/osf.io/mtps5.

Haidt, J., & Hersh, M. A. (2001). Sexual morality: The cultures and emotions of conservatives and liberals. *Journal of Applied Social Psychology*, *31*(1), 191–221. Available from https://doi.org/10.1111/j.1559-1816.2001.tb02489.x.

Hodge, D. R., Andereck, K., & Montoya, H. (2007). The protective influence of spiritual-religious lifestyle profiles on tobacco use, alcohol use, and gambling. *Social Work Research*, *31*(4), 211–219. Available from https://doi.org/10.1093/swr/31.4.211.

Hook, J. N., Farrell, J. E., Ramos, M. J., Davis, D. E., Karaga, S., Tongeren, D. R. V., & Grubbs, J. B. (2015). Religiousness and congruence between sexual values and behavior. *Journal of Psychology and Christianity*, *34*(2), 179–189.

Jakobsen, J. R., & Pellegrini, A. (2004). *Love the sin: Sexual regulation and the limits of religious tolerance*. Beacon Press.

Kafka, M. P. (2010). Hypersexual disorder: A proposed diagnosis for DSM-V. *Archives of Sexual Behavior*, *39*(2), 377–400. Available from https://doi.org/10.1007/s10508-009-9574-7.

Kelly, J. F., Hoeppner, B., Stout, R. L., & Pagano, M. (2012). Determining the relative importance of the mechanisms of behavior change within Alcoholics Anonymous: A multiple mediator analysis. *Addiction*, *107*(2), 289–299. Available from https://doi.org/10.1111/j.1360-0443.2011.03593.x.

Kendler, K. S., Liu, X.-Q., Gardner, C. O., McCullough, M. E., Larson, D., & Prescott, C. A. (2003). Dimensions of religiosity and their relationship to lifetime psychiatric and substance use disorders. *American Journal of Psychiatry*, *160*(3), 496–503. Available from https://doi.org/10.1176/appi.ajp.160.3.496.

Kim, H. S., Shifrin, A., Sztainert, T., & Wohl, M. J. A. (2018). Placing your faith on the betting floor: Religiosity predicts disordered gambling via gambling fallacies. *Journal of Behavioral Addictions*, 1–9. Available from https://doi.org/10.1556/2006.7.2018.23.

Kowalewska, E., Grubbs, J. B., Potenza, M. N., Gola, M., Draps, M., & Kraus, S. W. (2018). Neurocognitive mechanisms in compulsive sexual behavior disorder. *Current Sexual Health Reports*, *10*(4), 255–264. Available from https://doi.org/10.1007/s11930-018-0176-z.

Kraus, S. W., Meshberg-Cohen, S., Martino, S., Quinones, L. J., & Potenza, M. N. (2015). Treatment of compulsive pornography use with naltrexone: A case report. *American Journal of Psychiatry*, *172*(12), 1260–1261. Available from https://doi.org/10.1176/appi.ajp.2015.15060843.

Kraus, S. W., & Sweeney, P. J. (2019). Hitting the target: Considerations for differential diagnosis when treating individuals for problematic use of pornography. *Archives of Sexual Behavior*, *48*(2), 431–435. Available from https://doi.org/10.1007/s10508-018-1301-9.

Kraus, S. W., Voon, V., & Potenza, M. N. (2016a). Neurobiology of compulsive sexual behavior: Emerging science. *Neuropsychopharmacology: Official Publication of the American College of Neuropsychopharmacology*, *41*(1), 385–386. Available from https://doi.org/10.1038/npp.2015.300.

Kraus, S. W., Voon, V., & Potenza, M. N. (2016b). Should compulsive sexual behavior be considered an addiction? *Addiction (Abingdon, England)*, *111*(12), 2097–2106. Available from https://doi.org/10.1111/add.13297.

Kwee, W. A., Dominguez, A. W., & Ferrell, D. (2007). Sexual addiction and Christian college men: Conceptual, assessment, and treatment challenges. *Journal of Psychology and Christianity*, *26*, 3–13.

Lefkowitz, E. S., Gillen, M. M., Shearer, C. L., & Boone, T. L. (2004). Religiosity, sexual behaviors, and sexual attitudes during emerging adulthood. *The Journal of Sex Research*, *41*(2), 150–159. Available from https://doi.org/10.1080/00224490409552223.

Leonhardt, N. D., & Willoughby, B. J. (2017). Longitudinal links between pornography use, marital importance, and permissive sexuality during emerging adulthood. *Marriage & Family Review*, *54*(1), 64–84. Available from https://doi.org/10.1080/01494929.2017.1359811.

Mark, K., Rosenkrantz, D., & Kerner, I. (2014). "Bi"ing into monogamy: Attitudes toward monogamy in a sample of bisexual-identified adults. *Psychology of Sexual Orientation and Gender Diversity*, *1*(3), 263. Available from https://doi.org/10.1037/sgd0000051.

Montgomery, B. E. E., Stewart, K. E., Bryant, K. J., & Ounpraseuth, S. T. (2014). Dimensions of religion, depression symptomatology, and substance use among rural African American cocaine users. *Journal of Ethnicity in Substance Abuse*, *13*(1), 72–90. Available from https://doi.org/10.1080/15332640.2014.873605.

Oei, T. P. S., & Gordon, L. M. (2008). Psychosocial factors related to gambling abstinence and relapse in members of Gamblers Anonymous. *Journal of Gambling Studies*, *24*(1), 91–105. Available from https://doi.org/10.1007/s10899-007-9071-7.

Perry, S. L. (2018). Not practicing what you preach: Religion and incongruence between pornography beliefs and usage. *Journal of Sex Research*, *55*(3), 369–380. Available from https://doi.org/10.1080/00224499.2017.1333569.

Petry, N. M., Blanco, C., Auriacombe, M., Borges, G., Bucholz, K., Crowley, T. J., ... O'Brien, C. (2014). An overview of and rationale for changes proposed for pathological gambling in DSM-5. *Journal of Gambling Studies*, *30*(2), 493–502. Available from https://doi.org/10.1007/s10899-013-9370-0.

Pickthall, M. M. (Trans.). (2001). *The Glorious Qur'an*. Elmhurst: Tahrike Tarsile Qur'an.

Pirutinsky, S. (2018, December 12). *Religion and compulsive sexuality: A response to Efrati's (2019) God, I can't stop thinking about sex!* [Letter]. Retrieved from <https://www.tandfonline.com/doi/abs/10.1080/00224499.2018.1552751>.

Potenza, M. N. (2008). The neurobiology of pathological gambling and drug addiction: An overview and new findings. *Philosophical Transactions of the Royal Society B: Biological Sciences*, *363*(1507), 3181–3189. Available from https://doi.org/10.1098/rstb.2008.0100.

Potenza, M. N. (2013). Neurobiology of gambling behaviors. *Current Opinion in Neurobiology*, *23*(4), 660–667. Available from https://doi.org/10.1016/j.conb.2013.03.004.

Reid, R. C., Carpenter, B. N., & Hook, J. N. (2016). Investigating correlates of hypersexual behavior in religious patients. *Sexual Addiction & Compulsivity*, *23*(2–3), 296–312. Available from https://doi.org/10.1080/10720162.2015.1130002.

Reid, R. C., Carpenter, B. N., Hook, J. N., Garos, S., Manning, J. C., Gilliland, R., ... Fong, T. (2012). Report of findings in a DSM-5 field trial for hypersexual disorder. *The Journal of Sexual Medicine*, *9*(11), 2868–2877.

Reid, R. C., & Kafka, M. P. (2014). Controversies about hypersexual disorder and the DSM-5. *Current Sexual Health Reports*, *6*(4), 259–264.

Reilly, C., & Smith, N. (2013). *The evolving definition of pathological gambling in the DSM-5* (pp. 1–6). Washington, DC: National Center for Responsible Gaming.

Rosmarin, D. H., & Pirutinsky, S. (2019). Problematic sexual behavior and religion among adult Jewish males: An initial study. *American Journal of Men's Health, 13*(1). Available from https://doi.org/10.1177/1557988318823586, 155798831882358.

Rowatt, W. C., & Schmitt, D. P. (2003). Associations between religious orientation and varieties of sexual experience. *Journal for the Scientific Study of Religion, 42*(3), 455–465. Available from https://doi.org/10.1111/1468-5906.00194.

Scott, J. (1998). Changing attitudes to sexual morality: A cross-national comparison. *Sociology, 32*(4), 815–845.

Sinha, J. W., Cnaan, R. A., & Gelles, R. J. (2007). Adolescent risk behaviors and religion: Findings from a national study. *Journal of Adolescence, 30*(2), 231–249. Available from https://doi.org/10.1016/j.adolescence.2006.02.005.

Stauner, N., Exline, J. J., Grubbs, J. B., Pargament, K. I., Bradley, D. F., & Uzdavines, A. (2016). Bifactor models of religious and spiritual struggles: Distinct from religiousness and distress. *Religions*, 7(6), 68.

Thomas, J. N. (2013). Outsourcing moral authority: The internal secularization of evangelicals' anti-pornography narratives. *Journal for the Scientific Study of Religion, 52*. Available from https://doi.org/10.1111/jssr.12052.

Thomas, J. N. (2016). The development and deployment of the idea of pornography addiction within American evangelicalism. *Sexual Addiction & Compulsivity, 23*(2–3), 182–195. Available from https://doi.org/10.1080/10720162.2016.1140603.

van den Akker, H., van der Ploeg, R., & Scheepers, P. (2013). Disapproval of homosexuality: Comparative research on individual and national determinants of disapproval of homosexuality in 20 European countries. *International Journal of Public Opinion Research, 25*(1), 64–86. Available from https://doi.org/10.1093/ijpor/edr058.

Volk, F., Thomas, J., Sosin, L., Jacob, V., & Moen, C. (2016). Religiosity, developmental context, and sexual shame in pornography users: A serial mediation model. *Sexual Addiction & Compulsivity, 23*(2–3), 244–259. Available from https://doi.org/10.1080/10720162.2016.1151391.

Walton, M. T. (2019). Incongruence as a variable feature of problematic sexual behaviors in an online sample of self-reported "sex addiction". *Archives of Sexual Behavior, 48*(2), 443–447. Available from https://doi.org/10.1007/s10508-018-1305-5.

Weinstock, J., April, L. M., & Kallmi, S. (2017). Is subclinical gambling really subclinical? *Addictive Behaviors, 73*, 185–191. Available from https://doi.org/10.1016/j.addbeh.2017.05.014.

Welte, J. W., Barnes, G. M., Tidwell, M.-C. O., & Hoffman, J. H. (2008). The prevalence of problem gambling among U.S. adolescents and young adults: Results from a national survey. *Journal of Gambling Studies, 24*(2), 119–133. Available from https://doi.org/10.1007/s10899-007-9086-0.

White, W. L. (1998). *Slaying the dragon: The history of addiction treatment and recovery in America*. Bloomington, IL: Chestnut Health Systems/Lighthouse Institute.

Williams, D. J. (2017). The framing of frequent sexual behavior and/or pornography viewing as addiction: Some concerns for social work. *Journal of Social Work, 17*(5), 616–623. Available from https://doi.org/10.1177/1468017316644701.

Wilt, J. A., Grubbs, J. B., Exline, J., & Pargament, K. (2016). The big five, religious and spiritual struggles, and well-being. *Personality and Individual Differences, 101*, 527.

Wilt, J. A., Grubbs, J. B., Pargament, K. I., & Exline, J. J. (2017). Religious and spiritual struggles, past and present: Relations to the big five and well-being. *The International Journal for the Psychology of Religion, 27*(1), 51–64.

World Health Organization. (2018). *ICD-11*. Retrieved June 29, 2018, from <https://icd.who.int/>.

CHAPTER 9

Spirituality, religion, and marital/family issues

Annette Mahoney, Daniel D. Flint and James S. McGraw
Department of Psychology, Bowling Green State University, Bowling Green, OH, United States

Contents

Introduction

This chapter addresses ways that spirituality (S) and religion (R) could decrease or increase individual psychological distress by shaping close relationships. Such pathways of influence may be relevant to many couples and parents. For example, according to 2011–13 US surveys, 79% married mothers, 77% of single mothers, and 68% of cohabiting American mothers view religion as "somewhat" or "very important" to their daily life (National Center for Family and Marriage Research, 2017). Mothers and fathers in non-US countries also report that religion influences their parenting and is important in their lives (Bornstein et al., 2017). Furthermore, we estimate that over 500 peer-reviewed studies have been published in journals since 1980 that target links between S/R factors and marital or parental functioning. These studies span an enormous range of

Handbook of Spirituality, Religion, and Mental Health
DOI: https://doi.org/10.1016/B978-0-12-816766-3.00009-4

topics such as union formation, fertility, spousal gender roles, marital satisfaction and dynamics, divorce, domestic violence, infidelity, pregnancy, parenting infants, children and adolescents, and coping with family distress. Mahoney (2010, 2013) created the "Relational Spirituality Framework" (RSF) to synthesize this expansive literature, and in this chapter, we highlight some key findings from these and other in-depth reviews (Ellison & Xu, 2014; Mahoney & Boyatzis, 2019; Mahoney, Pargament, Swank, & Tarakeshwar, 2001). Specifically, we first present scientific evidence that S/R is tied to positive relationship functioning, and, in turn, the personal well-being of family members. We then discuss specific ways that S/R could intensify relational and personal distress. Next, we offer with two clinical vignettes to illustrate the roles S/R could play, for better or worse, for distressed clients dealing with relationship issues. Finally, we close with a summary of key points.

Spirituality/religion, relationships, and well-being

Religious community involvement and relational well-being

Most peer-reviewed, quantitative studies on the intersection of S/R and close relationships have examined links between general engagement in religious groups and marital and parent—child relational well-being. These studies typically use one or two items to assess S/R, such as how often a particular family member attends religious services or views religion as important to daily life, and (dis)similarity between two family members on such items.

For couples, greater religious attendance or involvement has been tied to a greater likelihood of getting married and mate selection (e.g., Blackwell & Lichter, 2004), less extramarital infidelity (e.g., Atkins & Kessel, 2008) and domestic violence (e.g., Ellison & Anderson, 2001), greater marital satisfaction (e.g., Mahoney et al., 2001), and a lower risk of divorce, especially for Caucasians or couples with similar religious involvement (e.g., Brown, Orbuch, & Bauermeister, 2008). The strength and consistency of these associations, however, are modest. More robust findings emerge in studies on couples that assess specific S/R beliefs about marriage which we illustrate later.

With regard to becoming and being a parent, higher religious attendance or overall importance of religion, regardless of place of worship, has been tied to a greater likelihood of becoming a mother (e.g., McQuillan, Greil, Shreffler, & Bedrous, 2015), less alcohol, marijuana and drug use during pregnancy (e.g., Page, Ellison, & Lee, 2009), and more satisfaction and less stress as a parent for married mothers and fathers and single mothers (e.g., Henderson, Uecker, & Stroope, 2016; Petts, 2012). When it comes to child-rearing attitudes and practices, higher religious attendance has been tied to less use of corporal punishment (e.g., Frechette & Romano, 2015; Petts, 2012), lower risk of child physical abuse (e.g., Brown, Cohen, Johnson, & Salzinger, 1998), and greater positive parent time spent with children (e.g., Jorgensen, Mancini, Yorgason, & Day, 2016; Perry & Snawder, 2017). Conservative Christian beliefs and affiliation have been tied to greater belief in and use of corporal punishment (e.g., Gershoff, Miller, & Holden, 1999; Hoffmann, Ellison, & Bartkowski, 2017) but not higher child physical abuse (e.g., Breyer & MacPhee, 2015).

With regard to coparenting between married heterosexuals, higher engagement in religious groups has been associated with more traditional division of infant and childcare activities (e.g., DeMaris, Mahoney, & Pargament, 2011). Inconclusive findings exist between participation in conservative Christian Protestant groups and non-egalitarian division of household labor or decision-making, despite teachings within this subculture that promote complementary gender roles (e.g., Edgell, 2005; Ellison & Bartkowski, 2002).

In summary, in families headed by married heterosexuals and single mothers, greater engagement in organized religion has been linked to desirable family outcomes (e.g., marital and parental satisfaction) as well as undesirable outcomes, depending on one's perspective (e.g., gendered parenting roles and corporal punishment). Scarce research exists on whether involvement in religious groups may help other types of families, including those headed by single fathers, cohabiting or same-sex couples, divorced or remarried coparents, or adoptive, foster, or grandparents. Despite "nontraditional" families being less likely to turn to religious communities for support (Ellison & Xu, 2014), such possibilities need to be explored in science and practice.

Spirituality/religion processes and relational well-being

It is important to recognize that religious groups across the theologically progressive to conservative spectrum may promote both helpful and harmful S/R beliefs or behaviors, with an increasing number of people distancing themselves from any faith community. Thus, researchers have begun to identify and disentangle specific S/R processes that may enhance relational well-being for people whose S/R journeys take place inside or outside a formal religious context. Next, we illustrate three such S/R processes.

Sanctification

Married heterosexual (e.g., Mahoney et al., 1999), same-sex (e.g., Phillips et al., 2017), and dating and cohabiting couples (Henderson, Ellison, & Glenn, 2018) often view their relationship as having sacred qualities and/or being a manifestation of a deity's presence. These two processes have been coined, respectively, as nontheistic and theistic sanctification (Pargament & Mahoney, 2005). Greater perceived sanctity of marriages and committed unions has been tied to greater relationship satisfaction, even after controlling for positive relationship behaviors such as forgiveness and sacrifice (e.g., Henderson et al., 2018; Russell et al., 2017; Sabey, Rauer, & Jensen, 2014) and stable traits of the spouses (Kusner, Mahoney, Pargament, & DeMaris, 2014). Greater sanctification also leads to more supportive behaviors between spouses which, in turn, are connected to marital happiness (Rusu, Hilpert, Beach, Turliuc, & Bodenmann, 2015). Furthermore, greater sanctity of marriage predicts better-observed communication skills by husbands and wives during conflictual marital interactions (Kusner et al., 2014; Rauer & Volling, 2015) and emotionally focused dialogs for couples (Padgett, Annette Mahoney, Pargament, & DeMaris, 2019).

Viewing parenting as sacred also appears to be commonplace, at least in the United States (e.g., Nelson & Uecker, 2017). Moreover, such perceptions by Americans increase the odds of feeling satisfied with being a parent of school-aged children by 77%, even after controlling for global religious involvement and other demographics (Nelson & Uecker, 2017). Sanctification has also been tied to more satisfaction with parent–child relationships by college students and their mothers and fathers (Brelsford, 2013). Beyond satisfaction, the sanctity of parenting appears to strengthen parents' commitment to their preferred child-rearing methods. For instance, during the transition to parenthood, greater sanctification of the parent–infant bond increased the traditional gender divisions of infant care between married heterosexuals (DeMaris et al., 2011). Focusing on disciplinary situations, sanctification by married parents was tied to greater contingent praise and teaching reparation, but not punitive techniques such as shaming or spanking (Volling, Mahoney, & Rauer, 2009).

Furthermore, the combination of stronger belief in the sanctity of parenting and greater nonpunitive strategies enhanced children's conscience development; this suggests parents who relied on both factors were more determined to instill their values in their offspring. Other studies on parenting (see Mahoney & Boyatzis, 2019) and marital sexuality (e.g., Hernandez-Kane & Mahoney, 2018) echo these findings on sanctification and relational well-being.

Spiritual disclosure and intimacy

Whereas sanctification captures a given individual's perception of a relationship, two people can engage in overt S/R behaviors with each other that appear to be helpful. For example, emerging research suggests that dyadic dialogs focused on S/R could enhance relational quality. In an initial study on this topic, Brelsford and Mahoney (2008) assessed how much college students and parents candidly talked with each other about their S/R views, resources, and struggles. This process was labeled spiritual disclosure, and it was tied to greater satisfaction and lower verbal hostility within the mother–child and father–child relationship. Because S/R experiences can easily be disputed, presumably many people may avoid revealing such information to loved ones for fear of being dismissed, ridiculed, or misunderstood (Brelsford & Mahoney, 2008; Mahoney, 2013). Kusner et al. (2014) therefore created a measure to assess spiritual disclosure and support (i.e., responding to a partner's spiritual disclosures in an empathic, nonjudgmental manner). This combined process was labeled "spiritual intimacy." Greater spiritual intimacy predicted both spouses' displaying less negativity and more positivity during observations of couples discussing major conflicts (Kusner et al., 2014) and talking about their fears and vulnerabilities about becoming parents (Padgett et al., 2019).

Prayer for a partner

Individuals can privately turn to a felt relationship with God to help them enact virtues to sustain their union with a partner (Fincham & Beach, 2014). One compelling program of research by Fincham and colleagues, for instance, shows that in generally well-functioning relationships, benevolent prayer for one's partner (PFP) clearly facilitates that relational quality (for review, see Fincham & Beach, 2013). In studies of dating college students, those who privately prayed for their romantic partner's well-being reported increased relationship satisfaction and decreased the risk of infidelity over time. Experimental studies have also found that praying for a person with whom one has a romantic or close relationship increases the prayer's levels of selfless concern, gratitude, and forgiveness of the other person. In addition, Beach et al. (2011) conducted a randomized experiment with a community sample of married African Americans to see if PFP strengthened marriages. Specifically, couples were randomly assigned to one of three conditions: (1) a marital education program previously found to protect marriages, (2) the same program supplemented with a module focused on PFP, and (3) self-help reading materials only. Over time, prayer for partner enhanced marital outcomes for wives, but not husbands, beyond the beneficial effects of an established marital education program or self-help efforts. However, PFP by both spouses predicted both partners' marital satisfaction, which also mediated PFP's association with marital commitment (Fincham & Beach, 2014).

Pathways from spirituality/religion to better relationships and mental health

To recap, both general involvement in religious groups and specific relational S/R processes have been directly tied to better marital or parent–child dynamics. Other research shows that greater S/R also lowers the risk of psychological maladjustment and substance misuse in adults and youths (e.g., Yonker, Schnabelrauch, & DeHaan, 2012; (e.g., references to other chapters) see Chapter 7, Spirituality, religion, and substance use disorders, of this text for a review of this topic). These two sets of direct linkages raise the question of whether indirect pathways of influence exist whereby greater S/R by a spouse(s) or parent(s) leads to better mental health functioning of the family member(s) by enhancing relational functioning.

Spouses' spirituality/religion to marital functioning to spouses' well-being

To our surprise, we could locate only two published, peer-reviewed studies that have examined indirect pathways of influence of S/R facilitating spouses' personal adjustment by improving marital dynamics. Among married Romanian, Orthodox Christian couples, Rusu et al. (2015) found that greater sanctification of marriage improved both spouses' sense of life purpose and satisfaction by increasing partners' engagement in supportive behaviors to help their spouse deal with problems. Holland, Lee, Marshak, and Martin (2016) found similar results using the same measure of psychological well-being in a sample of Seventh-day Adventists.

Specifically, a more supportive perceived relationship with God was tied to a closer and more supportive marital relationship which, in turn, led to greater personal well-being of each partner.

Parents' spirituality/religion to parenting to youth psychosocial well-being

When it comes to parenting, three compelling longitudinal studies exist on indirect pathways of influence from parents' S/R to parenting to youth's mental health adjustment. Notably, these studies assessed youth behavioral or emotional problems rather than psychosocial well-being per se. First, in a national US survey (Li, 2013), married parents' religious attendance and familial religious activities with 12–14-year-olds were directly tied to youth being less likely to exhibit delinquent behavior 2 years later. Much of this effect was due to teens' perceptions of less inter-parental conflict, better parenting practices, and stronger affection for parents. Preliminary analyses found similar results with single-parent households. In another study focused on African American teens (Landor, Simons, Simons, Brody, & Gibbons, 2011), greater parental S/R predicted 15–16-year-olds' reports of less risky sexual behavior 2 years later by increasing authoritative parenting, adolescent religiosity, and the adolescents' friendships with less sexually permissive peers. Third, Bornstein et al. (2017) assessed whether parents' S/R (i.e., overall importance of religion and its influence on parenting) when their children were 8 years old influenced child's internalizing and externalizing symptoms at age 10 by improving parenting when the children were age 9. On a positive note, initial parental S/R led to increased higher parental efficacy and warmth 1 year later, which then led to increased children's social competence and school performance 2 years later. On a negative note, greater parental S/R was longitudinally associated with stronger parent behavioral control of youth, with little opportunity for child autonomy, which led to more child internalizing and externalizing problems, although the children's difficulties fell well below clinical cut points. Greater initial parental S/R was, unfortunately, also tied to children's reports of parental rejection at age 9 and increases in children's adjustment difficulties at age 10. These mixed results did not vary due to religious denomination or nationality across nine countries.

We close this section by highlighting that we could locate only two studies that have directly investigated whether physical discipline of young children reduces behavioral or emotional problems within Conservative

Protestant Christian (CPC) families, as suggested by some leaders of this religious subgroup (Hoffmann et al., 2017). Using longitudinal data gathered between 1987 and 1994, Ellison, Musick, and Holden (2011) found that American 2–4-year-olds of CPC mothers exhibited minimal negative effects of corporal punishment 5 years later and less antisocial behavior if CPC mothers had initially used but later discontinued spanking. Updating this study with longitudinal data collected between 2001 and 2005 on two-parent US families, Petts and Kysar-Moon (2012) found that parents reported less misbehavior by their preschoolers over 4 years with very specific family dynamics: If only the father spanked and he spanked infrequently, and only if both parents were CPC. Prompted by persistent concerns about physical discipline within contemporary CPC families, Miller-Perrin and Perrin (2017a, 2017b) conducted two randomized experiments that demonstrated the effectiveness of a biblical education intervention to decrease support for spanking by CPC college students and parents of children.

In summary, a handful of intriguing longitudinal studies have uncovered indirect pathways of influence from adults' S/R to their own or offspring's better psychosocial functioning by enhancing marital or parent–child relationships, although some contrary findings have emerged for youth (i.e., Bornstein et al., 2017). More studies are obviously needed to replicate and expand these initial findings. Furthermore, current evidence is based on generally well-functioning national or community samples. As a result, findings suggestive of positive carry-over effects of S/R cannot be uncritically generalized to clinically distressed couples or parents where maladaptive S/R processes may be both more prevalent and likely to contribute to dysfunctional interpersonal processes and, in turn, mental health problems. We illustrate such possibilities next.

Spirituality/religion, relationships, and mental health maladjustment

S/R has the potential to contribute to mental health problems across the life span when people face dilemmas in creating or sustaining healthy relationships, or reforming or exiting dysfunctional relationships (Mahoney, 2010, 2013). Normative relationship situations where S/R could exacerbate personal distress include making choices about dating and marital partners, nonmarital sexuality and cohabitation, spousal and coparenting gender roles, contraception use and pregnancy, couple relationship dynamics, child-rearing styles, and elder care. Atypical or highly stressful relationship experiences may also trigger problematic manifestations of S/R that heighten individual distress. Salient examples include experiencing infertility, unwanted pregnancy, death of an infant or child, infidelity, domestic violence, child maltreatment, dysfunctional family dynamics, divorce or remarriage, or a family member's chronic developmental disabilities or mental health impairments. Remarkably scarce research has directly addressed ways that S/R could intensify individuals' psychological distress when coping with relationship stressors. Nevertheless, empirical findings on S/R dissimilarity between family members as well as spiritual struggles over family matters highlight the need for clinicians to be alert to S/R difficulties tied to relational issues.

Spirituality/religion dissimilarity

Dissimilarity between family dyads on S/R factors is tied to higher relational and child distress. Regarding domestic violence, for example, biblically conservative husbands married to biblically liberal wives have been found to be about four times more likely to engage in domestic violence toward wives than husbands married to wives with similar biblical views (Ellison, Bartkowski, & Anderson, 1999). Regarding adolescence, parents and teens who diverge greatly in their organized religious involvement tend to report more distance and dissatisfaction in their relationship (e.g., Stokes & Regnerus, 2009). Major disagreement between parents about religious attendance or beliefs also increases child adjustment problems (Bartkowski, Xu, & Levin, 2008). It is worth emphasizing, however, that major S/R discord between family members is relatively rare. For example, Ellison et al. found that only 7.5% of couples strongly disagree about the Bible, and Stokes and Regnerus (2009) found that only 11% of parents rated religion as much more important than their teens rated religion. Thus, major disputes between family members over faith appear to be infrequent but likely to increase distress when they do occur.

Spiritual struggles, desecration, and sacred loss

Negative S/R coping refers to ways that stressors trigger distressing S/R thoughts and feelings about supernatural figures (e.g., anger toward God, feeling punished by the devil), religious groups (e.g., conflicts with cobelievers), or the self (e.g., feeling morally conflicted), processes that are increasingly referred to as "spiritual struggles" (Exline, Pargament,

Grubbs, & Yali, 2014). Spiritual struggles generally lead to declines in individuals' psychological well-being, particularly if left unresolved, but can occasionally lead to greater personal growth, particularly if resolved (Exline et al., 2014; Pargament, 2007). Studies on divorce illustrate the need to address spiritual struggles centered on relationship problems. For example, most adults who had recently divorced experienced spiritual struggles internally, with God, and others over the divorce, as well as viewed the marital dissolution as the loss or desecration of a sacred bond; the more these negative S/R processes occurred, the more depressive and anxiety symptoms the divorcees experienced over time (Krumrei, Mahoney, & Pargament, 2011). Likewise, the more college students viewed a prior romantic breakup as a sacred loss/desecration and experienced spiritual struggles over the event, the more they reported current emotional distress; this pathway was particularly robust if students had engaged in more premarital sexual activity with their ex-partner and more often attended services and saw religion as important (Hawley, Mahoney, Pargament, & Gordon, 2015). Overall, viewing a relationship ending through a negative S/R lens appears to intensify personal maladjustment.

Parents also appear to be vulnerable to greater emotional distress if they encounter spiritual struggles while raising children. Such struggles range from doubts and anger at God about their children's problems to feelings of shame and guilt in the eyes of God or S/R cobelievers, or despair over a lack of help from those parties. In a study of parents of preterm infants, for example, negative S/R coping related to poorer family cohesion and greater use of maladaptive denial (Brelsford, Ramirez, Veneman, & Doheny, 2016). For parents of at-risk preschoolers (Dumas & Nissley-Tsiopinis, 2006) and children with autism (Tarakeshwar & Pargament, 2001), greater negative S/R coping correlated with more parental distress and depression. Weyand, O'Laughlin, and Bennett (2013), however, did not find negative S/R coping to intensify the link between parental distress and child maladjustment in a community sample. Thus, spiritual struggles may only adversely impact parents who face high levels of family or child difficulties.

Clinical implications

Resources for clinicians

Randomized clinical trials (RCTs) are needed to test the efficacy of S/Roriented interventions to improve marital dynamics for clinically distressed couples or parenting practices in families with children with clinically elevated psychological problems. Such studies are just to help inform clinical practice are just beginning to be conducted. One notable example is an RCT that compared a religiously accommodative intervention formaritally distressed and predominantly conservative Christian couples to a parallel nonreligious version of the same (HOPE) marital intervention, with no major differences found in outcomes (Ripley et al., 2014). Samta Pandya has also opened promising line of research for parents from diverse religious groups (e.g., Buddhist, Christian, Hindu, Islamic, Jewish) by developing a spiritually oriented intervention that fits into a Universalist or Unitarian spiritual system and is designed to build resilience in primary caregivers of children with autism spectrum disorders (Pandya, 2018) and acute anxiety problems (Pandya, 2019); based on RCTs conducted in multiple cities across the globe, parents showed significant improvement in positive parenting in both studies. We look forward to more controlled applied and basic studies on the pros or cons of integrating S/R into psychotherapy to address relationship problems which, in turn, may impact the well-being of partners, parents, or youth seeking counseling.

Valuable clinically informed resources are available to help therapists become informed and thoughtful about S/R when working with clients on relationship problems. Onedera's (2008) edited text, for instance, offers useful chapters on the theological positions on marriage and family life taken by a wide range of religious denominations. Walker and Hathaway (2013) and Walsh (2009) offer two edited texts filled with case studies and exercises to address S/R when working with distressed family systems. In addition, Ripley and Worthington (2014) have developed a religiously accommodative intervention for maritally distressed, predominantly conservative Christian couples in a book that integrates theory, basic research, and cases. For parent-focused referrals, Mahoney, LeRoy, Kusner, Padgett, and Grimes (2013) offer case examples to address parental perfectionism and rigidity, child physical abuse, and parent–adolescent clashes over sexuality. Finally, Gardner, Butler, and Seedall (2008) offer therapists' valuable insights on the toxic ways S/R can be triangulated into couples' and family system dynamics.

Clinical vignettes

Analogous to Pargament and Mahoney's (2017) conception of spirituality as the discovery, conservation, and transformation of the sacred, Mahoney

(2010, 2013) heuristically sorted S/R and family research literature in the RSF into three recursive, overlapping stages: (1) formation—creating and structuring a particular relationship, (2) maintenance—preserving and protecting an established relationship, and (3) transformation—reforming or exiting a distressed relationship. In addition, Mahoney proposed that S/R resources or struggles could be embedded in a client's relationships with: (1) supernatural figures (e.g., deity, immortal ancestor), (2) other individuals (e.g., a spouse, child), and (3) religious community that could impact personal well-being. We offer two clinical vignettes to illustrate addressing S/R relational processes.

Union formation and termination

Our first vignette involves, Andrea, a 25-year-old graduate student struggling with the ending of a troubled intimate relationship and dating. Six months before she sought psychotherapy, Andrea and her cohabiting partner had ended their 4-year long relationship after she discovered him having sex in their apartment with one of her friends. Her ex-partner attributed his behavior to Andrea's loss of interest in their sexual relationship. Talking about the breakup triggered a mix of complex emotions—anger at her ex-partner's infidelity, grief about the loss of the future family they had planned, and anxiety about her sexual attractiveness and a sexually transmitted infection (STI) he had given her. She was typically a high achiever academically and she entered therapy after nearly failing a graduate course. Andrea's treatment goals were to reduce her depressive and anxiety symptoms, complete her graduate program on time, and form a committed romantic relationship that she thought could evolve into a stable, satisfying marriage.

In exploring the S/R dimensions of Andrea's romantic relationship experiences, Andrea and her therapist uncovered that Andrea had experienced God as a supportive loving "Presence" until the past year. She also harbored what she disparagingly labeled "vague irrational fears" that her STI might be some kind of divine punishment. Exploring the concept of sanctification, Andrea realized she had experienced feelings of awe, love, and transcendent connection to her ex-partner, especially during sex, that she interpreted to mean that he was "the One" she was ultimately meant to marry. She also realized she experienced his infidelity as a desecration and sacred loss, as a wound that could not be healed and this made her frightened of future relationships. Prior to psychotherapy, she had an appointment with a campus minister who a friend had recommended that

Andrea talk to about her anger and forgiving her ex-partner. Although sympathetic, he recommended that Andrea commit to sexual celibacy until she got married. This response deepened her distrust and irritation with organized religious groups.

Over time, Andrea took more seriously her persistent feeling of being unfairly punished and reinterpreted her reaction as a sign that she was angry at God but wanted to feel reconnected to a divine Presence. She experimented with S/R focused introspective activities outside of attending religious services (e.g., journaling, nature walks, guided meditations, reading feminist Christian and Jewish writers) and rekindled a sense of connection to divine support and love. This helped her let go of hostile feelings toward her ex-partner and become more hopeful and self-confident about dating. She also generated more explicit criteria for what interpersonal behaviors would merit a "sacred union" with a partner; this facilitated her being more selective with potential dating partners and assertive in communicating about sexuality and commitment.

Family maintenance and transformation

Our second vignette involves a 41-year-old man, Joe, struggling to maintain his family's stability. Like his wife Belinda, Joe grew up in a family where his parents divorced due to alcoholism and domestic violence. The couple met at an alcohol anonymous (AA) group when they were both 28. They married 2 years later and, after struggling with infertility for several years, they were overjoyed to have twins. They strongly agreed that Belinda be a full-time homemaker, with Joe working long hours and backing up her authoritarian parenting style with paternal punishment when he was home. When the twins were 6, Joe was laid off and unable to find another full-time job with health insurance benefits, so Belinda had to go back into the paid labor force. Upset about this shift in gender roles, Joe began to lose often his temper with Belinda and the twins who began acting out. Joe sought psychotherapy after a marital argument escalated to him threatening to hit Belinda. He was deeply shaken by this incident. His treatment goals were to learn to manage his emotions more effectively, avoid divorce, and effectively help Belinda get both twins to behave better.

As one component of therapy, the family therapist explored S/R dimensions of Joe's family life. Joe clearly viewed his marriage as a miracle granted by God because he and Belinda had joined AA and recovered from alcohol abuse during their 20s. He deeply believed God had blessed them with children because neither lost faith in God throughout their infertility difficulties. Exploring sanctification, Joe viewed a family marked by traditional gender roles as fulfilling a "God-given" plan and felt resentful that insurmountable societal obstacles blocked their ability to maintain their complementary roles. At an early session that Belinda attended, Joe wondered aloud if demonic forces were conspiring to dismantle families like theirs, and Belinda teared up, saying she had similar worries. This spiritually intimate dialog defused Joe's anger and drew the couple together in a palatable state of anxiety. With regard to coparenting, Joe felt it was his sacred duty to teach his children to be responsible, hard-working, helpful, and well-mannered; he viewed a father's use of corporal punishment as a means to these ends. He and Belinda married in a conservative Christian church that reinforced Joe's S/R views of family life where he regularly attended services with Belinda until she entered the workforce.

In addressing the S/R elements of Joe's family life, the therapist expressed sincere interest in understanding Joe's views about the role God had played in his AA recovery and family life. As a result, Joe felt more trusting of the therapist's guidance about cognitive behavioral therapy—based marital and parenting strategies. Drawing upon Joe's desire to be a role model of divine love helped motivate him to learn to communicate more effectively with Belinda and engage in more child-directed interactions to marked by warmth and positive, effective coaching to elicit desired child behavior. As he gained more insight into his profound spiritual fears about the shift in the couple's gender roles, he was better able to slow down when he felt himself losing his temper during marital interactions. Over time, he was better able to recognize and share his deeper anxieties with Belinda and engage in more calm, effective problem-solving with her. The therapist also explored when and why Joe used corporal punishment; this typically only occurred when he felt overwhelmed and angry, rather than being a consistent or measured response to his children's misbehavior. He came to see his reactions as impulsive and became more open to other disciplinary options to reach his parenting goals. He realized he was avoiding attending religious services due to his embarrassment about Belinda working. He then sought out his pastor who helped him join a men's church group where he learned biblical ways to fulfill his felt "calling" to be the spiritual leader of the family besides by being the primary income earner.

Discussion

Given the salience of S/R across the globe, many millions of couples and parents could draw on S/R to form and maintain family relationships in ways that could facilitate their own and loved ones' psychological well-being. In this chapter, we summarized scientific evidence of such pathways, as well as specific S/R processes within the context of close relationships (e.g., sanctification, spiritual disclosure and intimacy, prayer for partner) that could be explored with clients as possible S/R resources to help them reach their treatment goals. In addition, we highlighted some specific ways that S/R may create tension within relationships (e.g., S/R dissimilarity between family members) and/or intensify personal distress tied to serious relationship problems or endings (e.g., desecration and sacred loss). We hope this chapter helps practitioners to be sensitive to the roles that S/R may play, for better and worse, in close relationships, and thereby be part of the problem or solution when addressing individuals' personal well-being.

References

Atkins, D. C., & Kessel, D. E. (2008). Religiousness and infidelity: Attendance, but not faith and prayer, predict marital fidelity. *Journal of Marriage and Family*, *70*, 407–418. Available from https://doi.org/10.1111/j.1741-3737.2008.00490.x.

Bartkowski, J. P., Xu, X., & Levin, M. L. (2008). Religion and child development: Evidence from the early childhood longitudinal study. *Social Science Research*, *37*, 18–36. Available from https://doi.org/10.1016/j.ssresearch.2007.02.001.

Beach, S. R. H., Hurt, T. R., Fincham, F. D., Franklin, K. J., McNair, L. M., & Stanley, S. M. (2011). Enhancing marital enrichment through spirituality: Efficacy data for prayer focused relationship enhancement. *Psychology of Religion and Spirituality*, *3*, 201–216. Available from https://doi.org/10.1037/a0022207.

Blackwell, D. L., & Lichter, D. T. (2004). Homogamy among dating, cohabiting, and married couples. *Sociological Quarterly*, *45*, 719–737. Available from https://doi.org/10.1111/j.1533-8525.2004.tb02311.x.

Bornstein, M. H., Putnick, D. L., Lansford, J. E., Al-Hassan, S. M., Bacchini, D., Bombi, A. S., ... Alampay, L. P. (2017). 'Mixed blessings': Parental religiousness, parenting, and child adjustment in global perspective. *The Journal of Child Psychology and Psychiatry*, *58*, 880–892. Available from https://doi.org/10.1111/jcpp.12705.

Brelsford, G. M. (2013). Sanctification and spiritual disclosure in parent-child relationships: Implications for family relationship quality. *Journal of Family Psychology*, *27*, 639–649. Available from https://doi.org/10.1037/a0033424.

Brelsford, G. M., & Mahoney, A. (2008). Spiritual disclosure between older adolescents and their mothers. *Journal of Family Psychology*, *22*, 62–70.

Brelsford, G. M., Ramirez, J., Veneman, K., & Doheny, K. K. (2016). Sacred spaces religious and secular coping and family relationships in the neonatal intensive care unit. *Advances in Neonatal Care*, *16*, 315–322. Available from https://doi.org/10.1097/ANC.0000000000000263.

Breyer, R. J., & MacPhee, D. (2015). Community characteristics, conservative ideology, and child abuse rates. *Child Abuse & Neglect, 41*, 126–135. Available from https://doi.org/10.1016/j.chiabu.2014.11.019.

Brown, E., Orbuch, T. L., & Bauermeister, J. A. (2008). Religiosity and marital stability among Black American and White American couples. *Family Relations, 57*, 186–197. Available from https://doi.org/10.1111/j.1741-3729.2008.00493.x.

Brown, J., Cohen, P., Johnson, J. G., & Salzinger, S. (1998). A longitudinal analysis of risk factors for child maltreatment: Findings of a 17-year prospective study of officially recorded and self-reported. *Child Abuse & Neglect, 22*, 1065–1078.

DeMaris, A., Mahoney, A., & Pargament, K. I. (2011). Doing the scut work of childcare: Does religiousness encourage greater father involvement? *Journal of Marriage and Family, 73*, 354–368. Available from https://doi.org/10.1111/j.1741-3737.2010.00811.x.

Dumas, J. E., & Nissley-Tsiopinis, J. (2006). Parental global religiousness, sanctification of parenting, and positive and negative religious coping as predictors of parental and child functioning. *International Journal for the Psychology of Religion, 16*, 289–310. Available from https://doi.org/10.1207/s15327582ijpr1604_4.

Edgell, P. (2005). *Religion and family in a changing society*. Princeton, NJ: Princeton University Press.

Ellison, C. G., & Anderson, K. L. (2001). Religious involvement and domestic violence among U.S. couples. *Journal for the Scientific Study of Religion, 40*, 269–286. Available from https://doi.org/10.1111/0021-8294.00055.

Ellison, C. G., & Bartkowski, J. P. (2002). Conservative Protestantism and the division of household labor among married couples. *Journal of Family Issues, 23*, 950–985.

Ellison, C. G., Bartkowski, J. P., & Anderson, K. L. (1999). Are there religious variations in domestic violence? *Journal of Family Issues, 20*, 87–113. Available from https://doi.org/10.1177/019251399020001005.

Ellison, C. G., Musick, M. A., & Holden, G. W. (2011). Does conservative Protestantism moderate the association between corporal punishment and child outcomes? *Journal of Marriage and Family, 73*, 946–961. Available from https://doi.org/10.1111/j.1741-3737.2011.00854.x.

Ellison, C. G., & Xu, X. (2014). Religion and families. In J. Treas, J. Scott, & M. Richards (Eds.), *Wiley Blackwell Companion to the Sociology of Families Book Series: Blackwell Companions to Sociology* (pp. 277–299). New York: Wiley.

Exline, J. J., Pargament, K. I., Grubbs, J. B., & Yali, A. M. (2014). The religious and spiritual struggles scale: Development and initial validation. *Psychology of Religion and Spirituality, 6*, 208–222. Available from https://doi.org/10.1037/a0036465.

Fincham, F. D., & Beach, S. R. H. (2013). Can religion and spirituality enhance prevention programs for couples? In K. I. Pargament, A. Mahoney, & E. Shafranske (Eds.), *APA handbook of psychology, religion, and spirituality* (Vol. 2, pp. 461–480). Washington, DC: American Psychological Association.

Fincham, F. D., & Beach, S. R. H. (2014). I say a little prayer for you: Praying for partner increases commitment in romantic relationships. *Journal of Family Psychology, 28*(5), 587–593. Available from https://doi.org/10.1037/a0034999.

Frechette, S., & Romano, E. (2015). Change in corporal punishment over time in a representative sample of Canadian parents. *Journal of Family Psychology, 29*, 507–517. Available from https://doi.org/10.1037/fam0000104.

Gardner, B. C., Butler, M. H., & Seedall, R. B. (2008). En-gendering the couple-deity relationship: Clinical implications of power and process. *Contemporary Family Therapy: An International Journal, 30*, 152–166. Available from https://doi.org/10.1007/s10591-008-9063-5.

Gershoff, E. T., Miller, P. C., & Holden, G. W. (1999). Parenting influences from the pulpit: Religious affiliation as a determinant of parental corporal punishment. *Journal of Family Psychology*, *13*, 307–320. Available from https://doi.org/10.1037/0893-3200.13.3.307.

Hawley, A. R., Mahoney, A., Pargament, K. I., & Gordon, A. K. (2015). Sexuality and spirituality as predictors of distress over a romantic breakup: Mediated and moderated pathways. *Spirituality in Clinical Practice*, *2*, 145–159. Available from https://doi.org/10.1037/scp0000034.

Henderson, A. K., Ellison, C. G., & Glenn, N. D. (2018). Religion and relationship quality among cohabiting and dating couples. *Journal of Family Issues*, *39*, 1904–1932. Available from https://doi.org/10.1177/0192513X17728982.

Henderson, W. M., Uecker, J. E., & Stroope, S. (2016). The role of religion in parenting satisfaction and parenting stress among young parents. *The Sociological Quarterly*, *57*, 675–710. Available from https://doi.org/10.1111/tsq.12147.

Hernandez-Kane, K. M., & Mahoney, A. (2018). Sex through a sacred lens: Longitudinal effects of sanctification of marital sexuality. *Journal of Family Psychology*, *32*, 425–434. Available from https://doi.org/org/10.1037/fam0000392.

Hoffmann, J., Ellison, C., & Bartkowski, J. (2017). Conservative Protestantism and attitudes toward corporal punishment, 1986–2014. *Social Science Research*, *63*, 81–94. Available from https://doi.org/10.1016/j.ssresearch.2016.09.010.

Holland, K. J., Lee, J. W., Marshak, H. H., & Martin, L. R. (2016). Spiritual intimacy, marital intimacy, and physical/psychological well-being: Spiritual meaning as a mediator. *Psychology of Religion and Spirituality*, *8*, 218–227.

Jorgensen, B., Mancini, J., Yorgason, J., & Day, R. (2016). Religious beliefs, practices, and family strengths: A comparison of husbands and wives. *Psychology of Religion and Spirituality*, *8*, 164–174. Available from https://doi.org/10.1037/rel0000052.

Krumrei, E. J., Mahoney, A., & Pargament, K. I. (2011). Spiritual stress and coping model of divorce: A longitudinal study of a community sample. *Journal of Family Psychology*, *25*, 973–985. Available from https://doi.org/10.1037/a0025879.

Kusner, K., Mahoney, A., Pargament, K. I., & DeMaris, A. (2014). Sanctification and spiritual intimacy predicting observed marital interactions across the transition to parenthood. *Journal of Family Psychology*, *28*, 604–614. Available from https://doi.org/10.1037/a0036989.

Landor, A., Simons, L. G., Simons, R. L., Brody, G. H., & Gibbons, F. X. (2011). The role of religiosity in the relationship between parents, peers, and adolescent risky sexual behavior. *Journal of Youth and Adolescence*, *40*, 296–309. Available from https://doi.org/10.1007/s10964-010-9598-2.

Li, S. D. (2013). Familial religiosity, family processes, and juvenile delinquency in a national sample of early adolescents. *The Journal of Early Adolescence*, *34*, 436–462. Available from https://doi.org/10.1177/0272431613495445.

Mahoney, A. (2010). Religion in families 1999–2009: A relational spirituality framework. *Journal of Marriage and Family*, *72*, 805–827. Available from https://doi.org/10.1111/j.1741-3737.2010.00732.x.

Mahoney, A. (2013). The spirituality of us: Relational spirituality in the context of family relationships. In K. Pargament, J. J. Exline, & J. Jones (Eds.), *APA handbook of psychology, religion, and spirituality* (Vol. 1, pp. 365–389). Washington, DC: American Psychological Association. Available from https://doi.org/10.1037/14045-020.

Mahoney, A., & Boyatzis, C. J. (2019). Parenting, religion, and spirituality. In M. Bornstein (Ed.), *Handbook of Parenting* (3rd ed.). New York: Routledge.

Mahoney, A., LeRoy, M., Kusner, K., Padgett, E., & Grimes, L. (2013). Addressing parental spirituality as part of the problem and solution in family psychotherapy.

In D. F. Walker, & W. Hathaway (Eds.), *Spiritual interventions in child and adolescent psychotherapy* (pp. 65–88). Washington, DC: American Psychological Association.

Mahoney, A., Pargament, K. I., Jewell, T., Swank, A. B., Scott, E., Emery, E., & Rye, M. (1999). Marriage and the spiritual realm: The role of proximal and distal religious constructs in marital functioning. *Journal of Family Psychology, 13*, 321–338. Available from https://doi.org/10.1037/0893-3200.13.3.321.

Mahoney, A., Pargament, K. I., Swank, A., & Tarakeshwar, N. (2001). Religion in the home in the 1980s and 90s: A meta-analytic review and conceptual analysis of religion, marriage, and parenting. *Journal of Family Psychology, 15*, 559–596. Available from https://doi.org/10.1037/0893-3200.15.4.559.

McQuillan, J., Greil, A. L., Shreffler, K. M., & Bedrous, A. V. (2015). The importance of motherhood and fertility intentions among U.S. women. *Sociological Perspectives, 58*, 20–35. Available from https://doi.org/10.1177/0731121414534393.

Miller-Perrin, C., & Perrin, R. (2017a). Changing attitudes about spanking among conservative Christians using interventions that focus on empirical research evidence and progressive biblical interpretations. *Child Abuse & Neglect, 71*, 69–79. Available from https://doi.org/10.1016/j.chiabu.2017.03.015.

Miller-Perrin, C. & Perrin, R. (2017b). Changing attitudes using alternative biblical interpretations. In *Paper presented at the 22nd international summit on violence, abuse and trauma*. La Jolla, CA.

National Center for Family and Marriage Research (2017). 2011–2013 National survey of family growth religiosity and family structure. Personal communication.

Nelson, J. J., & Uecker, J. E. (2017). Are religious parents more satisfied parents? Individual-and couple-level religious correlates of parenting satisfaction. *Journal of Family Issues, 39*, 1770–1796. Available from https://doi.org/10.1177/0192513x17728983.

Onedera, J. D. (Ed.), (2008). *The role of religion in marriage and family counseling*. New York: Routledge.

Padgett, E., Annette Mahoney, A., Pargament, K. I., & DeMaris, A. (2019). Marital sanctification and spiritual intimacy predicting married couples' observed intimacy skills across the transition to parenthood. *Religions, 10*, 177–193. Available from https://doi.org/10.3390/rel10030177.

Page, R. L., Ellison, C. G., & Lee, J. (2009). Does religiosity affect health risk behaviors in pregnant and postpartum women? *Maternal and Child Health Journal, 13*, 621–632. Available from https://doi.org/10.1007/s10995-008-0394-5.

Pandya, S. P. (2018). Spirituality to build resilience in primary caregiver parents of children with autism spectrum disorders: A cross-country experiment. *International Journal of Developmental Disabilities, 64*, 53–64. Available from https://doi.org/10.1080/20473869.2016.1222722.

Pandya, S. P. (2019). Spiritual education programme for primary caregiver parents to build resilience in children with acute anxiety symptoms: A multicity study. *Child & Family Social Work, 24*, 309–320. Available from https://doi.org/10.1111/CFS.12616.

Pargament, K. I. (2007). *Spiritually integrated psychotherapy: Understanding and addressing the sacred*. New York: Guilford Press.

Pargament, K. I., & Mahoney, A. (2005). Sacred matters: Sanctification as vital topic for the psychology of religion. *The International Journal of the Psychology of Religion, 15*, 179–198. Available from https://doi.org/10.1207/s15327582ijpr1503_1.

Pargament, K. I., & Mahoney, A. (2017). Spirituality: The search for the sacred. In S. J. Lopez, & C. R. Snyder (Eds.), *Oxford handbook of positive psychology* (3rd ed.). Online Publication Date: Feb 2017. <https://doi.org/10.1093/oxfordhb/9780199396511.013.5>.

Perry, S. L., & Snawder, K. J. (2017). Pornography, religion, and parent–child relationship quality. *Archives of Sexual Behavior*, *46*, 1747–1761. Available from https://doi.org/10.1007/s10508-016-0927-8.

Petts, R. J. (2012). Single mothers' religious participation and early childhood behavior. *Journal of Marriage and Family*, *74*, 251–268. Available from https://doi.org/10.1111/j.1741-3737.2011.00953.x.

Petts, R. J., & Kysar-Moon, A. E. (2012). Child discipline and conservative Protestantism: Why the relationship between corporal punishment and child behavior problems may vary by religious context. *Review of Religious Research*, *54*, 445–468. Available from https://doi.org/10.1007/s13644-012-0080-3.

Phillips, R. E., Kalp, D., Lucci, M., Maccarelli, A., Avant, S., Cenkner, D., & Herndon, R. (2017). Initial validation of measures of sanctification in same-sex romantic relationships and sexual behavior. *Journal for the Scientific Study of Religion*, *56*, 836–851. Available from https://doi.org/10.1111/jssr.12488.

Rauer, A., & Volling, B. (2015). The role of relational spirituality in happily-married couples' observed problem-solving. *Psychology of Religion and Spirituality*, *7*, 239–249.

Ripley, J. S., Leon, C., Worthington, E. L., Jr., Berry, J. W., Davis, E. B., Smith, A., ... Sierra, T. (2014). Efficacy of religion-accommodative strategic hope focused theory applied to couples therapy. *Couple & Family Psychology: Research and Practice*, *3*, 83–98. Available from https://doi.org/10.1037/cfp0000019.

Ripley, J. S., & Worthington, E. L. (2014). *Couple therapy: A new hope-focused approach*. Downers Grove, IL: InterVarsity Press.

Rusu, P. P., Hilpert, P., Beach, S. R. H., Turliuc, M. N., & Bodenmann, G. (2015). Dyadic coping mediates the association of sanctification with marital satisfaction and well-being. *Journal of Family Psychology*, *29*, 843–849. Available from https://doi.org/10.1037/fam0000108.

Sabey, A. K., Rauer, A. J., & Jensen, J. F. (2014). Compassionate love as a mechanism linking sacred qualities of marriage to older couples' marital satisfaction. *Journal of Family Psychology*, *28*, 594–603.

Stokes, C. E., & Regnerus, M. D. (2009). When faith divides family: Religious discord and adolescent reports of parent–child relations. *Social Science Research*, *38*, 155–167. Available from https://doi.org/10.1016/j.ssresearch.2008.05.002.

Tarakeshwar, N., & Pargament, K. I. (2001). Religious coping in families of children with autism. *Focus on Autism and Other Developmental Disabilities*, *16*, 247–260. Available from https://doi.org/10.1177/108835760101600408.

Volling, B. L., Mahoney, A., & Rauer, A. J. (2009). Sanctification of parenting, moral socialization, and young children's conscience development. *Psychology of Religion and Spirituality*, *1*, 53–68. Available from https://doi.org/10.1037/a0014958.

Walker, D. F., & Hathaway, W. (2013). *Spiritual interventions in child and adolescent psychotherapy*. Washington, DC: American Psychological Association Press.

Walsh, F. (2009). *Spiritual resources in family therapy* (2nd ed.). New York: Guilford Press.

Weyand, C., O'Laughlin, L., & Bennett, P. (2013). Dimensions of religiousness that influence parenting. *Psychology of Religion and Spirituality*, *5*, 182–191. Available from https://doi.org/10.1037/a0030627.

Yonker, J. E., Schnabelrauch, C. A., & DeHaan, L. G. (2012). The relationship between spirituality and religiosity on psychological outcomes in adolescents and emerging adults: A meta-analytic review. *Journal of Adolescence*, *35*, 299–314. Available from https://doi.org/10.1016/j.adolescence.2011.08.010.

CHAPTER 10

Spirituality/religion and pain

Christina Rush, Kaitlyn Vagnini and Amy Wachholtz
Department of Psychology, University of Colorado Denver, Denver, CO, United States

Contents

Introduction

The United States is in the midst of an opioid epidemic. An estimated 21%–29% of patients prescribed opioids for chronic pain misuse them, and in 2015, more than 33,000 Americans died as a result of an opioid overdose (National Institute on Drug Abuse, 2018). In response, the US Department of Health and Human Services and the National Institutes of Health have declared five priorities, including "advancing better practices for pain management" (National Institute on Drug Abuse, 2018). Nonpharmacological interventions for pain could possibly provide alternative or integrative approaches to pain management with fewer risks.

This chapter explores the role of spirituality/religion (S/R) in the management of pain, including chronic pain, arthritis, fibromyalgia, migraines, and pain related to select medical conditions. The role of S/R for cancer and end-of-life pain is discussed elsewhere in this book (see Chapter 11: Spirituality/religion and end-of-life care). First, we review the existing empirical evidence for S/R and pain, as well as limitations of

Handbook of Spirituality, Religion, and Mental Health
DOI: https://doi.org/10.1016/B978-0-12-816766-3.00010-0

current research and future directions. Next, we consider theory behind the relationship between S/R and pain, as well as mechanisms that explain the role the S/R plays in pain. Lastly, we review clinical considerations and applications of S/R in the treatment of pain.

Current empirical evidence: spirituality/religion and pain

Overview of spirituality/religion associations and pain outcomes

S/R is associated with pain outcomes that, at turns, agree and conflict. In a review of the S/R and pain literature, S/R in pain populations has been linked to meaning and purpose, self-efficacy, coping techniques such as prayer, social support, relaxation (and associated physiological changes), and feeling loved (Wachholtz, Pearce, & Koenig, 2007). Literature also indicates that S/R may be related to increased pain acceptance, happiness, and decreased guilt/worry (Glover-Graf, Marini, Baker, & Buck, 2007). Additionally, spirituality versus religion may differentially associate with pain outcomes (Baetz & Bowen, 2008), and demographic and cultural variables also appear to affect the relationship between S/R and pain outcomes (e.g., Defrin, Eli, & Pud, 2011). Furthermore, S/R is associated linearly as well as nonlinearly with outcomes in several medical populations experiencing pain (Harrison et al., 2005; O'Connell-Edwards et al., 2009; Taheri Kharame, Zamanian, Foroozanfar, & Afsahi, 2014). Taken together, these results suggest that S/R plays multiple roles in pain outcomes and that further exploration of mechanisms, timelines, and moderators of S/R effects is warranted to better understand the complex relationships between S/R and pain.

The "active ingredients" of spirituality/religion for pain

There is a reasonable body of research exploring the "active ingredients" of S/R that affect the perception of pain, that is, research that examines how different S/R components and approaches influence pain outcomes. Religious attendance, connection with religious figures (e.g., guardian angels, saints, God), forgiveness, prayer, meditation, and coping strategies may each affect the pain experience.

Religious attendance

Baetz and Bowen (2008) found that frequent religious attendance was linked to less chronic pain, but the directionality of this association is unclear (i.e., do frequent attenders have less pain, or does their attendance reduce pain?). However, among 219 older Taiwanese chronic pain patients, people who described themselves as "religious" tended to experience pain more frequently than those who were not religious ($\chi^2 = 7.00$, $P = .008$). The authors propose that religiosity can be a possible indicator of pain among older Taiwanese (Yu, Tang, Kuo, & Yu, 2006) due to the relationship between Buddhism and pain conceptualization, including the need to accept and embrace pain rather than avoid it.

In a longitudinal study among a Nordic population based in Norway, Sweden, Finland, and Denmark ($N = 25{,}177$), headache at baseline increased the odds of frequent religious attendance 11 years later (Tronvik et al., 2014). The authors conclude that those with headaches may be more likely to attend religious services frequently to cope and acknowledge that other factors could be involved, such as personality traits, genetic susceptibility, or other factors.

Connection with religious figures

Throughout history, people have turned to religious figures at times of suffering. Several studies indicate that connection with S/R figures is a possible response to pain. In a sample of 576 German chronic disease patients (75% with chronic pain), over half of patients (56%) thought of S/R imagery of guardian angels, including 38% of participants who denied religious or spiritual beliefs. This suggests that S/R is viewed by chronic pain patients as a coping resource that is not necessarily contingent on holding specific S/R beliefs (Büssing, Reiser, Michalsen, Zahn, & Baumann, 2015). Future work should explore the effectiveness of guardian angel imagery for pain management.

Wiech and colleagues (2009) explored the role of contemplating a religious figure versus not doing so (control) in religious and nonreligious groups. Results indicated that processing the religious image enabled the religious group to detach from their experience of pain, suggesting that connection to salient religious figures can modify one's experience of pain.

Furthermore, in a sample of 136 chronic pain patients, one's emotional experience of God had an influence on happiness both directly and indirectly through the pathway of positive disease interpretation. Positive God Image (having a positive image and emotional connection to God) was linked to better outcomes. Positive interpretation of disease mediated the relationship between positive God Image and happiness, irrespective of pain severity (Dezutter et al., 2010). Results suggest that connection with

God enables cognitive reframing to foster positive emotional states in persons experiencing pain.

Finally, in a study of 141 southern Appalachian physical therapy patients, feeling forgiven by God predicted better health-related social functioning whereas forgiveness of one's self predicted better overall health status. The authors concluded that forgiveness-based interventions may be useful in the context of rehabilitation (Svalina & Webb, 2012).

Considering these findings, it seems that a healthy, positive relationship and emotional connection to S/R figures and images can minimize the experience of pain as well as bolster the ability to cope and experience happiness, even in the presence of pain. Perhaps perceiving the presence of a loving, sacred, powerful being provides the person in pain with a sense of safety and hope in the midst of suffering and may support the ability to transcend suffering.

Prayer

Prayer is another common S/R strategy when faced with difficulties and can be linked to beneficial outcomes for pain. In a large national sample assessed in both 2001 and 2007, analyses indicated that the use of prayer to cope with health concerns increased during the 6-year period between 2001 and 2007, suggesting that prayer is becoming an increasingly more common source of coping with medical concerns (Wachholtz & Sambamoorthi, 2011). Similarly, in a review, Moreira-Almeida and Koenig (2008) found that there are sometimes associations between petitionary prayer and higher pain, which the authors suggest is because people use prayer to ask for help when pain increases. Given that people turn to prayer in the face of difficult medical concerns, several studies highlight the role of prayer for pain.

Among 202 Flemish chronic pain patients, prayer was related to pain tolerance, but not pain severity. Prayer appears to be more useful for religious than nonreligious pain patients in predicting pain severity and pain tolerance. This suggests that prayer needs to be meaningful to the patient to be a tool for pain management. Cognitive positive reappraisals have been shown to mediate the relationship between prayer and pain tolerance (Dezutter, Wachholtz, & Corveleyn, 2011).

In an Iranian study of the effects of prayer on migraine headache, 92 patients were randomized to receive either 40 mg of propranolol twice a day for 2 months or 40 mg of propranolol twice a day for 2 months plus prayer. At the beginning of the study and 3 months after intervention, patients' pain was measured using the visual analog scale. It was found that pain was significantly reduced in both groups at follow-up, but pain was significantly lower in the prayer group compared to the propranolol-only group (Tajadini et al., 2017).

These studies suggest that prayer can be used for coping with pain and is perhaps especially helpful when used in the context of a person's S/R beliefs. That is, prayer may be most effective if it is an approach that is embedded within one's broader beliefs and worldviews, as some people believe that prayer can help and is a way to seek solace with God, while others do not. Finally, petitionary prayer may be especially relevant and sought by those who are in the most acute pain, suggesting that asking for help is a favored course of action for those who have greater need.

Meditation

Meditation is yet another common approach both in S/R as well as secular contexts for mastery in the face of difficulty. As such, meditation has been studied for its effects on the experience of migraine pain. In a study examining the effects of a single exposure to meditation on migraine patients ($N = 27$), meditation significantly reduced migraine pain and emotional tension (Tonelli & Wachholtz, 2014).

In another meditation study of migraine sufferers, compared to three other groups (internally focused secular meditation, externally focused secular meditation, and progressive muscle relaxation), those who practiced spiritual meditation had greater decreases in the frequency of migraine headaches, anxiety, and negative affect, as well as greater increases in pain tolerance, headache-related self-efficacy, daily spiritual experiences, and existential well-being (Wachholtz & Pargament, 2008).

In a more recent study of the effects of meditation practice on migraine medication usage, results showed that migraine frequency decreased in the spiritual meditation group compared to other types of meditation groups. Headache severity ratings did not differ across groups. After adjusting for headache frequency, migraine medication use decreased in the spiritual meditation group compared to other groups. Spiritual meditation did not affect pain sensitivity, but it was associated with reduced headache-related analgesic medication use, which suggests an increase in pain tolerance (Wachholtz, Malone, & Pargament, 2017).

These findings suggest that meditation in various forms can benefit those suffering from migraines. However, spiritual meditation seems to be particularly potent for addressing migraine frequency, pain tolerance, and pain medication use, as well as coexisting psychological states such as anxiety, negative affect, and self-efficacy. Spiritual meditation may have the strongest effects due to fostering a sense of connection with a greater being and/or purpose, which could help migraineurs feel supported to transcend the pain experience. These possible mechanisms of action of spiritual meditation could be useful targets for future research.

Spirituality/religion coping styles

There is literature linking S/R coping styles to pain-related outcomes. Pargament et al. (1988) identified three forms of S/R coping. "Collaborative" coping involves sharing responsibility for one's own health with a higher power (e.g., "God and I are in this together. God will do his part and I'll do mine"). "Deferred" coping involves deferring responsibility of one's own health to his or her higher power (e.g., "It's all in God's hands and out of my control"). "Self-Directed" coping does not involve a higher power at all (e.g., "I will take care of this myself. I don't believe in God"). In addition, Phillips, Pargament, Lynn, and Crossley (2004) identified a fourth form of coping, "Abandoned," in which an individual feels fully responsible for his or her health because he or she has been abandoned or punished by God (e.g., "I'm on my own because God has abandoned me").

Empirical research regarding these four S/R coping styles has generally revealed the Collaborative form of coping to be associated with better mental and physical health outcomes compared to the others (Hathaway & Pargament, 1990; Pargament et al., 1988; Pargament, Smith, Koenig, & Perez, 1998). Findings are typically mixed regarding the Self-Directed coping approach, whereas the Abandoned coping style is most often associated with strong negative outcomes (Phillips et al., 2004). The Deferred approach tends to be associated with negative outcomes (Abraído-Lanza, Vásquez, & Echeverría, 2004; McLaughlin et al., 2013; Pargament et al., 1998).

Other methods of categorizing S/R strategies have been used in the literature, including problem-based versus emotion-based, and positive versus negative (for a review, see Wachholtz & Pearce, 2009). In a meta-synthesis qualitative summary of spiritual well-being in patients with rheumatoid arthritis, four adaptive coping themes emerged across ten studies: (1) living with the disease, (2) reclaiming control, (3) reframing the situation, and (4) bolstering courage (Lin, Gau, Lin, & Lin, 2011). In a cross-sectional study of 590 fibromyalgia patients, researchers found that problem-focused coping and social support mediate the relationship between spirituality and quality of life (Biccheri, Roussiau, & Mambet-Doue, 2016). Furthermore, in a sample of 200 Latinos with arthritis, religious coping was related to active coping. Active coping in this sample was mediated by acceptance of illness and self-efficacy, which predicted lower pain, lower depression, and greater psychological well-being. In another study, religious coping was directly related to greater psychological well-being (Abraído-Lanza et al., 2004). Finally, among a sample of Polish rheumatoid arthritis patients ($N = 250$), stress coping strategies (return to religion, acceptance), spirituality, and social support (need for support) were significantly and positively related to posttraumatic growth among participants (Rzeszutek, Oniszczenko, & Kwiatkowska, 2017).

It is important to acknowledge that S/R beliefs can be linked to maladaptive coping. In a review of research on S/R for pain, Unruh (2007) reviewed four possible misconceptions originally described by Koenig (2003), including: (1) belief that one should refuse medication; (2) belief that pain should be dealt with spiritually, and taking medication is going against God; (3) belief that pain is a path to spiritual growth and should not be relieved; and (4) belief that persistent pain is a sign of weak faith. Clinical implications for dealing with such misconceptions include respectful communication with patients about spirituality and pain, inclusion of spirituality in education and support programs, integration of spiritual preferences in pain management where feasible, consultation with pastoral care teams, and reflection by providers about spirituality in their own lives. These results suggest that S/R can edify patients against the burden of pain if S/R views are navigated respectfully and compassionately. Collectively, these findings indicate that in addition to assessing for the presence or absence of S/R coping, it is also important for clinicians to assess the type of S/R coping that patients employ.

Demographic and cultural influences on spirituality/religion and pain

Culture and religious background can influence how pain is experienced and interpreted. A few qualitative and cross-sectional studies explore S/R for pain and suffering in the context of specific cultures. Among 1005 Mexican Americans, attending religious services was associated with searching for the positive in suffering, which, in turn, was associated with a perceived closer relationship with God, more optimism, and better health (Krause & Bastida, 2009).

In a qualitative study of older Christian African Americans and their beliefs about pain, themes included: (1) pain-free indicates good health,

(2) God is the healer, (3) suffer pain in silence, and (4) depression, even if caused by pain, is bad (Booker, 2015). The author highlights that African Americans may face persistent pain and health care disparities, and pharmacological interventions may have differential effects for African Americans. For this population, pain seems to be understood as a challenge to be faced in silence, and negative emotions about pain are not permissible. Booker (2015) recommends that providers utilize spiritual approaches in tandem with pharmacological treatment and cites skilled faith-community nurses as possible appropriate professionals for bridging this gap between biomedicine and spiritual medicine.

In a qualitative study of Dominican patients with advanced osteoarthritis ($N = 20$), participants held strong religious beliefs that offered them strength to cope with chronic arthritis pain and prepare for acute pain following surgery (Yu et al., 2016). Patients exhibited a great deal of trust in others who held positions of authority, expecting God and doctors to cure their pain through surgery. Patients' view of God's role can be monitored to ensure that they are appropriately following self-care recommendations for pain management and recovery from procedures.

A study exploring the interaction among sex, ethnicity, religion, and gender role expectations among 548 participants of Jewish-, Christian-, and Muslim-Arab background found that gender was a stronger predictor of gender role expectations with regard to pain (GREP) than ethno-religious background (Defrin et al., 2011). Across the three groups, men were less willing to report pain and reported less sensitivity to pain. When conducting comparisons on the basis of religious background, Christian-Arabs held the strongest stereotyped views of GREP, that is, greatest expectations between both genders that men would report less pain and less pain sensitivity than women. Thus culture may influence how pain sufferers use S/R to interpret, express, and manage their pain.

These studies show that S/R plays a role in the interpretation and management of pain across various conditions and cultural contexts, and understanding these contexts is critical to understanding the influence and applications of S/R for pain in diverse populations.

Mechanisms: spirituality/religion and pain

Theoretical foundation

One model that provides a framework for understanding the complex interrelationship between S/R and pain is the biopsychosocial model of disease (Engel, 1977). This model emphasizes bidirectional pathways between biological, psychological, and environmental factors with regard to disease and also acknowledges that each of those three domains can positively or negatively affect the other domains. The application of this model to the conceptualization and treatment of pain disorders allows for understanding that individuals may experience pain in the absence of an identifiable pathophysiological etiology. The addition of S/R to the biopsychosocial model (i.e., biopsychosocial-spiritual model) may better reflect emerging evidence that highlights the influence of S/R on pain outcomes.

The gate control/neuromatrix theory of pain (Melzack, 1999; Melzack & Wall, 1965) describes how biological, psychological, and social factors can influence an individual's pain experience via descending pathways from the brain. Rather than conceptualizing the experience of pain as a mere biochemical transmission of a painful stimulus from a specific part of the body to the brain via the spinal cord, this theory acknowledges bidirectionality in the relationship between pain and cognition, emotion, and behavior.

Both the biopsychosocial model and the gate control/neuromatrix theory identify psychosocial variables as potential mediators and moderators of the pain experience. Several psychosocial mediators of pain have been identified, including mood, anxiety, social support, self-efficacy, coping strategies, and meaning-making. Potential pathways linking S/R to pain that are consistent with the biopsychosocial and gate control/neuromatrix models are identified in Fig. 10.1.

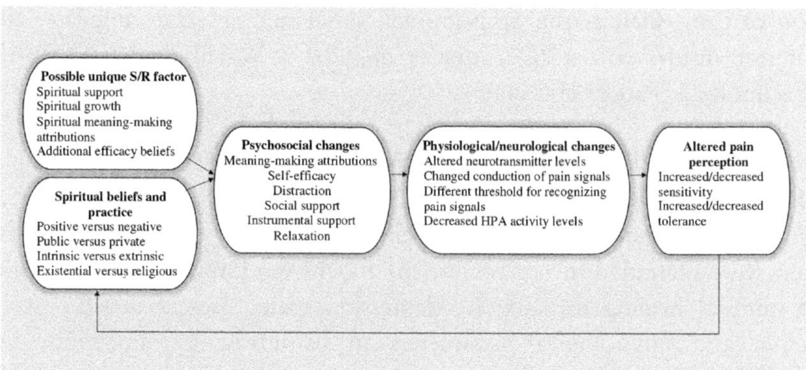

Figure 10.1 Potential pathways between spirituality/religion and pain. *HPA*, Hypothalamus-pituitary-adrenal axis; *S/R*, spirituality/religion. *Adapted from Wachholtz, A. B., Pearce, M. J., & Koenig, H. (2007). Exploring the relationship between spirituality, coping, and pain.* Journal of Behavioral Medicine, 30, *311–318. <https://doi.org/10.1007/s10865-007-9114-7>.*

Neurobiological underpinnings

There are several potential neurobiological pathways through which S/R may affect the experience of pain (Seybold, 2007). Evidence suggests that the density of serotonin receptors in the brain is related to engagement with S/R, raising the possibility that S/R may influence serotonin pathways in the brain that regulate mood and the experience of pain (Borg, Andrée, Soderstrom, & Farde, 2003).

Moreover, several studies have found S/R variables to be related to the modulation of pain via cognition. For example, in a functional magnetic resonance imaging (fMRI) study examining practicing Catholics and avowed atheists and agnostics ($n = 24$), the authors found that only religious participants engaged in a context-dependent form of analgesia that was triggered by the presentation of a religious image (i.e., an image of the Virgin Mary) and was not triggered by the presentation of a secular image (i.e., "Lady with an Ermine" by Leonardo da Vinci) during painful stimulation by engaging the right ventrolateral prefrontal cortex (Wiech et al., 2009).

Using fMRI and psychophysical evaluation of experimental pain, Zeidan et al. (2015) found in a sample of 75 subjects that those randomly assigned to engage in mindfulness meditation experienced less pain intensity ($P = .032$) and pain unpleasantness ($P < .001$) more than those allocated to placebo or sham mindfulness meditation ($P = .030$; $P = .043$). The pain relief associated with mindfulness meditation was related to greater activation in brain regions associated with the cognitive modulation of pain, such as the orbitofrontal, subgenual anterior cingulate, and anterior insular cortex (Dezutter et al., 2011; Wachholtz et al., 2017; Wachholtz & Pargament, 2005).

Available spirituality/religion-based clinical programs/approaches for pain

Only a few studies of S/R-based clinical programs and approaches for pain were identified in our review. In a 2017 randomized controlled trial of spiritual healing for anxiety, depression, pain, muscle tension, well-being, and physiological parameters in cardiovascular inpatients, the authors compared three interventions (spiritual healing, sham, control). Results indicated that spiritual healing was associated with perceived reduced muscle tension, among other beneficial outcomes, compared to sham or no intervention (Carneiro et al., 2017).

Protocols for S/R meditation with demonstrated efficacy for migraine include a 20-minute daily Buddhist "Loving-Kindness"-focused meditation (Tonelli & Wachholtz, 2014) and a 20-minute daily spiritual meditation (e.g., focusing on the phrase "God is good") (Wachholtz et al., 2017; Wachholtz & Pargament, 2008). A similar protocol was tested in healthy college students and revealed that those in the spiritual meditation group tolerated pain almost twice as long as the other two groups (Wachholtz & Pargament, 2005).

Additionally, there are Internet-based support group S/R resources available for chronic pain. To our knowledge, the support programs have not been empirically evaluated (Wachholtz et al., 2011). Of these, only Chronic Pain Anonymous has an S/R framework following a 12-step program for chronic pain (https://chronicpainanonymous.org/). The 12-step programming emphasizes S/R aspects of healing and the importance of social support and fellowship. For people who are facing S/R struggles in response to pain, this program may be particularly salient.

These sources indicate that there is some S/R-based programming available for those seeking to manage their pain. Empirical evidence is sparse (with the exception of spiritual meditation for migraine pain) but promising. As described above, some studies indicate that spiritual approaches are linked to greater pain tolerance, muscle relaxation, positive mood, spiritual health, spiritual experiences, and decreases in anxiety. Nevertheless, few structured clinical S/R pain programs exist, none appear to be routinely offered as the standard of care, and only one support group emphasizes the role of S/R in pain management.

Limitations of current research and future directions

These findings highlight the potential benefit of S/R on pain outcomes, but they also indicate that outcomes can be differentially influenced by spirituality versus religion. One widely identified limitation to S/R research is the heterogeneity of S/R construct definitions. Standardized definitions of these constructs are needed. Moreover, investigators' decision to study spirituality and religion separately or together as one construct (i.e., S/R) should have an empirical and theoretical basis (Park et al., 2017). The studies described here reveal various factors that may underlie the relationship between S/R and pain outcomes, including cultural expectations, gender roles, and individual personality factors. This calls for more precise identification and understanding of the mediators and moderators that may underlie outcomes. More methodologically rigorous studies are also needed in order to facilitate interpretation of findings. Cross-lagged analyses could elucidate whether S/R precedes pain and assists individuals in coping with pain, or whether pain urges individuals to seek S/R or become more spiritual or religious. Park et al. (2017) suggest strengthening the research by using prospective designs, experimental approaches, strong sampling methods, psychometrically robust measures of S/R and health outcomes, appropriate statistical analyses with adequate power for moderator analyses, and controlling for established protective factors.

Clinical considerations and applications: spirituality/religion and pain

Given the powerful impact that S/R can have on the pain experience, it is crucial that providers address S/R when providing care to their patients. It is our hope that in this chapter, you have gained an understanding of the many ways in which S/R can differentially affect patients' experience of pain. Moreover, we hope that by understanding patients from a biopsychosocial-spiritual framework, health care providers will better address the needs of their patients who suffer from acute or chronic pain. We acknowledge that addressing S/R with patients may feel unfamiliar and uncomfortable to many health care providers. Moreover, we recognize that health care providers have important concerns regarding the clinical application of S/R with patients, such as lack of time or training, fear of projecting one's own beliefs, difficulty identifying which patients would desire a conversation about S/R, assuming that patients will find spiritual resources on their own, and the lack of provider S/R beliefs affecting the value that they place on such approaches (Kristeller, Zumbrun, & Schilling, 1999). However, with a guided interview approach and/or appropriate training, those issues do not need to interfere with assessing a patient's need for further S/R-related treatment. This section will provide practical recommendations regarding the clinical application of S/R that we hope will mitigate some of these concerns. We highlight here important clinical considerations that can be noted when considering target outcomes for programming and treatment of patients suffering from pain disorders.

Spirituality/religion clinical application recommendations

Identify spirituality/religion practices and beliefs

Given that the role of S/R for pain is not well understood and S/R practices and beliefs are unique to each individual, it is not possible to "prescribe" a specific S/R approach to help a patient manage pain. Instead, it is more useful to explore with patients their own S/R practices and beliefs and how those may be applicable to their pain experience. What do they find meaningful and helpful? Explore with the patient ways to increase anything that they identify as useful. Refer to the "Active Ingredients" section of this chapter for guidance on specific areas to inquire about with the patient (e.g., religious attendance, S/R social support, attachment to S/R figures, S/R practices such as prayer or meditation, and cultural considerations for the patient's perception and interpretation of pain). If the patient is unsure of their S/R beliefs and desiring to explore their S/R identity, that can be a useful first target of treatment. On the other hand, if the patient is certain that S/R approaches are not applicable to them, it is important to honor this and instead explore other pain management options that are salient to and compatible with the patient's worldviews.

Conduct psychoeducation

As with any form of treatment, it is important to assess the patient's understanding of chronic pain and current psychological pain management interventions. Highlight research findings (in lay terms) to the patient, such as S/R associations with increased well-being and quality of life, as described in the first section of this chapter. It is also important to highlight that the ways that S/R helps with pain are not yet fully understood.

Discuss pain severity versus pain tolerance

Much of the research on S/R and pain suggests that S/R practices have a greater influence on pain tolerance than on pain sensitivity (see Wachholtz & Pearce, 2009, for a review on S/R coping). That is, S/R might not necessarily decrease an individual's perception of pain severity, but can provide the person with internal resources to develop a greater tolerance and management of pain. For example, a patient may say, "My pain is still at a 7, but it doesn't seem to bother me as much as it used to." Thus, it is important to assess patients' expectations of treatment and inform them that although the existence and even intensity of pain may not greatly change, it is possible to target increasing one's tolerance of pain, which can then permit greater focus on expanding other valued areas in life.

Identify spirituality/religion coping strategies

Identify with the patient their current S/R coping style. For example, adaptive S/R coping strategies are an expression of a sense of spirituality, a secure relationship with a benevolent God, a belief that there is meaning in life, and a sense of spiritual connection with others (Pargament et al., 1998). Maladaptive S/R coping strategies are an expression of a less secure relationship with God, a tenuous and pessimistic view of the world, a feeling of punishment, and a religious struggle in the search for significance and can have a significant negative effect on mental and physical health outcomes. Psycho-spiritual therapy to enhance the Collaborative coping style can be encouraged. If the patient tends to use other coping styles, identify with them cognitions around these styles (e.g., "God is punishing me by making me feel pain"). If possible, gently challenge such cognitions and encourage adaptive reframing. Alternatively, refer the patient to professionals who can help them to navigate their S/R struggles. Doing so has implications for your patients' health, well-being, and pain experience, considering the relationship between maladaptive coping and depression, emotional distress, poor physical health, and poor quality of life (Koenig, George, & Titus, 2004; Mickley, Pargament, Brant, & Hipp, 1998; Nooney & Woodrum, 2002; Pargament et al., 1998).

Activate beneficial spirituality/religion mechanisms

Research identifies various mechanisms explaining how S/R beliefs and practices may impact pain outcomes, including mood, social support, self-efficacy, coping, cognitive reappraisal and positive, realistic expectations, meaning-making, and healthy attachment to identified religious figures or images (see Fig. 10.1). Assessing how each of these areas interact with S/R beliefs and practices, may help the provider target beneficial changes in these areas, and identify other providers to include in the patient's care.

Consider cultural and ethical concerns

Culture and S/R-specific factors may play a role in the patient's experience and interpretation of chronic or acute pain and suffering. The provider must consider the patient's cultural and S/R-specific beliefs about his or her pain experience when identifying treatment needs and developing a treatment plan. For example, some faith traditions may lead patients to refuse certain pain medications due to the value that their faith tradition places on maintaining clarity of mind, especially during life-limiting illnesses or injuries. Other faith traditions may lead patients to prolong aggressive and painful medical interventions due to belief in the possibility of a miracle (Wachholtz & Makowski, 2012). It is important to recognize that S/R-specific values, beliefs, and practices can influence a patient's medical decision-making. Moreover, it is just as important to refrain from making generalizations regarding a patient's beliefs, values, practices, and potential decision-making choices based on their faith tradition. Rather, it is essential to understand that just as there is variability in the beliefs and practices of members of different faith traditions, there is also variability in the beliefs and practices within members of the same faith traditions. Each patient's pain experience can be uniquely shaped by his or her S/R and other biological, psychological, and social influences.

Use structured or semistructured spirituality/religion assessment tools as a guide

Inquiring about S/R does not need to be demanding, take a large amount of time, or involve a great deal of training. Assessing S/R in patients can be a brief act, the intent of which is outlined below:

- To support the patient through the experience of chronic or acute pain by listening actively, nonjudgmentally, and empathetically.
- To document the patient's spiritual preferences in order to promote continuity of care.
- To identify potential barriers to pain management by assessing for negative S/R coping.
- To ensure that the patient's S/R preferences are honored in the treatment plan.
- To foster overall wellness by encouraging S/R patients to access their internal and external S/R resources.
- To demonstrate to the patient your interest in their entire clinical picture.
- To assess the S/R needs of patients in order to consult the appropriate professionals.

There are several assessment tools that physicians and other health care providers can use to guide S/R assessment with their patients. It is beyond the scope of this chapter to discuss these tools in great detail; however, we will provide a brief description of the three most prevalent qualitative assessment tools below.

HOPE

The HOPE assessment uses an acronym that guides providers through a four-step spiritual assessment interview (Anandarajah & Hight, 2001). The "H" stands for *H*ope and includes questions about where the patient finds hope, strength, comfort, peace, or feelings of connectedness. The "O" stands for *O*rganized religion and guides the provider in understanding the patient's religious or spiritual affiliation and social support. The "P" stands for *P*ersonal spirituality and practices and may include questions about the use of prayer, meditation, or other practices that may relate to their health issues. The "E" stands for *E*ffects on medical decisions. This allows the provider to identify how a patient's medical care may be affected by his or her S/R beliefs. The HOPE assessment tool can be used to gather information about a patient's S/R beliefs and practices while also identifying the patient's preferences for integrating S/R into their treatment plan. Due to the interview format of this assessment, there are no explicit validation studies for this measure and there are limited empirically validated recommendations based on the results of this S/R assessment (Anandarajah & Hight, 2001).

FICA

Similar to HOPE, this S/R assessment also utilizes an acronym to guide providers through an S/R history-taking process (Puchalski, 2001; Puchalski & Romer, 2000). The "F" stands for *F*aith/beliefs and encourages the provider to use an unstructured statement to elicit patient S/R-related information. The "I" stands for *I*mportance/*I*nfluence and identifies the impact that S/R has on the patient's life. The "C" stands for *C*ommunity and assesses for S/R social support and group S/R practices. The "A" stands for *A*ddress in care and assesses patient preferences for integrating this information into their care. This measure has been validated, demonstrating that FICA quantitative ratings and qualitative comments correlate with items from quality of life tools assessing aspects of S/R (Borneman, Ferrell, & Puchalski, 2010).

OASIS

The OASIS project (Oncologist Assisted Spiritual Intervention Study; Kristeller, Rhodes, Cripe, & Sheets, 2005) is a seven-step S/R semistructured interview that includes (1) introducing the issue in a neutral inquiring manner, (2) inquiring further and adjusting inquiry to patient's initial response, (3) continuing to explore further as indicated, (4) inquiring about ways of finding meaning and a sense of peace, (5) inquiring about resources, (6) offering assistance as appropriate and available, and (7) bringing the inquiry to a close. This is one of the few qualitative S/R assessments that have been empirically validated in both physician and patient populations. Patient receptivity to this assessment was strong; immediately following the assessment and during a series of follow-up assessments, patients never expressed a negative response to the interview, regardless of their endorsement of any S/R beliefs. Moreover, 98% of patients felt that the discussion was at least a little helpful, and patients in the spiritual interview group had greater increases in their satisfaction with the care provided by their physician, compared with those who did not receive the spiritual interview (Kristeller et al., 2005).

Refer patients to appropriate professionals

Physicians and other health professionals are not expected to solve patients' spiritual struggles or meet their spiritual needs by engaging in spiritual counseling. In fact, physicians and other medical health providers should not attempt to provide S/R counseling if they are not trained to do so. However, they are responsible for assessing these needs and consulting with the appropriate professionals to ensure that their patients receive the necessary treatment because S/R may affect their health, pain levels, and opioid consumption. It is important not to assume that patients suffering from S/R-related concerns will self-refer. It is the clinician's responsibility to make referrals to appropriate professionals, just as they would make referrals to psychologists, physical therapists, dieticians, medical specialists, or other treatment providers. We encourage providers to note that most clergy receive minimal training in mental health counseling and no training on health conditions. We therefore recommend referrals to licensed mental health professionals who have training in S/R forms of psychotherapy or chaplains with specific training in health chaplaincy.

Discussion

It should be noted that although complementary, alternative, and integrative medicine (CAIM) bridges S/R and secular beliefs, CAIM approaches were only addressed in this chapter if they were explicitly of an S/R nature (e.g., spiritual meditation). Given the varied approaches and interpretations of CAIM, it was not possible to capture all CAIM research relevant to S/R and pain. In particular, secular CAIM approaches, while a worthy area of exploration, were beyond the scope of this chapter.

Considering the research highlighted here, it is evident that S/R plays a role in the pain experience. If assessed appropriately, applied thoughtfully, and adapted to patient's individual circumstances, a patient's S/R beliefs may be part of a comprehensive treatment plan to facilitate improved pain management. When carefully navigated, S/R approaches may, in some cases, bring increased mastery over pain without any of the deleterious risks associated with opioid medications. More research elucidating approaches to working within the patient's S/R worldview to maximize potential benefits of S/R is needed and more rigorous empirical evaluation of existing S/R pain management programming, such as Chronic Pain Anonymous, could be useful to patients seeking to reconcile their difficult pain experiences with their S/R beliefs. Person-centered approaches, including S/R, may offer safe additive or alternative options for the management of pain. Such considerations should be part of the call to advance better practices for pain management.

References

Abraído-Lanza, A. F., Vásquez, E., & Echeverría, S. E. (2004). En las manos de dios [in God's Hands]: Religious and other forms of coping among Latinos with arthritis. *Journal of Consulting and Clinical Psychology, 72*, 91–102. Available from https://doi.org/10.1037/0022-006X.72.1.91.

Anandarajah, G., & Hight, E. (2001). Spirituality and medical practice: Using the HOPE questions as a practical tool for spiritual assessment. *American Family Physician, 63*, 81–89. Available from https://doi.org/10.1016/S1443-8461(01)80044-7.

Baetz, M., & Bowen, R. (2008). Chronic pain and fatigue: Associations with religion and spirituality. *Pain Research and Management, 13*(5), 383–388.

Biccheri, E., Roussiau, N., & Mambet-Doue, C. (2016). Fibromyalgia, spirituality, coping and quality of life. *Journal of Religion and Health, 55*, 1189–1197. Available from https://doi.org/10.1007/s10943-016-0216-9.

Booker, S. Q. (2015). Older African Americans' beliefs about pain, biomedicine, and spiritual medicine. *Journal of Christian Nursing, 32*, 148–155. Available from https://doi.org/10.1097/CNJ.0000000000000152.

Borg, J., Andrée, B., Soderstrom, H., & Farde, L. (2003). The serotonin system and spiritual experiences. *American Journal of Psychiatry, 160*, 1965–1969. Available from https://doi.org/10.1176/appi.ajp.160.11.1965.

Borneman, T., Ferrell, B., & Puchalski, C. M. (2010). Evaluation of the FICA tool for spiritual assessment. *Journal of Pain and Symptom Management, 40*, 163–173. Available from https://doi.org/10.1016/j.jpainsymman.2009.12.019.

Büssing, A., Reiser, F., Michalsen, A., Zahn, A., & Baumann, K. (2015). Do patients with chronic pain diseases believe in guardian angels: Even in a secular society? A cross-sectional study among german patients with chronic diseases. *Journal of Religion and Health, 54*(1), 76–86. Available from https://doi.org/10.1007/s10943-013-9735-9.

Carneiro, É. M., Barbosa, L. P., Marson, J. M., Terra, J. A., Martins, C. J. P., Modesto, D., ... de Borges, M. F. (2017). Effectiveness of spiritist "passe" (spiritual healing) for anxiety levels, depression, pain, muscle tension, well-being, and physiological parameters in cardiovascular inpatients: A randomized controlled trial. *Complementary Therapies in Medicine*, *30*, 73–78. Available from https://doi.org/10.1016/j.ctim.2016.11.008.

Defrin, R., Eli, I., & Pud, D. (2011). Interactions among sex, ethnicity, religion, and gender role expectations of pain. *Gender Medicine*, *8*, 172–183. Available from https://doi.org/10.1016/j.genm.2011.04.001.

Dezutter, J., Luyckx, K., Schaap-Jonker, H., Büssing, A., Corveleyn, J., & Hutsebaut, D. (2010). God image and happiness in chronic pain patients: The mediating role of disease interpretation. *Pain Medicine*, *11*, 765–773. Available from https://doi.org/10.1111/j.1526-4637.2010.00827.x.

Dezutter, J., Wachholtz, A. B., & Corveleyn, J. (2011). Prayer and pain: The mediating role of positive re-appraisal. *Journal of Behavioral Medicine*, *34*, 542–549. Available from https://doi.org/10.1007/s10865-011-9348-2.

Engel, G. L. (1977). The need for a new medical model: A challenge for biomedicine. *Science (New York, N.Y.)*, *196*, 129–136. Available from https://doi.org/10.1126/science.847460.

Glover-Graf, N. M., Marini, I., Baker, J., & Buck, T. (2007). Religious and spiritual beliefs and practices of persons with chronic pain. *Rehabilitation Counseling Bulletin*, *51*, 21–33. Available from https://doi.org/10.1177/00343552070510010501.

Harrison, M. O., Edwards, C. L., Koenig, H. G., Bosworth, H. B., Decastro, L., & Wood, M. (2005). Religiosity/spirituality and pain in patients with sickle cell disease. *The Journal of Nervous and Mental Disease*, *193*, 250–257. Available from https://doi.org/10.1097/01.nmd.0000158375.73779.50.

Hathaway, W. L., & Pargament, K. I. (1990). Intrinsic religiousness, religious coping, and psychosocial competence: A covariance structure analysis. *Journal for the Scientific Study of religion*, *29*, 423–441.

Koenig, H. G. (2003). Chronic pain: Biomedical and spiritual approaches. Chronic pain: Biomedical and spiritual approaches. New York: Haworth Pastoral Press. Available from https://doi.org/10.4324/9780203048993.

Koenig, H. G., George, L. K., & Titus, P. (2004). Religion, spirituality, and health in medically ill hospitalized older patients. *Journal of the American Geriatrics Society*, *52*, 554–562. Available from https://doi.org/10.1111/j.1532-5415.2004.52161.x.

Krause, N., & Bastida, E. (2009). Religion, suffering, and health among older Mexican Americans. *Journal of Aging Studies*, *23*, 114–123. Available from https://doi.org/10.1016/j.jaging.2008.11.002.

Kristeller, J. L., Rhodes, M., Cripe, L. D., & Sheets, V. (2005). Oncologist assisted spiritual intervention study (OASIS): Patient acceptability and initial evidence of effects. *The International Journal of Psychiatry in Medicine*, *35*, 329–347. Available from https://doi.org/10.2190/8AE4-F01C-60M0-85C8.

Kristeller, J. L., Zumbrun, C. S., & Schilling, R. F. (1999). "I would if I could": How oncologists and oncology nurses address spiritual distress in cancer patients. *Psycho-Oncology*, *8*, 451–458. Available from https://doi.org/10.1002/(SICI)1099-1611(199909/10)8:5<451::AID-PON422>3.0.CO;2-3.

Lin, W. C., Gau, M. L., Lin, H. C., & Lin, H. R. (2011). Spiritual well-being in patients with rheumatoid arthritis. *Journal of Nursing Research*, *19*(1), 1–12.

McLaughlin, B., Yoo, W., D'Angelo, J., Tsang, S., Shaw, B., Shah, D., ... Gustafson, D. (2013). It is out of my hands: How deferring control to God can decrease quality of life for breast cancer patients. *Psycho-Oncology*, *22*, 2747–2754. Available from https://doi.org/10.1002/pon.3356.

Melzack, R. (1999). From the gate to the neuromatrix. *Pain*, *82*, S121–S126. Available from https://doi.org/10.1016/S0304-3959(99)00145-1.

Melzack, R., & Wall, P. D. (1965). Pain mechanisms: A new theory. *Science*, *150*, 971–979. Available from https://doi.org/10.1126/science.150.3699.971.

Mickley, J. R., Pargament, K., Brant, C. R., & Hipp, K. M. (1998). God and the search for meaning among hospice caregivers. *The Hospice Journal*, *13*, 1–17. Available from https://doi.org/10.1300/J011v13n04_01.

Moreira-Almeida, A., & Koenig, H. G. (2008). Religiousness and spirituality in fibromyalgia and chronic pain patients. *Current Pain and Headache Reports*, *12*, 327–332. Available from https://doi.org/10.1007/s11916-008-0055-9.

National Institute on Drug Abuse. (2018). *Opioid overdose crisis*. Retrieved from <https://www.drugabuse.gov/drugs-abuse/opioids/opioid-overdose-crisis>.

Nooney, J., & Woodrum, E. (2002). Religious coping and church-based social support as predictors of mental health outcomes: Testing a conceptual model. *Journal for the Scientific Study of Religion*, *41*, 359–368. Available from https://doi.org/10.1111/1468-5906.00122.

O'Connell-Edwards, C. F., Edwards, C. L., Pearce, M., Wachholtz, A. B., Wood, M., Muhammad, M., ... Robinson, E. (2009). Religious coping and pain associated with sickle cell disease: Exploration of a non-linear model. *Journal of African American Studies*, *13*(1), 1–13.

Pargament, K. I., Kennell, J., Hathaway, W., Grevengoed, N., Newman, J., & Jones, W. (1988). Religion and the problem-solving process: Three styles of coping. *Journal for the Scientific Study of Religion*, *27*, 90–104. Available from https://doi.org/10.2307/1387404.

Pargament, K. I., Smith, B. W., Koenig, H. G., & Perez, L. (1998). Patterns of positive and negative religious coping with major life stressors. *Journal for the Scientific Study of Religion*, *37*, 710–724. Available from https://doi.org/10.2307/1388152.

Park, C. L., Masters, K. S., Salsman, J. M., Wachholtz, A. B., Clements, A. D., Salmoirago-Blotcher, E., ... Wischenka, D. M. (2017). Advancing our understanding of religion and spirituality in the context of behavioral medicine. *Journal of Behavioral Medicine*, *40*, 39–51. Available from https://doi.org/10.1007/s10865-016-9755-5.

Phillips, R. E., Pargament, K. I., Lynn, Q. K., & Crossley, C. D. (2004). Self-directing religious coping: A deistic god, abandoning god, or no god at all? *Journal for the Scientific Study of Religion*, *43*, 409–418. Available from https://doi.org/10.1111/j.1468-5906.2004.00243.x.

Puchalski, C. M. (2001). Spirituality and health: The art of compassionate medicine. *Hospital Physician*, *37*(3), 30–36.

Puchalski, C. M., & Romer, A. L. (2000). Taking a spiritual history allows clinicians to understand patients more fully. *Journal of Palliative Medicine*, *3*(1), 129–137.

Rzeszutek, M., Oniszczenko, W., & Kwiatkowska, B. (2017). Stress coping strategies, spirituality, social support and posttraumatic growth in a Polish sample of rheumatoid arthritis patients. *Psychology, Health and Medicine*, *22*, 1082–1088. Available from https://doi.org/10.1080/13548506.2017.1280174.

Seybold, K. S. (2007). Physiological mechanisms involved in religiosity/spirituality and health. *Journal of Behavioral Medicine*, *30*, 303–309. Available from https://doi.org/10.1007/s10865-007-9115-6.

Svalina, S. S., & Webb, J. R. (2012). Forgiveness and health among people in outpatient physical therapy. *Disability and Rehabilitation*, *34*(5), 383–392.

Taheri Kharame, Z., Zamanian, H., Foroozanfar, S., & Afsahi, S. (2014). Religious well-being as a predictor for quality of life in Iranian hemodialysis patients. *Global Journal of Health Science*, *6*, 261–269. Available from https://doi.org/10.5539/gjhs.v6n4p261.

Tajadini, H., Zangiabadi, N., Divsalar, K., Safizadeh, H., Esmaili, Z., & Rafiei, H. (2017). Effect of prayer on intensity of migraine headache: A randomized clinical trial. *Journal of Evidence-Based Complementary and Alternative Medicine*, *22*, 37–40. Available from https://doi.org/10.1177/2156587215627551.

Tonelli, M. E., & Wachholtz, A. B. (2014). Meditation-based treatment yielding immediate relief for meditation-naïve migraineurs. *Pain Management Nursing, 15*, 36–40. Available from https://doi.org/10.1016/j.pmn.2012.04.002.

Tronvik, E., Sørensen, T., Linde, M., Bendtsen, L., Artto, V., Laurell, K., ... Hagen, K. (2014). The relationship between headache and religious attendance (the Nord-Trøndelag health study- HUNT). *Journal of Headache and Pain, 15*, 1. Available from https://doi.org/10.1186/1129-2377-15-1.

Unruh, A. M. (2007). Spirituality, religion, and pain. *Canadian Journal of Nursing Research, 39*(2), 66–86.

Wachholtz, A. B., Gonzalez., Boyer., Naqvi., Rosenbaum., & Ziedonis. (2011). Intersection of chronic pain treatment and opioid analgesic misuse: Causes, treatments, and policy strategies. *Substance Abuse and Rehabilitation, 2*, 145–162. Available from https://doi.org/10.2147/SAR.S12944.

Wachholtz, A. B., & Makowski, S. (2012). Spiritual dimensions of pain and suffering. In R. Moore (Ed.), *Handbook of pain and palliative care: Biobehavioral approaches for the life course* (pp. 697–713). New York: Springer. Available from https://doi.org/10.1007/978-1-4419-1651-8_36.

Wachholtz, A. B., Malone, C. D., & Pargament, K. I. (2017). Effect of different meditation types on migraine headache medication use. *Behavioral Medicine, 43*, 1–8. Available from https://doi.org/10.1080/08964289.2015.1024601.

Wachholtz, A. B., & Pargament, K. I. (2005). Is spirituality a critical ingredient of meditation? Comparing the effects of spiritual meditation, secular meditation, and relaxation on spiritual, psychological, cardiac, and pain outcomes. *Journal of Behavioral Medicine, 28*, 369–384. Available from https://doi.org/10.1007/s10865-005-9008-5.

Wachholtz, A. B., & Pargament, K. I. (2008). Migraines and meditation: Does spirituality matter? *Journal of Behavioral Medicine, 31*, 351–366. Available from https://doi.org/10.1007/s10865-008-9159-2.

Wachholtz, A. B., & Pearce, M. J. (2009). Does spirituality as a coping mechanism help or hinder coping with chronic pain? *Current Pain and Headache Reports, 13*, 127–132. Available from https://doi.org/10.1007/s11916-009-0022-0.

Wachholtz, A. B., Pearce, M. J., & Koenig, H. (2007). Exploring the relationship between spirituality, coping, and pain. *Journal of Behavioral Medicine, 30*, 311–318. Available from https://doi.org/10.1007/s10865-007-9114-7.

Wachholtz, A. B., & Sambamoorthi, U. (2011). National trends in prayer use as a coping mechanism for heath concerns: Changes from 2002 to 2007. *Psychology of Religion and Spirituality, 3*(2), 67–77.

Wiech, K., Farias, M., Kahane, G., Shackel, N., Tiede, W., & Tracey, I. (2009). An fMRI study measuring analgesia enhanced by religion as a belief system. *Pain, 139*, 467–476. Available from https://doi.org/10.1016/j.pain.2008.07.030.

Yu, A., Devine, C. A., Kasdin, R. G., Orizondo, M., Perdomo, W., Davis, A. M., ... Katz, J. N. (2016). Pain management among Dominican patients with advanced osteoarthritis: A qualitative study. *BMC Musculoskeletal Disorders, 17*, 211. Available from https://doi.org/10.1186/s12891-016-1075-y.

Yu, H. Y., Tang, F. I., Kuo, B. I. T., & Yu, S. (2006). Prevalence, interference, and risk factors for chronic pain among taiwanese community older people. *Pain Management Nursing, 7*, 2–11. Available from https://doi.org/10.1016/j.pmn.2005.12.002.

Zeidan, F., Emerson, N. M., Farris, S. R., Ray, J. N., Jung, Y., McHaffie, J. G., & Coghill, R. C. (2015). Mindfulness meditation-based pain relief employs different neural mechanisms than placebo and sham mindfulness meditation-induced analgesia. *Journal of Neuroscience, 35*, 15307–15325. Available from https://doi.org/10.1523/JNEUROSCI.2542-15.2015.

CHAPTER 11

Spirituality/religion and end-of-life care

John Peteet
Department of Psychaitry, Harvard Medical School, Boston, MA, United States

Contents

Introduction

The relevance of spirituality/religion (S/R) for medicine is nowhere clearer than in the care of seriously ill and dying patients. In this chapter, we explore the place of S/R in life-threatening illness and end-of-life (EOL) care and examine clinical approaches to the diagnosis and treatment of these patients' existential distress and related disorders, using a case example of spiritually informed treatment. We conclude by noting the ethical, educational, and research challenges involved in dealing with S/R at the EOL. Life-threatening illness raises existential questions for which many individuals seek spiritual/religious answers. These questions concern identity (What most defines me?), hope (What is the ultimate basis of my hope?), meaning/purpose (Are my goals still valuable? What is the meaning of my life?), morality (Do I need to forgive or be forgiven?), and connection (Am I ultimately alone?).

Research on spirituality/religion at the end of life

Recent research has helped to clarify the importance of S/R to seriously ill patients, spiritual needs of patients at the EOL, what kinds of spiritual

Handbook of Spirituality, Religion, and Mental Health
DOI: https://doi.org/10.1016/B978-0-12-816766-3.00011-2

care they want and receive, what impact their S/R concerns have on their quality of life (QOL) and treatment decisions, and what impact spiritual care has on outcomes.

The *Coping with Cancer* study is a prospective, multiinstitutional interview study of patients with advanced cancer designed to investigate how psychosocial factors, including spiritual care, influence patients' EOL care and QOL near death. In this study, Balboni, Vanderwerker, and Block (2007) found that (88%) of participants ($N=230$) considered religion to be at least somewhat important. However, 47% reported that their spiritual needs were minimally or not at all supported by a religious community, and 72% reported that their spiritual needs were supported minimally or not at all by the medical system. In a subsequent study of 68 randomly selected advanced cancer patients, Alcorn et al. (2010) found that S/R was important to the cancer experience in 78% of patients and identified five principal themes ($N=53$) (Table 11.1).

S/R has also been linked to patients' QOL. Steinhauser et al. (2000) found in a national survey of 1885 seriously ill patients that of 44 attributes of QOL near death, being at peace with God was ranked second in importance to freedom from pain.

With respect to decision-making, Silvestri, Knittig, Zoller, and Nietert (2003) found that when 100 patients with advanced lung cancer, their caregivers, and 257 medical oncologists were asked to rank factors they felt important to patients when making treatment decisions, S/R was ranked second by patients/families (after oncologists' treatment recommendations), but seventh (last) by physicians. Going further to explore the role of patient spirituality and medical decision-making, Phelps et al. (2009) described a significant and unexpected relationship between religious coping and receipt of aggressive medical care at the EOL. While religious patients might have been expected to be more accepting of terminal illness and prepared for death, instead they were found they were more likely to want aggressive care at the EOL. Focusing on the role of spiritual support, Balboni, Balboni, et al. (2013), Balboni, Paulk, and Balboni (2010), and Balboni, Sullivan, et al. (2013) found that high spiritual support from the medical team was associated with greater use of hospice, less aggressive interventions, and fewer ICU deaths. The impact of spiritual support on EOL care was largely seen in patients who scored high on religious coping. By contrast, high spiritual support from patients' religious communities was associated with less hospice use, more aggressive interventions, and more ICU deaths. These findings were stronger

Table 11.1 Qualitatively grounded religious/spiritual themes in patients' experiences of advanced cancer ($n = 53$).

Theme	*n* (%)	Representative quote
Coping through S/R	39 (74)	*I don't know if I will survive this cancer, but without God it is hard to stay sane sometimes. For me, religion and spirituality keeps me going.*
S/R practices	31 (58)	*I pray a lot. It helps. You find yourself praying an awful lot. Not for myself, but for those you leave behind. There will be a lot more praying.*
S/R beliefs	28 (53)	*It is God's will, not my will. My job is to do what I can to stay healthy—eat right, think positively, get to appointments on time, and also to do what I can to become healthy again like make sure that I have the best doctors to take care of me. After this, it is up to God.*
S/R transformation	20 (38)	*Since I have an incurable disease that will shorten my life, it has made me focus on issues of mortality and sharpened my curiosity on religion/spirituality and what the various traditions have to say about that. I've spent a lot of time thinking about those issues, and it has enriched my psychological, intellectual, and spiritual experience of this time.*
S/R community	11 (21)	*Well, I depend a lot upon my faith community for support. It's proven incredibly helpful for me.*

among racial/ethnic minority groups and patients scoring high on religious coping, suggesting that religious beliefs about EOL medical care are significantly more common among racial/ethnic minority patients, are related to greater preference for aggressive EOL medical care, and may be an important factor in understanding the relationship between race and greater aggressive care at life's end.

In an effort to better understand the contributions of community clergy to this process, investigators in the *National Clergy Project on End-of-Life Care* conducted a cross-sectional study of a random sample of US community clergy designed to measure the prevalence of clergy beliefs and practices concerning EOL care (Balboni et al., 2017). The study found that clergy hold a number of religious values related to patients' medical considerations at the EOL: a majority of clergy reported belief in a divine miracle in the face of a terminal diagnosis and in the sanctity of life requiring pursuit of all means to stay alive. Just over a quarter of clergy endorsed at least some belief that faith justifies deferring future medical decisions and that divine testing supports endurance of painful EOL medical procedures. These life-prolonging religious values were more prevalent among religious leaders who were black, evangelical, Pentecostal, and those serving lower-income congregations. The study also found that clergy actively engage in conversations (92%) with dying congregants about medical decisions, including discussions about hospice, do not resuscitate orders, pain medications, and stopping or foregoing treatment. Clergy who were more likely to endorse life-prolonging religious values were both more likely to agree that doctors should always extend life and less likely to report having an EOL conversation with a dying congregant. The lack of a clergy-congregant hospice discussion significantly reduced the odds of receiving hospice care and increased odds of receiving ICU care in the last week of life. These data suggest that clergy play a role in how some congregants approach EOL medical decisions and that there is a need for the medical community to engage and partner with community religious leaders in EOL care.

Spiritual needs of advanced cancer patients, defined as both distressing spiritual struggles and spiritual seeking (e.g., thinking about what gives meaning to life, seeking forgiveness, etc.), were found by Winkelman, Lauderdale, and Balboni (2011) in 86% and by Pearce, Coan, Herndon, Koenig, and Abernethy (2012) in 91% of patients studied. Unmet spiritual needs in a number of studies, including negative religious coping (e.g., anger at God) (Tarakeshwar et al., 2006), have been associated with lower QOL (Astrow, Wexler, Texeira, He, & Sulmasy, 2007; Kang, Shin, & Choi, 2012; Winkelman et al., 2011) and poorer psychological adjustment (Pearce et al., 2012). A challenge in such research is to distinguish the role of psychological and spiritual/religious factors. For example, is a patient struggling to believe in God because s/he is depressed, or depressed because of a crisis in belief? Is this spiritual struggle or its associated psychological distress more important in influencing QOL?

A majority of patients, when asked, say that they consider attention to spiritual concerns an important part of cancer care by physicians and nurses (Balboni, Balboni, et al., 2013; Balboni, Sullivan, et al., 2013; Kang et al., 2012). However, in a sample of 150 patients with advanced cancer in a southeastern US medical center, Pearce et al. (2012) found that more patients reported they desired spiritual care (defined as support for specific spiritual needs) than those who actually received it from their health care providers (67% and 17% overall, respectively: 78% and 11% from their religious community; 45% and 40% from a hospital chaplain).

By comparison, in a multicenter US study of advanced cancer patients, 47% indicated that their spiritual needs were being minimally or not met by their religious community, and 72% that their spiritual needs were being minimally or not met by the medical system (Balboni et al., 2007).

Spiritual care, as measured by patients' reports that the health care team supported their S/R needs, has been correlated with better satisfaction with care (Pearce et al., 2012), greater QOL (Chen et al., 2018), fewer depressive symptoms and more meaning/peace (Pearce et al., 2012), and less aggressive care at the EOL (Balboni et al., 2010), as well as with lower EOL costs, particularly among racial/ethnic minorities and high religious coping patients (Balboni, Balboni, & Paulk, 2011). By comparison, S/R support from religious communities has been found to predict more aggressive care at the EOL, suggesting (as discussed above) that collaboration with and education of religious communities may be strategies to help reduce such aggressive care (Balboni, Balboni, et al., 2013; Balboni et al., 2017; Balboni, Sullivan, et al., 2013). Of interest, in a cross-sectional survey of 3585 hospitals, significantly lower rates of hospital deaths and higher rates of hospice enrollment were reported in those who received chaplaincy services (Flannelly et al., 2012).

Why is spiritual care infrequent at the EOL? In a survey-based, multisite study of 75 eligible patients with advanced cancer receiving palliative radiation therapy, along with oncology physicians and nurses at four Boston academic centers (Balboni, Balboni, et al., 2013; Balboni, Sullivan, et al., 2013), a majority of the 339 nurses and physicians viewed spiritual care as an important, appropriate, and a beneficial component of EOL care. The study identified lack of training as the most frequent reason for its infrequency. However, ethical concerns also often surface in discussions of the clinician's role in providing spiritual care. In a cross-sectional, multisite, mixed methods study of patients with advanced cancer ($n = 70$), oncology physicians ($n = 206$), and oncology nurses, Balboni et al. (2011) found that most cancer patients (71%), nurses (83%), and physicians (65%) believed that patient-initiated patient–practitioner prayer was at least occasionally appropriate and most patients viewed prayer as spiritually supportive. The authors concluded that the appropriateness of patient-specific prayer is case-specific and requires consideration of multiple factors including a preexisting relationship, knowledge of patient openness toward S/R, and S/R concordance in the patient–practitioner relationship.

Over the past 30 years, the importance of caring for the spiritual needs of patients has begun to be formally recognized by professional spiritual care providers, palliative care clinicians, health care councils and regulatory agencies such as the Joint Commission (2011), the National Consensus Project Guidelines for Quality Palliative Care (2013), and health care delivery systems. However, in part because of the difficulty of generating widely accepted research-based definitions of spirituality and spiritual care for use in outcome studies, research on spiritual care (Edwards, Pang, Shiu, & Chan, 2010) and chaplaincy care (Jankowski, Handzo, & Flannelly, 2011) has only recently begun. Existing research (Sinclair, Mysak, & Hagen, 2009) has shown that spiritual care programs that are centrally located within the cancer center, reflect a multifaith approach, provide guidance to senior leaders, and have an academic aspect are utilized more frequently, better funded, and more often viewed as an integral component of interdisciplinary care.

A growing literature describes the use of specific spiritually oriented interventions in oncology, the best studied of which are mindfulness-based stress reduction (MBSR) and mindfulness-based cognitive behavior therapy (Foley, Farmer, & Petronis, 2006; Garland, Carlson, Cook, Lansdell, & Speca, 2007; Harrison, Koenig, Hays, Eme-Akwari, & Pargament, 2009). MBSR approaches have been found in randomized controlled trials (RCTs) to improve psychological functioning and well-being (Cramer, Lauche, Paul, & Dobos, 2012; Ott, Norris, & Bauer-Wu, 2006). However, a Cochrane Review (Candy et al., 2012) of five RCTs ($n = 1130$ participants) of other spiritual and religious interventions for well-being in the terminal phase of illness, including those provided by chaplains, found inconclusive evidence of benefit and called for more rigorous research.

Randomized clinical trials have shown efficacy for meaning-centered therapy in less seriously ill oncology patients. For example, Breitbart et al. (2010) piloted a group intervention based on Victor Frankl's logotherapy and, along with Lee, Robin Cohen, Edgar, Laizner, and Gagnon (2006), demonstrated improvements in self-esteem, self-efficacy, and optimism compared to controls utilizing a four-session individual intervention designed to address existential issues by exploring meaning-making coping strategies. In a study of 441 terminally ill patients randomized to dignity-conserving therapy, standard palliative care, or client-centered care, Chochinov et al. (2005) found that dignity therapy significantly improved measures of spiritual well-being and greater satisfaction when compared to standard palliative care. It is also clear that interfaith chaplains are often a helpful resource to clinicians in understanding and providing for specific spiritual needs at the

EOL. For example, while Hindus have a strong preference for dying at home, Muslims want to die facing Mecca and be surrounded by loved ones, and Buddhists wish to chant or hear others chanting when near death (Sloan, Bagiella, & VandeCreek, 2000).

Finally, studies have shown that S/R and life philosophy play an important role in the lives of most but not all family members of patients with cancer (Peteet & Balboni, 2013). A large-scale survey of former palliative caregivers found that 4.7% reported that additional spiritual support would have been helpful (Hegarty, Abernethy, Olver, & Currow, 2011). These individuals were also more likely to say that a number of other additional supports would have been helpful, emphasizing the importance of stress and its timing. Similarly, spirituality plays an important role for some though not all bereaved individuals (Currier, Mallot, Martinez, Charlotte, & Neimeyer, 2012). Since bereavement is a crisis that challenges one's assumptions about existence and provides the grounds for spiritual change, it is not surprising that spiritual beliefs and practices can influence the process of grieving, reassessing one's identity, reengaging in life, and struggling from a religious standpoint (e.g., anger at God). Religious struggles of this type have been associated with worse adjustment to cancer and bereavement. Meert, Thurston, and Briller (2005) note that health care providers can help parents of pediatric patients deal with their spiritual needs by providing a safe environment, opportunities to stay connected with their child at the time of death, and ways to remember their child in the future. Studies have also shown MBSR to be helpful to the caregivers of cancer patients (Minor, Carlson, Mackenzie, Zernicke, & Jones, 2006).

Clinical implications

What is the role of mental health professionals in dealing with intertwined emotional and S/R concerns of patients and their caregivers near the EOL? As Harrison et al. (2009) have shown, patients who are prone to experience their spirituality in negative ways (using negative rather than positive religious coping) may be particularly vulnerable to anxiety and depression. Distressing religious or spiritual struggles as a type of religious or spiritual problem (DSM-5V Code 62.89) are an appropriate focus for attention from mental health professionals.

Arguably, the first task of clinicians is diagnostic—most notably, distinguishing depression from demoralization, expected adjustment, or religious/spiritual struggle. Recognition and treatment of depression are important to patients' QOL and decision-making, but major depression can be more difficult to diagnose in this setting due to the prevalence of vegetative symptoms related to physical illness and its treatment. Accordingly, it is crucial that clinicians assess the patient's history, cognitive and affective symptoms, and capacity for enjoyment (Block, 2000). At the same time, depression often has a spiritual dimension in that religious/spiritual struggles can both worsen and/or be worsened by a disordered mood (Peteet, 2010). As Robinson, Kissane, and Brooker (2016) have pointed out, many seriously ill patients who feel hopeless and overwhelmed facing the existential threat of death are better described as demoralized than depressed.

A growing number of evidence-based treatments have emerged for individuals with existential distress in the face of death. Spiegel and his colleagues at Stanford have demonstrated improved distress and coping through the use of supportive-expressive group therapy for women with metastatic breast cancer (Spiegel, Bloom, & Yalom, 1981). As noted above, Breitbart et al. (2010) have shown efficacy for meaning-centered therapy for oncology outpatients, based on Victor Frankl's logotherapy. Similarly, Lee et al. (2006) demonstrated benefits in self-esteem, self-efficacy, and optimism compared to controls using four individual sessions designed to address existential issues by exploring meaning-making coping strategies. Chochinov, Kristjanson, and Breitbart (2011), in a study of 441 terminally ill patients randomized to dignity-conserving therapy (which invites terminally ill patients to discuss issues that matter most or that they would most want to be remembered for), standard palliative care, or client-centered care, found that dignity therapy significantly improved measures of spiritual well-being, such as dignity, meaning and purpose, and satisfaction with care.

Cole et al. (2011), in a randomized trial of spiritually focused meditation for patients with metastatic melanoma, found that many patients preferred programs that included a spiritual component, which is consistent with other studies of spiritually integrated psychotherapy. Acceptance and commitment therapy (Hayes, Luoma, Bond, Masuda, & Lillis, 2006), which has been shown to help demoralized patients to take ownership of their lives and to help with the existential and spiritual task of finding direction, is now being applied to patients with cancer.

In addition, interest and research have grown into psychedelic medication—assisted treatment for anxiety and existential distress at the EOL

(Pollan, 2018). Parenthetically, like many of those who report therapeutic, if not transformative experiences of transcendence through the use of psychedelic substances, and a number of individuals draw meaning from moving near-death experiences, data on the nature and outcome of these experiences are limited (Bailey & Yates, 2013; Musgrave, 1997).

A step-by-step approach to addressing spirituality/religion in end-of-life care

Given this variety in published approaches to existential/spiritual distress in patients with serious illness, how should clinicians attempt to integrate and implement them in caring for suffering patients (cf. Harris, Amonoo, Abrahm, Murphy, & Peteet, 2019)?

The first step is to provide comfort by connecting with the patient as a human being (Cayley, 2006; Druss, 2003). Given the way that existential suffering can overwhelm and threaten one's identity and connections, simply helping the patient feel that a clinician understands their pain, cares and will follow through may provide powerful reassurance that they are not alone in the world or abandoned.

A second step is to consider why their stressors are so threatening and what their suffering means to them. Do the circumstances challenge their concept of self-identity and self-worth? Do they feel betrayed, ill-fated, or trapped? Is their worldview changing such that they feel they are being punished, or that the universe has it in for them, and if so why? Perhaps stressors have upended what they had believed had been rules by which the universe operated (e.g., "If I'm a good person, nothing bad will happen to me").

A third step is to assess what internal resources support their resilience. Griffith (2018) has helpfully categorized these into problem solving, emotional regulation, identity activation, and relational coping. Which have they drawn upon to deal with existential assaults in the past?

A fourth step is to query about distorted, emotionally driven and disabling perceptions (e.g., that nothing can change). Taking a narrative life history can help patients both feel understood and begin to reframe recent precipitating events (Viederman & Perry, 1980).

A fifth step is to help the patient actively enlist sources of resilience to reshape their approach to suffering: Can they recall what has given their life meaning in the past? What explanatory frameworks have they called upon, and what may they not have considered? If Christian, what does it mean to them that Jesus suffered and called on his followers to "pick up their cross"? If they believe suffering should be somehow redemptive, or could be character building, in what way? If Muslim, do they believe their suffering is a task given to them by God, thereby challenging them to respond in some way? If Buddhist, how do they understand the renunciation of desire? If they have valued being true to themselves, can they articulate their core values? Griffith (2018) advocates individualizing "hope modules" to help such individuals mobilize these resources.

A sixth task, once the sufferer is no longer acutely demoralized, is to decide on a plan of action for the time they have remaining. This involves taking into account core values, prior experiences, and the emotional context which may be influencing judgment. How do they want to redirect their efforts, and what is most important for them to preserve? The emotional component of the hopelessness of a patient just given weeks to live is likely to be more prominent and acute than that of a slowly declining elderly patient questioning the value of her remaining life. And yet, lifelong patterns of responding to adversity, for example, with cynicism and feelings of betrayal, are still important to recognize and reassess.

Finally, a seventh step is to help patients continue living in accordance with their re-evaluated faith or values (e.g., by reengaging with a faith community or a spiritual practice).

Often, however, psychiatrists are asked to see seriously ill hospitalized patients without either the time to implement these steps or the opportunity to enlist a chaplain. Consider the example of an 85-year-old, married, Catholic, semiretired real estate agent with a 14-year history of prostate cancer, undergoing androgen deprivation treatment, with nephrostomy tubes, who was hospitalized for a urinary tract infection and poor pain control. He became confused with higher doses of opiates and acknowledged that he had sometimes used pain meds to deal with his anxiety, which he experienced as waves of physical tension. When interviewed on lower doses of opiate medication, he was alert and aware of his situation, though vague on some details. He voiced concern about what would happen to his wife when he died and also wondered if God might be punishing him for something. The consulting psychiatrist explored how he pictured God and discovered that the patient imagined a loving God who, on reflection, probably was not trying to punish, but possibly to teach him something. He then asked the patient to imagine breathing God deeply into his lungs and letting Him settle his anxiety. The patient found this exercise so relaxing that this helped him sleep and continued to use it during his hospitalization. The consulting psychiatrist in this case integrated behavioral, dynamic, and spiritual perspectives to address the patient's acute, multifactorial distress.

Ethical considerations

A growing number of jurisdictions now allow physician-assisted suicide (PAS), a practice which remains controversial to many in part due to deeply held religious convictions. Advocates contend that patients deserve the right to die with means provided by their physicians and that there is little evidence, as yet, of abuse. Opponents express a number of concerns—that PAS has proven to be a slippery slope, that it conveys that patients' lives are no longer worth living, and that it undermines the physician's role to offer hope that patient's suffering has dignity, will be shared, and can be made more bearable. Some opponents point to the example of countries such as Belgium and the Netherlands, which have extended the logic of the right to die to the provision of euthanasia for individuals with mental illness, including personality disorders (Kim, DeVries, & Peteet, 2016). Psychiatrists who personally oppose PAS also struggle with whether to serve as consultants in the role of assessing capacity to consent to PAS.

Dying and the loss of control associated with it represent frightening prospects. The impressive growth of palliative care and the sensitivity of well-known physicians, such as Atul Gawande in *Being Mortal* (2014), have not allayed the fears of many that an increasingly scientific, impersonal medical system will fail and even abandon them in the end. This is reflected in studies which show that most individuals who request PAS do so not to escape intolerable physical symptoms, but to reestablish a sense of dignity and control. The plight of these individuals underscores the importance of the physician's role in going beyond the relief of physical suffering to helping them take charge of the time they do have. As suggested above, clinicians can help patients establish realistic hopes by expanding their possibilities, to bear suffering by assuring them that it is understood and by remaining with them, and to achieve perspective by reviewing their lives and their priorities. Physicians' responsibility to take these opportunities has its roots in the ancient, but increasingly relevant, traditions of beneficence, virtue, and of patient autonomy understood as mastery rather than freedom from influence. Wherever psychiatrists land on the permissibility of PAS, their painful inability to meet all of their patients' needs does not detract from the importance of the psychological, personal, and pastoral aspects of the doctor–patient relationship (Peteet, 1994).

In addition to ethical struggles involving PAS, psychiatrists may be asked to see patients whose treatment decision-making has religious components (Phelps et al., 2009), for example, that of members of a faith tradition such as Christian Science. Careful assessment of the patient's motivation and consultation with experts and/or practitioners of the tradition involved are generally indicated to help the team both establish capacity and understand the patient's specific needs for support (Herschkopf & Peteet, 2018). With regard to best practices, the expanding use of spiritually integrated interventions, such as mindfulness, meditation, and prayer near the EOL, raises the question of whether these can be divorced from the spiritual traditions from which they came (Brown, 2013). Some have wondered whether patients are at risk of becoming confused about whether their potential benefits are psychological, medical, or spiritual (Moczynski, Haler, & Bentele, 2009). A related question is how important it is for patients to receive tradition-specific, rather than more generic, multifaith pastoral care.

It is also important to note that educating mental health clinicians in addressing existential distress and providing spiritually sensitive care remain challenging for several reasons. Psychiatry lags behind palliative medicine in identifying spiritual care as an aim. No consensus exists on core competencies for dealing with existential S/R issues in psychiatry and only a minority of psychiatric residency programs includes formal instruction in this area. In settings where recognition of the importance of S/R exists, there can be a tendency to defer and instead refer patients to hospital chaplains, with few venues available for consultation and dialog about patients between psychiatric and spiritual care providers (Kao, Lokko, Gallivan, O'Brien, & Peteet, 2017). Fortunately, recently funded efforts to develop a core curriculum in spiritually integrated psychotherapy (Pearce, Pargament, Oxhandler, Vieten, & Wong, 2019) and educational efforts such as Griffith's (2018) to teach "hope modules" represents progress. Since religious coping has been associated with more aggressive care at the EOL, there is also need for clinicians to help educate faith leaders and congregations on the role of advance directives and goals of care discussions (Balboni et al., 2017; Sanders et al., 2017). The *Conversation Project*, dedicated to helping members of congregations talk about their wishes for EOL care, is an example.

Discussion

The evidence we have reviewed in this chapter supports several conclusions: (1) S/R is important to many oncology patients and family members, and this domain plays a larger role in medical decision-making than many clinicians may appreciate; (2) patients' spiritual needs can be significant source of distress, and meeting them can influence both QOL and aggressive care at the EOL; (3) lack of training is a major reason why clinicians provide spiritual care infrequently; and (4) evidence-based approaches to meeting patients' existential and spiritual needs include meaning-centered and dignity-promoting therapy.

A number of questions remain for those interested in addressing the whole person facing the EOL. One of the most basic is how to define spirituality in a way that takes into account its breadth and complexity, but allows for measurement (by researchers, clinicians, and administrators) (Salander, 2012). Notably, no studies have examined the neural correlates of spirituality in the context of EOL. Another question is how spiritual care providers can demonstrate the value of what they do and best collaborate with other members of the team to provide spiritually and psychologically integrated care. More specifically, how can they consult with psychiatrists and other medical providers in ways that sharpen and encourage the spiritual caregiving capacities of these providers? How can mental health clinicians, in turn, help other members of the team to understand and work with the psychological subtleties of patients' spiritual and existential struggles? Although a few models for such training and collaboration exist (Kao et al., 2017; Todres, Catlin, & Thiel, 2005), more needs to be done to understand and demonstrate what makes them effective.

References

Alcorn, S. R., Balboni, M. J., Prigerson, H. G., Reynolds, A., Phelps, A. C., Wright, A. A., et al. (2010). "If God wanted me yesterday, I wouldn't be here today": Religious and spiritual themes in patients' experiences of advanced cancer. *Journal of Palliative Medicine, 13*(5), 581–588.

Astrow, A. B., Wexler, A., Texeira, K., He, M. K., & Sulmasy, D. P. (2007). Is failure to meet spiritual needs associated with cancer patients' perceptions of quality of care and their satisfaction with care? *Journal of Clinical Oncology, 25*(36), 5753–5757.

Bailey, L. W., & Yates, Y. (2013). *The near death experience: A reader*. Taylor and Francis.

Balboni, M. J., Sullivan, A., Amobi, A., Phelps, A. C., Gorman, D. P., Zollfrank, A., et al. (2013). Why is spiritual care infrequent at the end of life? Spiritual care perceptions among patients, nurses, and physicians and the role of training. *Journal of Clinical Oncology, 31*(4), 461–467.

Balboni, M. J., Sullivan, A., Enzinger, A. C., Smith, P. T., Mitchell, C., Peteet, J. R., et al. (2017). United States clergy religious values and relationships to end-of-life discussions and care. *Journal of Pain and Symptom Management, 53*(6), 999–1009.

Balboni, T., Balboni, M., Paulk, M. E., Phelps, A., Wright, A., Peteet, J., et al. (2011). Support of cancer patients' spiritual needs and associations with medical care costs at the end of life. *Cancer, 117*(23), 5383–5391.

Balboni, T. A., Balboni, M., Phelps, A. C., Gallivan, K., Paulk, M. E., Wright, A. A., et al. (2013). Provision of spiritual support to advanced cancer patients by religious communities and associations with medical care at the end of life. *JAMA Internal Medicine, 173*(12), 1109–1117.

Balboni, T. A., Paulk, M. E., Balboni, M. J., et al. (2010). Provision of spiritual care to patients with advanced cancer: Associations with medical care and quality of life near death. *Journal of Clinical Oncology, 28*(3), 445–452.

Balboni, T. A., Paulk, M. E., Balboni, M. J., Phelps, A. C., Loggers, E. T., Wright, A. A., et al. (2009). Provision of spiritual care to advanced cancer patients: Associations with medical care and quality of life near death. *Journal of Clinical Oncology, 27*, 1–7.

Balboni, T. A., Vanderwerker, L. C., Block, S. D., Paulk, M. E., Lathan, C. S., Peteet, J. R., et al. (2007). Religiousness and spiritual support among advanced cancer patients and associations with end-of-life treatment preferences and quality of life. *Journal of Clinical Oncology, 25*(5), 555–560.

Block, S. (2000). Assessing and managing depression in the terminally patient. *Annals of Internal Medicine, 132*(3), 209–218.

Breitbart, W., Rosenfeld, B., Pessin, H., Poppito, S., Nelson, C., Tomarken, A., et al. (2010). Meaning-centered group psychotherapy for patients with advanced cancer: A pilot randomized controlled trial. *Psychooncology, 19*, 21–28.

Brown, C. G. (2013). *The healing Gods: Complementary and alternative medicine in Christian America*. New York: Oxford University Press.

Candy, B., Jones, L., Varagunam, M., Speck, P., Tookman, A., & King, M. (2012). Spiritual and religious interventions for well-being of adults in the terminal phase of disease. *Cochrane Database of Systematic Reviews, 5*, CD007544.

Cayley, W. E. (2006). Comfort always. *Family Practice Management, 13*, 74.

Chen, J., Lin, Y., Yan, J., Wu, Y., & Hu, R. (2018). The effects of spiritual care on quality of life and spiritual well-being among patients with terminal illness: a systematic review. *Palliative Medicine, 32*(7), 1167–1179.

Chochinov, H. M., Hack, T., Hassard, T., Kristjanson, L. J., McClement, S., & Harlos, M. (2005). Dignity therapy: A novel psychotherapeutic intervention for patients near the end of life. *Journal of Clinical Oncology, 23*, 5520–5525.

Chochinov, H. M., Kristjanson, L. J., Breitbart, W., McClement, S., Hack, T. F., Hassard, T., et al. (2011). Effect of dignity therapy on distress and end-of-life experience in terminally ill patients: A randomised controlled trial. *Lancet Oncology., 12*(8), 753–762.

Cole, B. S., Hopkins, C. M., Spiegel, J., Tisak, J., Agarwala, S., & Kirkwood, J. M. (2011). A randomised clinical trial of the effects of spiritually focused meditation for people with metastatic melanoma. *Mental Health, Religion & Culture, 15*(2), 161–174.

Cramer, H., Lauche, R., Paul, A., & Dobos, G. (2012). Mindfulness-based stress reduction for breast cancer—A systematic review and meta-analysis. *Current Oncology, 19*(5), e343–e352.

Currier, J. M., Mallot, J., Martinez, T. E., Charlotte, S., & Neimeyer, R. A. (2012). Bereavement, religion, and posttraumatic growth: A matched control group investigation. *Psychology of Religion and Spirituality., 5*, 69–77.

Druss, R. G. (2003). To comfort always. *American Journal of Psychiatry, 160*, 25–26.

Edwards, A., Pang, N., Shiu, V., & Chan, C. (2010). The understanding of spirituality and the potential role of spiritual care in end-of-life and palliative care: A meta-study of qualitative research. *Palliative Medicine, 24*(8), 753–770.

Flannelly, K. J., Emanuel, L. L., Handzo, G. F., Galek, K., Silton, N. R., & Carlson, M. (2012). A national study of chaplaincy services and end-of-life outcomes. *BMC Palliative Care*, *11*, 10.

Foley, K. L., Farmer, D. F., Petronis, V. M., Smith, R. G., McGraw, S., Smith, K., et al. (2006). A qualitative exploration of the cancer experience among long-term survivors: Comparisons by cancer type, ethnicity, gender, and age. *Psychooncology*, *15*(3), 248–258.

Garland, S. N., Carlson, L. E., Cook, S., Lansdell, L., & Speca, M. (2007). A non-randomized comparison of mindfulness-based stress reduction and healing arts programs for facilitating post-traumatic growth and spirituality in cancer outpatients. *Support Care Cancer*, *15*(8), 949–961.

Gawande, A. (2014). *Being mortal: Medicine and what matters in the end*. New York: Metropolitan.

Griffith, J. (2018). Hope modules: Brief psychotherapeutic interventions to counter demoralization from daily stressors of chronic illness. *Academic Psychiatry*, *42*(1), 135–145.

Harris, J. H., Amonoo, H. L., Abrahm, J. L., Murphy, W. S., & Peteet, J. R. (2019). The physician's role in responding to existential suffering: What does it mean to comfort always? *Journal of Palliative Care*, Apr 10:825859719839332.

Harrison, M. O., Koenig, H. G., Hays, J. C., Eme-Akwari, A. G., & Pargament, K. I. (2009). The epidemiology of religious coping: A review of recent literature. *International Review of Psychiatry*, *13*(2), 86–93. Available from https://doi.org/10.1080/09540260124356.

Hayes, S. C., Luoma, J. B., Bond, F. W., Masuda, A., & Lillis, J. (2006). Acceptance and commitment therapy: Model, processes and outcomes. *Behaviour Research and Therapy*, *31*, 1–25.

Hegarty, M. M., Abernethy, A. P., Olver, I., & Currow, D. C. (2011). Former palliative caregivers who identify that additional spiritual support would have been helpful in a population survey. *Palliative Medicine.*, *25*, 266–277.

Herschkopf, M., & Peteet, J. R. (2018). Consultation-liaison psychiatry. In J. R. Peteet, M. L. Dell, & W. L. A. Fung (Eds.), *Ethical considerations at the interface of psychiatry and religion* (pp. 138–149). New York: Oxford University Press.

Jankowski, K. R., Handzo, G. F., & Flannelly, K. J. (2011). Testing the efficacy of chaplaincy care. *Journal of Health Care Chaplaincy*, *17*(3–4), 100–125.

Kang, J., Shin, D. W., Choi, J. Y., Park, C. H., Baek, Y. J., Mo, H. N., et al. (2012). Addressing the religious and spiritual needs of dying patients by healthcare staff in Korea: Patient perspectives in a multi-religious Asian country. *Psychooncology*, *21*(4), 374–381.

Kao, L. E., Lokko, H. N., Gallivan, K., O'Brien, V., & Peteet, J. R. (2017). A model of collaborative spiritual and psychiatric care of oncology patients. *Psychosomatics*, *58*, 614–623.

Kim, S. Y. H., DeVries, R., & Peteet, J. R. (2016). Euthanasia and assisted suicide of patients with psychiatric disorders in the Netherlands 2011-2014. *JAMA Psychiatry*, *73*, 362–368.

Lee, V., Robin Cohen, S., Edgar, L., Laizner, A. M., & Gagnon, A. J. (2006). Meaning-making intervention during breast or colorectal cancer treatment improves self-esteem, optimism, and self-efficacy. *Social Science & Medicine*, *62*(12), 3133–3145.

Meert, K. L., Thurston, C. S., & Briller, S. H. (2005). The spiritual needs of parents at the time of their child's death in the pediatric intensive care unit and during bereavement: A qualitative study. *Pediatric Critical Care Medicine*, *6*, 420–427.

Minor, H. G., Carlson, L. E., Mackenzie, M. J., Zernicke, K., & Jones, L. (2006). Evaluation of a Mindfulness-Based Stress Reduction (MBSR) program for caregivers of children with chronic conditions. *Social Work in Health Care.*, *43*, 91–109.

Moczynski, W., Haler, H., & Bentele, K. (2009). *Medical ethics in health care chaplaincy*. Berlin: Verlag.

Musgrave, C. (1997). The near-death experience: A study of spiritual transformation. *Journal of Near-Death Studies*, *15*, 187–201.

NCP Clinical Practice Guidelines for Quality Palliative Care. (2013). *National consensus project*. <http://www.nationalcoalitionhpc.org/ncp-guidelines-2013/> Accessed 09.06.18.

Ott, M. J., Norris, R. L., & Bauer-Wu, S. M. (2006). Mindfulness meditation for oncology patients: A discussion and critical review. *Integrative Cancer Therapies*, *5*(2), 98–108.

Pearce, M. J., Coan, A. D., Herndon, J. E., 2nd, Koenig, H. G., & Abernethy, A. P. (2012). Unmet spiritual care needs impact emotional and spiritual well-being in advanced cancer patients. *Support Care Cancer*, *20*(10), 2269–2276, K.

Pearce, M. J., Pargament, K. I., Oxhandler, H. K., Vieten, C., & Wong, S. (2019). A novel training program for mental health providers in religious and spiritual competencies. *Spirituality in Clinical Practice*, *6*(2), 73–82. Available from https://doi.org/10.1037/scp0000195.

Peteet, J. R. (1994). Patients who request assisted suicide: A closer look at the physician's role. *Archives of Family Medicine*, *3*, 723–727.

Peteet, J. R. (2010). *Depression and the soul. A guide to spiritually integrated treatment*. New York: Routledge.

Peteet, J. R., & Balboni, M. J. (2013). Spirituality and religion in oncology. *CA Cancer Journal for Clinicians*, *63*, 280–289.

Phelps, A. C., Maciejewski, P. J., Wright, A. A., Balboni, T. A., Paulk, M. E., et al. (2009). Religious coping and use of intensive life-prolonging care near death among patients with advanced cancer. *JAMA*, *301*, 1140–1147.

Pollan, M. (2018). *How to change your mind: What the new science of psychedelics teaches us about consciousness, dying, addiction, depression, and transcendence*. New York: Penguin Press.

Robinson, S., Kissane, D. W., & Brooker, J. (2016). A review of the construct of demoralization: History, definitions and future directions for palliative care. *American Journal of Hospice and Palliative Medicine*, *33*, 93–101.

Salander, P. (2012). The emperor's new clothes: Spirituality. A concept based on questionable ontology and circular findings. *Archive for the Psychology of Religion*, *34*, 17–32.

Sanders, J. J., Chow, V., Enzinger, A. C., Lam, T., Smith, P. T., Quiñones, R., et al. (2017). Seeking and accepting: U.S. Clergy theological and moral perspectives informing decision making at the end of life. *Journal of Palliative Medicine*, *20*, 1059–1067. Available from https://doi.org/10.1089/jpm.2016.0545.

Silvestri, G. A., Knittig, S., Zoller, J. S., & Nietert, P. J. (2003). Importance of faith on medical decisions regarding cancer care. *Journal of Clinical Oncology*, *21*(7), 1379–1382.

Sinclair, S., Mysak, M., & Hagen, N. A. (2009). What are the core elements of oncology spiritual care programs? *Palliative & Supportive Care*, 7(4), 415–422.

Sloan, R. P., Bagiella, E., VanderCreek, L., Hover, M., Casalone, C., Hirsch, J. T., et al. (2000). Should physicians prescribe religious activities? *The New England Journal of Medicine*, *342*(25), 1913–1916.

Spiegel, D., Bloom, J. R., & Yalom, I. (1981). Group support for patients with metastatic breast cancer. *Archives of General Psychiatry*, *38*, 527–533.

Steinhauser, K. E., Christakis, N. A., Clipp, E. C., McNeilly, M., McIntyre, L., & Tulsky, J. A. (2000). Factors considered important at the end of life by patients, family, physicians, and other care providers. *JAMA*, *284*(19), 2476–2482.

Tarakeshwar, N., Vanderwerker, L. C., Paulk, E., Pearce, M. J., Kasl, S. V., & Prigerson, H. G. (2006). Religious coping is associated with the quality of life of patients with advanced cancer. *Journal of Palliative Medicine*, *9*(3), 646–657.

The Conversation Project, <https://theconversationproject.org/> Accessed 02.06.18. The Joint Commission: Edition, 2011:PC.02.02.13.

Todres, I. D., Catlin, E. A., & Thiel, M. M. (2005). The intensivist in a spiritual care training program adapted for clinicians. *Critical Care Medicine*, *33*(12), 2733–2736.

Viederman, M., & Perry, S. W., 3rd (1980). Use of a psychodynamic life narrative in the treatment of depression in the physically ill. *General Hospital Psychiatry*, *46*, 177–185.

Winkelman, W. D., Lauderdale, K., Balboni, M. J., Phelps, A. C., Peteet, J. R., Block, S. D., et al. (2011). The relationship of spiritual concerns to the quality of life of advanced cancer patients: Preliminary findings. *Journal of Palliative Medicine*, *14*(9), 1022–1028.

Index

Note: Page numbers followed by "*f*" and "*t*" refer to figures and tables, respectively.

E

M

N

O

S

9780128167663